SUBMARINES

1914–PRESENT

THE ESSENTIAL
NAVAL IDENTIFICATION GUIDE

SUBMARINES

1914–PRESENT

DAVID ROSS

amber
BOOKS

This edition published in 2012 by
Amber Books Ltd
Bradley's Close
74–77 White Lion Street
London N1 9PF
United Kingdom
www.amberbooks.co.uk

A catalogue record for this book is available from the British Library.

ISBN: 978-1-908696-66-3

Project Editor: Michael Spilling
Design: Colin Hawes
Picture Research: Terry Forshaw

Printed in China

PICTURE CREDITS
Art-Tech/Aerospace: 10, 44, 45, 67, 68, 77, 81, 86, 170
Cody Images: 6, 8, 11, 20, 28, 31, 41, 42, 69, 74, 76, 80, 91, 105, 113, 118
Getty Images: 163
Royal Navy Submarine Museum: 124
U.S. Department of Defense: 7, 116, 119, 135, 166, 168, 185

All artworks Art-Tech except for the following
Amber Books: 121, 122 top, 139 bottom, 153 top, 173 both, 174 centre & bottom,
   176, 179 both, 180 bottom, 181 bottom, 182–183 all
BAE Systems: 177 top

Contents

Introduction

The emergence of the submarine from August 1914 as a major strategic weapon was swift, and, to many, unexpected. Its early successes forced the warring navies into a drastic reconsideration of how war should be carried on at sea.

Hardly more than a month into World War I, the basis of naval warfare was changed for ever. On 5 September 1914, a British light cruiser, HMS *Pathfinder*, was sunk by the German submarine *U-21*, becoming the first victim of a free-fired torpedo. On the morning of 22 September three Royal Navy armoured cruisers, *Aboukir*, *Cressy* and *Hogue*, of Cruiser Force C, based at Harwich, were sunk in just over an an hour by *U-9*, a petrol-engined boat launched in 1910.

These events exposed a huge and potentially fatal gap in Britain's defences. The British Admiralty had underestimated the threat of submarines. Now, suddenly and glaringly, the vulnerability of surface ships was exposed. After decades of experiment, and dismissal of its value by many senior officers, the age of the submarine had arrived.

The submarines of 1914–18 could not travel underwater for long, or go very deep. In effect they were surface ships capable of submersion for relatively brief periods. But their crucial feature was their ability to approach unseen and fire weapons from below the surface, striking the relatively unprotected undersides of far bigger ships. This invisibility and potential destructiveness created a submarine 'mystique' from the start. Many naval officers considered it a 'sneak' weapon, but whatever their attitude, they could not forgo the use of submarines as long as the other side had them.

The Submariners

Conditions on board these submarines were unpleasant in the extreme, especially during the periods of submergence. The boat was formed

▲ **K-class (Royal Navy)**
HMS *K12* was commissioned in August 1917. The K-class submarines were large, fast, steam-propelled vessels designed to operate as part of a surface battle fleet.

▲ **Ballistic missile submarine**
This photograph shows a port view of a Soviet Navy Alfa-class nuclear-powered ballistic missile submarine (SSN) leaving Soviet waters.

around an engine room, flotation tanks and torpedo tubes. Somewhere, accommodation and living space got fitted in for the men who made it all work. Tiny, cramped living space, damp, mould, bad air, dependence on temperamental machinery – together these made for a tough environment.

Submariners in all navies were something of a separate breed. Their world was a tiny one and in all operating conditions it was highly dependent on team spirit, co-operation and trust. The formality of the surface navy could not be replicated on board a submarine, yet discipline and determination were vital in order for the boat to be an effective fighting unit. Much depended on the leadership given by the captain. Submariners of all nations were more at risk than surface sailors. In Germany's World War II *Kriegsmarine*, out of 40,000 men who served in U-boats, more than 32,000 perished.

The Nuclear Era

Up to the mid-1950s, conditions on board submarines changed little. The advent of the nuclear vessel brought changes, for two reasons: firstly it had more available space; and secondly its capacity for remaining underwater and for extended cruises meant that more attention had to be given to crew amenities. But submarines remained a tight and risky environment. Submariners were no less dependent on

technology to sustain their lives than astronauts. Soviet Russia, in its haste to catch up with the American lead in nuclear propulsion, either underestimated or ignored the dangers associated with nuclear reactors. Its first generations of crews paid a heavy price in radiation burns and sickness. In the United States, Admiral Rickover, the 'father' of the nuclear submarine, was as obsessive about safety as he was about everything else, and the radiation safety record of US nuclear submarines is unmatched.

Arms Limitation

Since the first London Naval Treaty of 1930, respect for the power of the submarine has been shown by international bargaining to keep the numbers down. The SALT (Strategic Arms Limitation Treaty) agreements of the 1970s showed that the Americans and Soviets were at least willing to consider some restriction in their submarine fleets. But it was a real political event, the collapse of the Soviet Union and the end of the Cold War in 1989–90, that prompted a major shift in the role of submarines. In the twenty-first century, nuclear-powered submarines, their strategic role as intercontinental ballistic missile carriers cut back, remain the prime attacking craft. But new developments in non-nuclear propulsion have ensured that the 'conventional' submarine, which is quiet, extremely hard to detect and much less expensive to build and dismantle, still has a vital role to play in the confrontations and tactical theatres of the world's hot-spots, where military muscle is deployed to back up political and diplomatic persuasion.

Chapter 1

World War I:
1914–18

Most of the submarines in action in 1914 were
of a primitive type, but from the earliest days of the war their
capacity for surprise attack and destruction became clear.
Yet, although operations in the North Sea, the Atlantic and
the Baltic, by both British and German boats, revealed the
submarine's huge strategic value, the naval authorities on
both sides remained preoccupied by surface warfare
and battleship engagements.

The German U-boat offensive came close to cutting
off Great Britain's main supply lines. But the submarine
remained essentially a surface vessel with the capacity to
submerge for relatively brief periods. Its gun was seen to be
as essential as its torpedoes. And its very success focused
attention on the means of detecting and destroying it.

◀ **Deck gun**
British submariners drill with a 12-pounder deck gun aboard a British E-class submarine.

Introduction

By 1914, the submarine or submersible boat had quite a long history, going all the way back to the eighteenth century.

THE ANTECEDENTS of the World War I submarine really start with the inclusion of the torpedo as part of its armament in 1879, and, around the same time, the development of electric accumulators and motors of sufficient power to propel a boat underwater. Even at this stage there were two views of what a navy needed: one was a boat that could operate wholly and continuously submerged; the other was for a boat that was primarily a surface craft but which could submerge and travel underwater for relatively brief periods.

This second view prevailed, partly because it was technically more feasible and partly because it was easier for the naval strategists of the time to understand. It was this approach that led to the adoption of the long, narrow torpedo-boat hull rather than the more bulbous, fish-shaped hull of many early submersibles. This hull design would prevail right into the 1950s.

Another influence was the improvement of naval guns, especially the development of the quick-firing gun, which made surface torpedo-boats vulnerable. France produced the first effective naval submarine, the electric-powered *Gustave Zédé* (1893), named for its designer.

The US Navy led during the 1890s in promoting experiments with gasoline and electric engines, and John Holland's *Holland* (1900), with gasoline and electric motors, was a major step forward. In 1900, six navies possessed a total of 10 submarines, with 11 under construction. The British Royal and German Imperial Navies were not among them. France had 14 built or on the stocks, the United States had two, Turkey had two (of 1880s vintage), and Italy, Spain and Portugal had one each.

New Century

During the 1900s, some important developments took place. Great Britain decided it had to have submarines and its first five were built to Holland's design. Home-designed B- C- and D-classes followed, each one larger than its predecessor. The

▲ **British D- and E-class**
Royal Navy submarines, including *E1* and *D2*, sit in a dockyard somewhere on the English coast. *E1* served mainly in the Baltic and was scuttled to avoid capture by advancing German forces near Helsinki, Finland. *D2* served in the North Sea before being sunk with all hands in November 1914.

▲ **USS** *Seal*
One of four G-class boats, commissioned on 28 October 1912, the USS *Seal* was allocated the unusual hull number of 19 from June 1916 until 1920. During World War I it was used almost exclusively as a training boat.

German Navy, though sceptical, began to build submarines from 1906 and took a lead in using heavy oil rather than vaporous and flammable gasoline, or cumbrous steam machinery, for surface travel. From 1907, the Germans and the British were both building 'overseas' submarines intended primarily for operations in the North Sea, and between 1908 and 1914 the Germans ordered 42 of these, of which 29 were available for service in August 1914. Boats of this type displaced around 508 tonnes (500 tons) and with the D-class (1906) the British too began to use paired diesel engines and twin propellers.

Up to the start of the war, the biggest submarine fleet was the French. The French Navy saw its submarines as compensating for its lack of large capital ships, and naval exercises from the days of *Gustave Zédé* onwards convinced them that the submarine had a role as a potential destroyer of surface warships. By 1906, submarine flotillas were established at Dunkirk, Cherbourg, Rochefort and Toulon – all important naval ports – with the purpose of operating defensively against any approaching hostile fleet. The French were also the first to send submarines to remote colonial bases, for the same purpose. This French perception of the submarine's role was influential and in other navies it was also seen essentially as a defensive craft. Britain followed the French example by establishing flotilla bases at Devonport, Portsmouth, Harwich and Dundee, to maintain a watch in the western approaches, the English Channel and the North Sea.

United States Left Behind

These European developments, part of the 'arms race' of the 1900s, left the United States somewhat behind after its early start. US submarines remained small and were used only for patrols close to the coast. But the European nations were preparing for a war, while the United States was not. Nobody, however, appears to have appreciated the possibilities of the submarine as a wide-ranging commerce raider and certainly none of the pre-1914 boats were designed with this role in mind.

Naval exercises had shown convincingly by 1910 that a submarine could approach a battleship undetected and fire torpedoes at it, and this aspect of a submarine's offensive power was appreciated by the more perceptive naval strategists; but they still had much to learn about its potential.

Submarine forces
1914

By the eve of World War I, 16 navies included submarines in their fleets, with a total of around 400, but these craft were relatively small and generally intended for short sea operations, not for venturing out into the oceans.

ALMOST EVERY EUROPEAN power maintained a submarine fleet, although as yet submarines had not been tested in a full-scale war. But they would prove to have a decisive influence in naval combat.

Denmark and Sweden

Submarine construction was a specialized activity and the Fiat-San Giorgio yard at La Spezia, Italy, built boats for several navies. Typical was the petrol-engined *Dykkeren*, bought by the Danish Navy in 1909 and used for inshore patrols. In World War I Denmark was neutral, and coastal patrol was essential to ensure belligerent vessels did not enter territorial waters. Sunk in a collision with a Norwegian steamer in 1916, *Dykkeren* was salvaged but broken up in 1918. Pre-war submarines had been armed with self-propelled torpedoes for attacking enemy ships, but *Dykkeren* had no deck gun, as this was not a feature of pre-war submarines.

During the war the belligerent powers fitted their boats with deck guns. This permitted them to approach enemy merchant ships on the surface and signal them to stop for searching (an early war policy), and later to sink small or unarmed ships that did not warrant expenditure of torpedoes. Up to 1914 most submarines carried no more than two to four torpedoes. Most war-built submarines had one and sometimes two guns of 75mm or 100mm (3- or 4in) calibre; however, the tendency was for deck guns to become bigger, and several later German submarines carried 150mm (5.9in) guns.

Sweden was to remain neutral in both world wars, but always maintained a strong defensive fleet. Its submarine tradition began in 1902 with *Hajen*, rebuilt and extended in 1916, but still a relatively primitive boat with a paraffin engine for surface work and a single 457mm (18in) torpedo tube.

France

The French had been pioneers in submarine design and began the war with a fleet of over 60 submarines in a range of types, including the 16-strong Brumaire

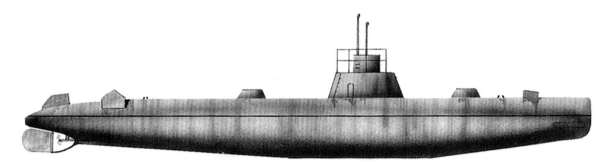

▲ **Dykkeren**

Danish Navy, coastal submarine, 1909

Dykkeren proved to have many mechanical and structural problems, and the Danish Navy did not look to Fiat-San Giorgio for further boats, instead building other Italian designs, from Whitehead, under licence in Denmark, as the Havmanden and Aegir classes. These had diesel engines rather than *Dykkeren's* kerosene motors.

Specifications

Crew: 35	Displacement: Surfaced: 107 tonnes (105 tons)
Powerplant: Twin screw petrol engine;	Submerged: 134 tonnes (132 tons)
one electric motor	Dimensions (length/beam/draught): 34.7m x
Max Speed: Surfaced: 12 knots;	3.3m x 2m (113ft 10in x 10ft 10in x 6ft 6in)
Submerged: 7.5 knots	Commissioned: June 1909
Surface Range: 185km (100nm) at 12 knots	Armament: Two 457mm (18in) torpedo tubes

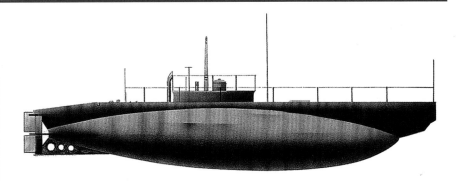

Specifications

Crew: 15

Powerplant: Single screw paraffin engine;
electric motor

Max Speed: Surfaced: 9.5 knots; Submerged:
7 knots

Surface Range: Not known

Displacement: Surfaced: 108 tonnes (107 tons);
Submerged: 130 tonnes (127 tons)

Dimensions (length/beam/draught): 19.8m x
3.6m x 3m (65ft x 11ft 10in x 9ft 10in)

Commissioned: July 1904

Armament: One 457mm (18in) torpedo tube

▲ Hajen

Swedish Navy, coastal submarine, 1900s

Hajen was in essence a Holland boat whose designer, Carl Richson, had studied submarine building in the United States.
Two reload torpedoes could be carried, and two similar boats were built in 1909. In 1916, Hajen was given diesel engines,
and a deck platform to raise the minimal bridge structure. Decommissioned in 1922, it is kept as a museum boat.

Specifications

Crew: 29

Powerplant: Two-shaft diesel engines; electric
motors

Max Speed: Surfaced: 13 knots; Submerged:
8 knots

Surface Range: 3150km (1700nm) at 10 knots

Displacement: Surfaced: 403 tonnes (397 tons);
Submerged: 560 tonnes (551 tons)

Dimensions (length/beam/draught): 52.1m x
5.14m x 3.1m (170ft 11in x 17ft 9in x 10ft 2in)

Commissioned: August 1911

Armament: Six 450mm (17.7in) torpedo tubes

▲ Frimaire

French Navy, patrol submarine, World War I

Possession of a shallow keel prevented the Brumaire-class submarines from
excessive rolling, but they were difficult to operate in anything other than a calm
sea. They had limited success in warfare, though *Bernouilli* penetrated the naval
base at Cattaro and torpedoed an Austrian destroyer. Three were lost in 1914–18.

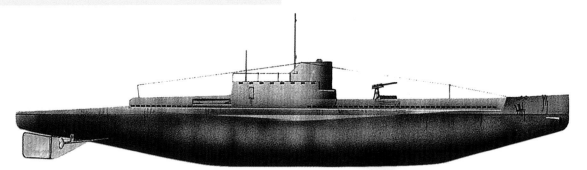

▲ Gustave Zédé

French Navy, patrol submarine, 1914

With eight torpedo tubes, *Gustave Zédé* was well armed for a 1914 submarine.
The deck gun was a wartime addition. The two reciprocating steam engines
developed 1640hp (1223kW). They were oil-fired, enabling rapid shutdown on
diving. Steam could be retained in the two boilers for a surface restart.

Specifications

Crew: 32

Powerplant: Twin screw reciprocating engines;
electric motors

Max Speed: Surfaced: 9.2 knots; Submerged:
6.5 knots

Surface Range: 2660km (1433nm) at 10 knots

Displacement: Surfaced: 862 tonnes (849 tons);
Submerged: 1115 tonnes (1098 tons)

Dimensions (length/beam/draught): 74m x 6m x
3.7m (242ft 9in x 19ft 8in x 12ft 2in)

Commissioned: May 1913

Armament: Eight 450mm (17.7in) torpedo tubes

class, of which *Frimaire*, launched in 1911, was one of the first. Active in the Mediterranean throughout the war, it was stricken in 1923. The most unusual feature of the class was its lack of a conning-tower, which gave it a minimal surface profile but also made it very 'wet' and restricted the range of vision. Essentially it was a torpedo-boat hull with capacity for brief submergence.

Although by 1914 diesel fuel, far less flammable than petrol, was becoming standard, experimentation with steam turbines continued, partly through the quest for speed and partly because early diesel engines

lacked power and reliability. The second *Gustave Zédé*, completed in 1914, could make 10 knots on the surface, but its reciprocating steam turbines were exchanged in 1921–22 for German diesels cannibalized from *U-165*. It followed what was to be the standard submarine design, with a conning tower, and a 75mm (3in) gun on the foredeck.

Germany and Austria-Hungary

The Imperial German Navy had 30 U-boats in service at the start of the war. The first U-boat came into service in 1906, and *U-1* had the double hull

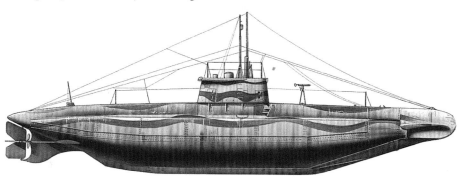

Specifications

Crew: 14	Submerged: 144 tonnes (142 tons)
Powerplant: Single screw; diesel/electric motors	Dimensions (length/beam/draught): 28m x 2.9m
Max Speed: Surfaced: 6.5 knots; Submerged:	x 3m (92ft 3in x 9ft 9in x 10ft)
5.5 knots	Commissioned: April 1915
Surface Range: 2778km (1599nm) at 5 knots	Armament: Two 457mm (18in) torpedo tubes
Displacement: Surfaced: 129 tonnes (127 tons);	

▲ **UB-4**

Imperial German Navy, coastal submarine, North and Adriatic Seas, 1914

Built and then disassembled in sections, these compact vessels were transported by rail to their base-ports, reassembled and put on active service. Most worked in the North Sea from German-held Antwerp, or from Pola on the Adriatic. Four of the eight UB-4 class were lost in the war.

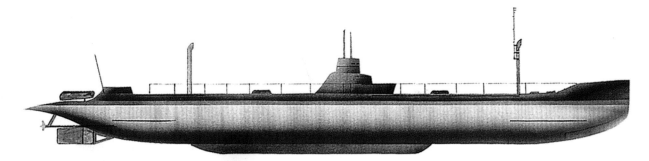

Specifications

Crew: 22	Displacement: Surfaced: 241 tonnes (238 tons);
Powerplant: Twin screws; heavy oil	Submerged: 287 tonnes (283 tons)
(kerosene)/electric motors	Dimensions (length/beam/draught): 42.4m x
Max Speed: Surfaced: 10.8 knots; Submerged:	3.8m x 3.2m (139ft x 12ft 6in x 10ft 6in)
8.7 knots	Commissioned: August 1906
Surface Range: 2850km (1536nm) at 10 knots	Armament: One 450mm (17.7in) torpedo tube

▲ **U-1**

Imperial German Navy, coastal submarine, North Sea, 1915

Designed by Krupps, *U-1* was an improved version of their Karp- and Forelle-type submarines sold to Russia in 1904. Trim tanks were fitted, as well as the Körting kerosene engines (which had the disadvantage of not being reversible). The profile clearly shows the torpedo-boat ancestry of submarines of this period.

and twin screws that would be typical of twentieth-century German submarines. It had only a single torpedo tube. *U-1* served throughout the war, but as a training and test boat only. Some German boats ran on petrol or kerosene at first, but diesel engines were introduced from 1908.

Like other navies, the German *Marinamt* initially saw submarines as short-range craft, with the North Sea as the prime theatre of operation. None of the early U-boat classes numbered more than four, and the U-31 class, introduced in 1913, was the first to number more than 10. By this time, intensive future planning was going on but the work was going into the UB-class, developed from 1914 and intended for coastal and short-range operations – it would be deployed in the North Sea, the Mediterranean-Adriatic and the Black Sea – and the UC-class, intended for minelaying.

The war-plan for Germany's U-boats was that they should be distributed in flotillas of 12, with each responsible for a 96.6km (60-mile) wide front. Kiel was the prime base. One flotilla at sea would patrol the Heligoland Bight, while a second would act as relief. Another flotilla would guard the approaches to Kiel, and a fourth, based at Emden, would undertake longer-range patrols using 'overseas boats'. A fifth flotilla would be held at Kiel as a reserve force. But the numbers available in August 1914 fell far short of what the plan required.

The Austro-Hungarian Empire had six submarines in 1914, numbered German-style as *U-1* to *U-6*. All were built in 1909–11 and were based at Adriatic ports, with Pola serving as the prime base; all would see action in the Adriatic. Austria also had the world's first torpedo factory, the Whitehead works at Fiume, but long before 1914, Whitehead (a British engineer-entrepreneur) had established works in both Britain and France.

Great Britain

By the start of World War I, the Royal Navy had 87 submarines in service, the largest fleet of all. The pioneer class were the A-boats of 1902, and the 11-strong B-class followed in 1904. They were fitted with two 457mm (18in) torpedo tubes. The C-class of 19 boats followed in 1906–10. Britain did not wholly dispense with petrol engines until 1913, and it was reported that all RN petrol submarines carried a cage of white mice, whose squeaks would give warning against escaping fumes.

The form of things to come was established by the eight D-class boats built between 1908 and 1912, with diesel engines and a range of 4630km (2880 miles). Radio was a standard fitment for the first time on a British submarine, using a retractable aerial attached to the conning tower mast.

In 1913, the E-class, which was perhaps the Royal Navy's most successful World War I submarine, was

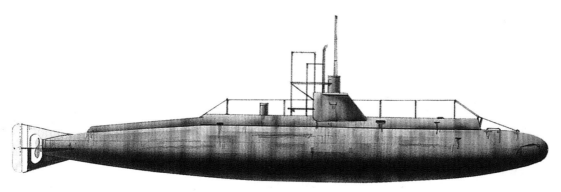

▲ B-1

Royal Navy, coastal submarine, Baltic and Dardanelles, 1914–15

The B-class were first intended to be stationed at Dover for Channel defence, though draft war plans also envisaged operations in the Baltic. By 1914 they were really obsolete, but saw active war service as far afield as the Dardanelles. Note the small hydroplanes fitted to the conning tower sides.

Specifications

Crew: 16

Powerplant: Single screw petrol engine, one electric motor

Max Speed: Surfaced: 13 knots; Submerged: 7 knots

Surface Range: 2779km (1500nm) at 8 knots

Displacement: Surfaced: 284 tonnes (280 tons); Submerged: 319 tonnes (314 tons)

Dimensions (length/beam/draught): 41m x 4.1m x 3m (135ft x 13ft 6in x 9ft 10in)

Commissioned: October 1904

Armament: Two 475mm (18in) torpedo tubes

introduced. Diesel-powered, and based on the D-class, this was a substantially larger and more formidable craft than its predecessors, displacing 677 tonnes (667 tons) on the surface and 820 tonnes (807 tons) submerged, and with five 457mm (18in) torpedo tubes and a 12-pounder deck gun. (The first eight, *E-1* to *E-7* plus two built for the Royal Australian Navy, *AE-1* and *AE-2*, had only four tubes and no deck gun.) A total of 55 were built, at 12 different yards, including

six adapted as minelayers. Various modifications were introduced up to the completion of *E-56* in June 1916, including more powerful electric motors, giving a marginally increased submerged speed of 10 knots compared to 9.5.

In 1914, British submarines were deployed in eight flotillas of unequal numbers: Flotilla No. 1 at Devonport had two boats; No. 2 at Portsmouth had four; Nos. 3 and 4, both at Dover, had six and eight

▲ **C-25**

Royal Navy, patrol submarine, North Sea, 1918

The C was the first large British class, with 37 boats in service by 1910. They were mostly deployed in the North Sea and English Channel, in the hope of intercepting U-boats in transit to the Atlantic, or engaged in minelaying. *C3* was packed with explosive and blown up as part of the operation to block the German base at Zeebrugge, on 23 April 1918.

Specifications

Crew: 16	Displacement: Surfaced: 295 tonnes (290 tons);
Powerplant: Single screw petrol engine; one	Submerged: 325 tonnes (320 tons)
electric motor	Dimensions (length/beam/draught): 43m x 4m x
Max Speed: Surfaced: 12 knots; Submerged:	3.5m (141ft x 13ft 1in x 11ft 4in)
7.5 knots	Commissioned: 1909
Surface Range: 2414km (1431nm) at 8 knots	Armament: Two 457mm (18in) torpedo tubes

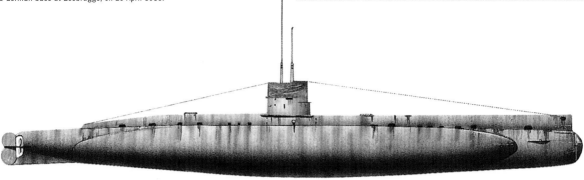

Specifications

Crew: 25	Submerged: 604 tonnes (595 tons)
Powerplant: Twin screw diesel engines; electric	Dimensions (length/beam/draught): 50m x 6m x
motors	3m (163ft x 20ft 6in x 10ft 5in)
Max Speed: Surfaced: 14 knots; Submerged:	Commissioned: August 1908
9 knots	Armament: Three 457mm (18in) torpedo tubes,
Surface Range: 2038km (1100nm) at 10 knots	one 12-pounder gun
Displacement: Surfaced: 490 tonnes (483 tons);	

▲ **D-1**

Royal Navy, patrol submarine, North Sea, 1916

D-class boats could transmit by radio as well as receive. External ballast tanks gave improved buoyancy, and battery capacity enabled them to remain submerged through the daylight hours. D-1 'torpedoed' two cruisers during a 1910 naval exercise, helping to convince the Royal Navy of the offensive power of submarines.

respectively; No. 5, at The Nore, had six; No. 6 on the Humber had six; No. 7 had three boats on the Tyne and three at Leith; No. 8, at Harwich, had 19, including all the newest and largest.

A further five flotillas and numerous additional bases would be added in the course of the war, but this disposition clearly shows the great majority of Royal Navy submarines placed to counter any venture by the German Navy across the North Sea towards British shores. As with France, some boats were deployed to colonial stations. Six of the B-class

boats were sent to Gibraltar and Malta in 1906, and in 1910 six of the C-class were towed to Hong Kong. In August 1914, three of these were still with the China Squadron.

Italy

The Italian Navy had only one submarine in 1900, but, spurred on by developments in France, submarine construction started from around 1904, using Italian-originated designs and concentrating on the small boats that would be most useful around the

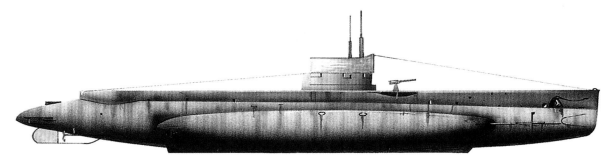

Specifications	
Crew: 30	Displacement: Surfaced: 677 tonnes (667 tons);
Powerplant: Two twin-shaft diesel engines; two	Submerged: 820 tonnes (807 tons)
electric motors	Dimensions (length/beam/draught): 55.17m x
Max Speed: Surfaced: 14 knots; Submerged:	6.91m x 3.81m (181ft x 22ft 8in x 12ft 6in)
9 knots	Commissioned: 1913
Surface Range: 6035km (3579nm)	Armament: Five 457mm (18in) torpedo tubes;
	one 12-pounder gun

▲ **E-11**

Royal Navy, patrol submarine, Baltic Sea, Dardanelles, 1915

In October 1914, *E-11* failed to gain entry to the Kattegat, but in August 1915, during a 29-day patrol in the Dardanelles and the Sea of Marmara, it sank the Turkish battleship *Barvarousse Haireddine*, a gunboat, seven transports and 23 sailing craft. The smaller vessels were sunk using the newly fitted deck gun.

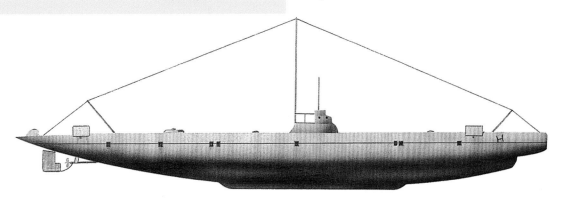

▲ **Fisalia**

Italian Navy, patrol submarine, Adriatic, World War I

Fisalia was one of the first of a class of eight boats that were among the first Italian submarines to have diesel engines. They were good sea boats with excellent manoeuvrability. *Fisalia* served in the Adriatic during World War I.

Specifications	
Crew: 40	Displacement: Surfaced: 256 tonnes (252 tons);
Powerplant: Twin screw diesel engines; electric	Submerged: 310 tonnes (305 tons)
motors	Dimensions (length/beam/draught): 45m x 4.2m
Max Speed: Surfaced: 12 knots; Submerged:	x 3m (148ft 2in x 13ft 9in x 9ft 10in)
8 knots	Commissioned: February 1912
Surface Range: Not known	Armament: Two 450mm (17.7in) torpedo tubes

BRITISH SUBMARINE CLASSES 1914–18, PRE-WAR BUILD			
Class	Number	Launched	Note
A	10	1903–05	
B	10	1904–06	
C	41	1906–10	
D	8	1908–11	First GB diesel-engined
E	11	1911–14	
V	1	1914	

BRITISH SUBMARINE CLASSES 1914–18, WARTIME BUILD			
Class	Number	Launched	Note
E	40	1914–18	
S	3	1914–15	Trans to Italy Oct 1915
V	2	1915	
W	4	1914–15	Trans to Italy Aug 1916
F	3	1915–16	
G	14	1916–17	
J	7	1915–17	Trans to Australia; 1 sank
K	17	1916–17	
M	3	1917–18	
H	43	1915–19	
L	32	1917–18	
R	10	1918	First 'hunter-killer' sub

Italian coast and in the inlets of the Adriatic. The first Italian class was named after the lead boat *Glauco* in 1905 and five were built between 1905 and 1909. Italy began to build diesel/electric powered submarines with the eight boats of the Medusa class, including *Fisalia*, in 1910–12.

By 1914, there were 20 boats in Italy's submarine squadron, including the pioneer *Delfino* of 1892. Also there were two experimental midget submarines of the Alfa class, built in 1913. They did not last beyond 1916, but the Italian Navy retained an interest in midget craft and built more from 1915. In the course of the war its prime adversary was the Austro-Hungarian fleet in the Adriatic. Intended for inshore and shallow-sea service, Italy's World War I submarines, though effective, were quite small. The most effective boats in 1914 were *Nereide* and *Nautilus*; *Nereide* was sunk in the Adriatic on 5 August 1915 by the Austrian *U-5*.

Japan and Russia

Japan and Russia had fought a naval war in 1904–05 and although submarines did not play a significant part, the war stimulated the interest of both navies in submarines as anti-warship and coastal defence units. Imperial Japan's first submarine squadron consisted of six small submarines of the American Holland type and a Japanese variant. Intended for coastal work,

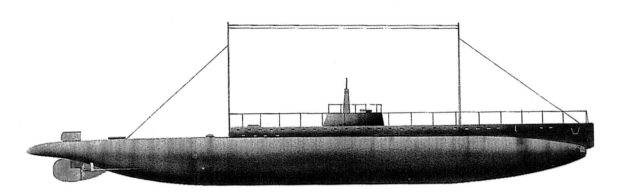

▲ Nereide

Italian Navy, patrol submarine, Adriatic, 1915

Nereide was designed by Curio Bernardis, whose influence on Italian submarine design was to be very strong. A deck-mounted third torpedo tube, though part of the design, was not installed. Despite a reputation for efficiency, *Nereide*'s war record appears to have been uneventful until its fatal duel with *U-5*.

Specifications

Crew: 35

Powerplant: Twin screws; diesel/electric motors

Max Speed: Surfaced: 13.2 knots; Submerged: 8 knots

Surface Range: 7412km (4000nm) at 10 knots

Displacement: Surfaced: 228 tonnes (225 tons);

Submerged: 325 tonnes (320 tons)

Dimensions (length/beam/draught): 40m x 4.3m x 2.8m (134ft 2in x 14ft 1in x 9ft 2in)

Commissioned: July 1913

Armament: Two 450mm (17in) torpedo tubes

they played no part in oceanic operations. In 1914, the Japanese had 12 submarines, of which the largest were five C1-C2 Vickers class boats, built in 1909–11, displacing from 295 to 325 tonnes (290 to 320 tons) on the surface, with two 457mm (18in) torpedo tubes. The others were considerably smaller. Japan's submarine base was the Kure naval yard on the Inland Sea.

In the later nineteenth century, Russia's Tsarist government had taken a keen interest in submarines, with a view to the protection of naval harbours. In 1914, Imperial Russia had between 30 and 40 small submarines on active duty, with a maximum range of around 241km (150 miles), based at Baltic and Black Sea ports. Most had been purchased from the United States, Britain, France and Germany, although some were built in Russian yards.

In the Baltic Sea, Russia had 11 submarines in 1914, organized in three divisions: two active, with four boats each; and one for training. Of these, only one, the one-off *Akula* of 1908, was really capable of longer-range missions.

United States

In the early twentieth century, the designer John Holland had given the United States a world lead in submarine design, but by 1917 several European fleets could boast submarines of greater performance and endurance than the United States possessed. In April 1917, when it entered the war against Germany, the United States had 12 classes of submarine and a total of 42 boats. *Grayling*, one of three D-class boats built in 1909–10, was petrol-engined, with four 457mm (18in) torpedo tubes.

America's first diesel-powered submarine was *E-1*, commissioned at Groton in February 1912. The US Navy was to make relatively little use of its submarines in the war; their operational range was limited and the Navy, mistakenly, did not anticipate hostile action close to the American coast. Grayling was in service until 1922.

The E- and F-classes of 1911–12 were diesel-engined with four torpedo tubes; all were re-engineered in 1915. *F-4* sank in March 1915 off Pearl Harbor, but the wreck was successfully salvaged from 91m (299ft) in a pioneering deep-water retrieval operation.

Limitations

The submarines of 1914 had many shortcomings. Perhaps the most serious was their lack of punch. The 457mm (18in) torpedo would not penetrate the armour plating of a Dreadnought-type battleship, though it could and did sink armoured cruisers and pre-Dreadnoughts. The torpedo stock was limited, and with only one or two forward-facing tubes, a destructive salvo could not be fired. Their speed was slow on the surface and even slower under water. This prevented them from keeping up with surface ships, whether friendly or hostile. Their low silhouettes,

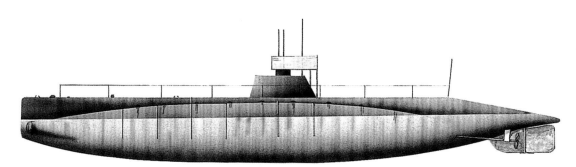

▲ USS Grayling

US Navy, patrol submarine, Atlantic, 1917–18

Grayling was flagboat of Submarine Division 3 of the Atlantic Fleet in 1910. It and the other D-class boats were used in offshore patrols on the east coast, but had no success in intercepting the long-range U-boats that appeared late in the war. On 14 September 1917 it sank at the dock but was lifted and remained in commission until 1922.

Specifications

Crew: 15	Displacement: Surfaced: 292 tonnes (288 tons);
Powerplant: Two twin screw petrol engines; two	Submerged: 342 tonnes (337 tons)
electric motors	Dimensions (length/beam/draught): 41m x 4.2m
Max Speed: Surfaced: 12 knots; Submerged:	x 3.6m (135ft x 13ft 9in x 12ft)
9.5 knots	Commissioned: June 1909
Surface Range: 2356km (1270nm) at 10 knots	Armament: Four 457mm (18in) torpedo tubes

while making them hard to detect on the surface, had the disadvantages of making them hard to steer and navigate in anything other than calm conditions, and of making them susceptible to accidental ramming by ships that had simply failed to notice them. Many had only the most rudimentary kind of bridge structure. Their small size and limited space restricted the amount of stores that could be carried. Their capacity for underwater navigation and manoeuvre was very limited. Nevertheless they had the huge advantage of stealth. In 1914, there was no way of detecting a submerged submarine. It was a completely new piece on the chessboard of naval war, and it did not conform to the old rules.

At international conferences between 1899 and 1907, certain rules of naval warfare had been agreed by the European powers. A warship encountering an enemy merchant vessel was expected to seize it as a 'prize' and sink it only as a last resort. Its crew should be taken prisoner. A neutral vessel suspected of carrying war goods to the enemy should be stopped, searched and seized in the same way if its cargo was suspect. This protocol, going back to the days of sail, took no account of the way in which a submarine was organized and managed.

The capacity to attack from a submerged position was the whole point. To surface and investigate was

▲ **Royal Navy E-class**

Submarines travelled on the surface whenever possible and consequently, for many years, surface performance was given priority in design.

to invite retaliation from an armed merchantman; or, quite possibly faster than the submarine, it could just zig-zag away. Also, a submarine had no space whatsoever for holding prisoners. These were some of the reasons why admirals decided to discount or ignore the potential of the submarine as a commerce raider, and to see it as part of the defensive line against hostile warships.

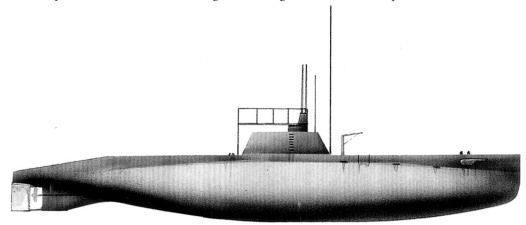

Specifications

Crew: 35	Submerged: 406 tonnes (400 tons)
Powerplant: Twin screw diesels; electric motors	Dimensions (length/beam/draught): 43.5m x
Max Speed: Surfaced: 13.5 knots; Submerged:	4.7m x 3.7m (142ft 9in x 15ft 5in x 12ft 2in)
5 knots	Commissioned: January 1912
Surface Range: 4260km (2300nm) at 11 knots	Armament: Four torpedo tubes
Displacement: Surfaced: 335 tonnes (330 tons);	

▲ **F 4**

US Navy, F-class coastal submarine, Pacific Fleet, 1914

F-4, originally to be named Skate, was launched in January 1912. From August 1914 it was attached to the First Submarine Group, Pacific Torpedo Flotilla. The cause of its disastrous dive was tentatively suggested as seepage of seawater into the battery compartment, causing power failure and loss of control.

Operations in European seas
1914–18

Much submarine action went on in the seas around the European continent, in particular the Baltic Sea, North Sea and Mediterranean.

IN THE BATLIC SEA submarines played a key strategic role for a time, and in the Dardanelles they participated effectively in the first big combined military operation.

Baltic Sea

Danzig (now Gdansk) was a German city in 1913 when the four boats of the U-19 class were completed there. *U-21* of this class was the first submarine to sink a ship with a self-propelling torpedo, when it hit the cruiser HMS *Pathfinder* on 5 September 1914. A new armament variation was to adapt a submarine to lay mines off an enemy harbour or across a shipping route.

The German Navy constructed several specialized submarines with vertical mine-launching tubes through their hulls: *UC-74*, launched in October 1917, was one of six. In 1918 it was transferred to the Austrian Navy for Adriatic operations against Italy but kept its German crew; the others in the class served in the North Sea and the Baltic; only two survived the war. Eighteen mines were carried, and the class also had three 508mm (20in) torpedo tubes and a 86mm (3.4in) deck gun.

GERMAN SUBMARINE CLASSES 1914–18, PRE-WAR BUILD			
Class	Number	Launched	Note
U1	1	1906	Petrol engine
U2	1	1908	Petrol engine
U3	2	1909	Petrol engine
U5	4	1910	Petrol engine
U9	4	1910–11	Petrol engine
U13	3	1910–11	Petrol engine
U16	1	1911	Petrol engine
U17	2	1912	Petrol engine
U19	4	1912–13	Diesel; ocean-going
U23	4	1913	Diesel; ocean-going
U27	4	1913	Diesel; ocean-going
U31	11	1913	Diesel; ocean-going

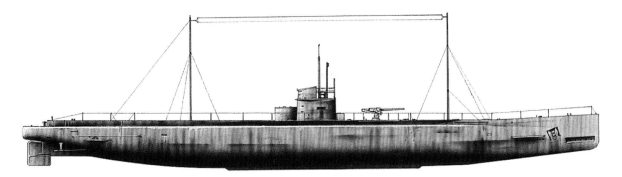

Specifications

Crew: 35

Powerplant: Two shafts; diesel/electric motors

Max Speed: Surfaced: 15.4 knots; Submerged: 9.5 knots

Surface Range: 9265km (5500nm) at 10 knots

Displacement: Surfaced: 660 tonnes (650 tons);

Submerged: 850 tonnes (837 tons)

Dimensions (length/beam/draught): 64.2m x 6.1m x 3.5m (210ft 6in x 20ft x 11ft 9in)

Commissioned: February 1913

Armament: Four 508mm (20in) torpedo tubes; one 86mm (3.4in) gun

▲ **U-21**

Imperial German Navy, patrol submarine, Mediterranean, 1916

One of the most successful World War I U-boats, *U-21* was unusual in having a single captain, Otto Hersing, throughout the war. It returned from its Mediterranean exploits to rejoin the High Seas Fleet at Kiel in March 1917. It foundered in the North Sea on 22 February 1919 while being towed to Britain to be handed over.

In the course of the war, the majority of new British submarines were built for open-sea work, but a small class of coastal submarines was built in 1913–15 as the F-class, and used extensively on coastal patrols. A second batch was cancelled in 1914, in favour of the longer-range E-class boats. *F-1* had a short service life, being broken up in 1920.

In October 1914, three British E-boats were dispatched to the Baltic and two got through, to support the Russians against the German Baltic Fleet. In August to September, four more were sent (one lost on the way), and four C-class boats were towed to

Archangel and delivered to the Baltic via canal barges. Originally intended to hinder German landing operations, they also were used to prevent shipments of iron ore from neutral Sweden to Germany. The E-boats were armed with five 457mm (18in) torpedo tubes plus a 5.4kg (12-pounder) deck gun. They had good surface speed, but their wireless sets had limited range and their captains had to rely on carrier pigeons while on remote patrols. The E-boats were also much less reliable than their German equivalents.

The British flotilla was based at Reval (now Tallinn) and its presence in the Baltic intimidated the

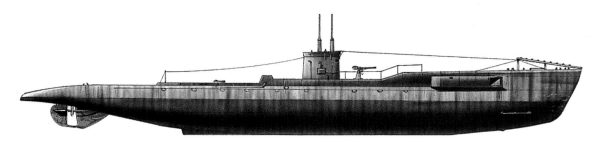

Specifications

Crew: 26

Powerplant: Two-shafts; diesel/electric motors

Max Speed: Surfaced: 11.8 knots; Submerged: 7.3 knots

Surface Range: 18,520km (10,000nm) at 10 knots

Displacement: Surfaced: 416 tonnes (410 tons); Submerged: 500 tonnes (492 tons)

Dimensions (length/beam/draught): 50.6m x 5.1m x 3.6m ((166ft x 17ft x 12ft)

Commissioned: October 1916

Armament: Three 508mm (20in) torpedo tubes; one 86mm (3.4in) gun; 18 mines

▲ UC-74

Imperial German Navy, minelayer, Adriatic, World War I

The mine-tubes were set in the forward part of the hull, below the raised fairing. The boat's Austrian service was arranged to assist the Austrian fleet even though Germany and Italy were not in a state of war at the time. At the end of the war, *UC-74* was ceded to France and was scrapped in 1921.

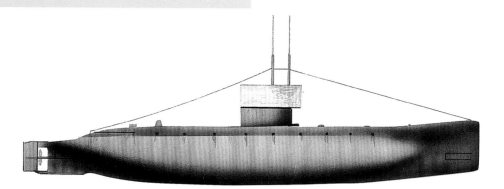

▲ F-1

Royal Navy, F-class coastal submarine, 1915

The three F-class were double-hulled. Diving depth was 30m (99ft). It does not seem that any was fitted with a deck gun, probably because of their small size and limited crew number. With limited endurance and offensive power, they were used only for inshore patrols, and no major encounters are recorded. All were broken up by 1922.

Specifications

Crew: 20

Powerplant: Twin screw diesel engines; electric motors

Max Speed: Surfaced: 14 knots; Submerged: 8.7 knots

Surface Range: 5556km (3000nm) at 9 knots

Displacement: Surfaced: 368 tonnes (363 tons); Submerged: 533 tonnes (525 tons)

Dimensions (length/beam/draught): 46m x 4.9m x 3.2m (151ft x 16ft x 10ft 6in)

Commissioned: March 1915

Armament: Three 457mm (18in) torpedo tubes

Germans, who quickly organized convoys to protect merchantmen. German propaganda blasted 'British pirate submarines' in the Baltic, just as British newspapers did about the U-boats in the North Sea. However, until well into 1915, all the sinkings of German vessels in the Baltic were due to mines.

The E-boats began to show more results in the summer of 1915. On 19 August, *E-1* fired a torpedo into the cruiser *Moltke*, and although it failed to sink it, the Germans abandoned their planned occupation

of Riga. By September, there were five E-boats in Baltic waters.

In October, *E-8* sank the German cruiser *Prinz Adelbert*, already damaged in July by *E-9*, and in the next month *E-19* sank the light cruiser *Undine*. Tight defence of the Kattegat eventually kept the E-boats at bay, except for those already in the Baltic. When Russia signed a peace treaty with Germany in 1918, four British E-class and three C-class submarines were scuttled by their crews off Helsinki.

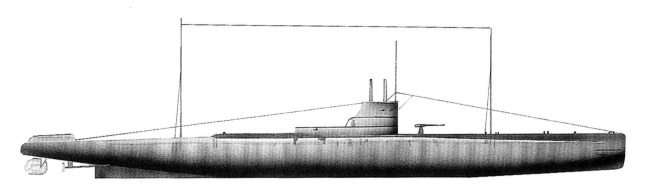

▲ **G-1**

Royal Navy, patrol submarine, North Sea, 1915–18

In autumn 1915, a new flotilla of G- and E-class boats was formed at Blyth, Northumberland, to operate with units of the Grand Fleet, but their slow speed made this an impossible project. *G-7* was the last British submarine lost in World War I, failing to return from a North Sea patrol on 1 November 1918.

Specifications

Crew: 31

Powerplant: Twin screw diesel; electric motors

Max Speed: Surfaced: 14.25 knots; Submerged: 9 knots

Surface Range: 4445km (2400nm) at 12.5 knots

Displacement: Surfaced: 704 tonnes (693 tons); Submerged: 850 tonnes (836 tons)

Dimensions (length/beam/draught): 57m x 6.9m x 4.1m (187ft x 22ft x 13ft 6in)

Commissioned: August 1915

Armament: Four 457mm (18in) torpedo tubes; one 533mm (21in) torpedo tube; one 76mm (3in) gun

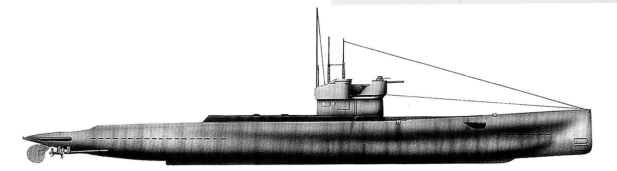

Specifications

Crew: 44

Powerplant: Triple screw diesel; electric motors

Max Speed: Surfaced: 17 knots; Submerged: 9.5 knots

Surface Range: 9500km (5120nm) at 12.5 knots

Displacement: Surfaced: 1223 tonnes (1204 tons); Submerged: 1849 tonnes (1820 tons)

Dimensions (length/beam/draught): 84m x 7m x 4.3m (275ft 7in x 23ft x 14ft)

Commissioned: November 1915

Armament: Six 457mm (18in) torpedo tubes; one 76mm (3in) gun

▲ **J-1**

Royal Navy, fast submarine, 1918

With three 12-cylinder diesel engines, producing 3600hp (2685kW), this was the Royal Navy's most powerful submarine yet, although its speed was not enough to keep up with the Fleet. The J-class also had better sea endurance than previous British classes. After the war, the six surviving boats were passed on to the Royal Australian Navy.

The Dardanelles, May 1915 to January 1916

The Gallipoli campaign, centred on the Dardanelles Straits, was the first major naval campaign in which submarines played an active supporting role. French and British, and one Australian, contended with U-boats and surface vessels. The first British boats despatched were five B-class, too small and underpowered to be really effective in the powerful currents, though *B-11* sank the Turkish battleship *Messoudieh* in December 1915; they were followed by five E-class boats plus the Australian Navy's *AE-2*. Four French submarines also took part. The disastrous Allied campaign ended in January 1916, when the British withdrew their forces.

The activities of Allied submarines were a bright spot in the dismal story, though all four French and four British submarines were lost in the effort. However, they had sunk seven Turkish warships, 16 transports and supply ships, plus 230 steamers and small vessels.

On the other side, *U-21* sank HMS *Triumph* off Anzac Bay on 25 May 1915, and another battleship, HMS *Majestic*, two days later. *U-21*'s feat in voyaging from Kiel to Pola without refuelling was remarkable. *U-21* joined the German U-boat flotilla based at Cattaro (now Kotor) on the Adriatic, in July 1915. On 8 February 1916 it sank a French armoured cruiser off the Syrian coast.

U-21 survived the war, having sunk some 40 Allied ships. *UB-14*, notionally transferred to the Austrian Navy but with an all-German crew, was, like other UB- and UC-boats, transported overland in sections to Pola, and in a highly successful career sank numerous merchant ships. It took HMS *E-20* by surprise on 6 November 1915, surfacing and sinking the British submarine with a single torpedo fired from 500m (547yds), in one of the few sub-versus-sub engagements to occur in the first years of the war.

North Sea

Perhaps one of the most famous and effective actions by a U-boat occurred in the North Sea in the first few months of the war. The British Admiralty sought to keep the German High Seas Fleet bottled up in its ports, which required an aggressive deployment of cruisers and light warships in the North Sea. Cruiser Force C, consisting of HMS *Aboukir*, HMS *Hogue* and HMS *Cressy*, were sent out on patrol, as part of this strategy. All the cruisers were at least 10 years old and obsolete, even by the standards of 1914.

On 22 September 1914 the fleet was spotted by *U-9*, one of the fastest and most advanced submarine types of its time. The slow-moving cruisers presented an easy target and each was sunk in turn by torpedo within the space of just an hour. The action proved the effectiveness of the new U-boats against slow-moving cruisers.

Despite their early successes, the North Sea became increasingly difficult for U-boats to traverse. The British *E-9* sank the German light cruiser *Hela* and the German destroyer *S-116* in the North Sea in mid-September 1914. Though the German High

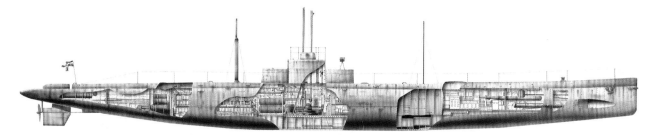

▲ U-9

Imperial German Navy, patrol submarine, 1914

U-9 had four Körting kerosene engines, which tended to make smoke and required a dismountable funnel. This was the first submarine on which the torpedo tubes were successfully reloaded while the boat was submerged. Its despatch of the British cruisers on 22 September 1914 with its six torpedoes demonstrated early in the war the power of the type.

Specifications

Crew: 29	601 tons
Powerplant: Four kerosene engines; electric motors	Dimensions (length/beam/draught): 57.3m
Max Speed: Surfaced: 26.3 km/h (14.2 knots);	(188ft) x 6m (19.7ft) x 3.5m (11.5ft)
Submerged: 14.8km/h (8.0kn)	Commissioned: April 1910
Surface Range: 6216km (3356nm) at	Armament: four 45cm (17.7in) torpedo tubes
15.9km/h (8.6 knots)	(two bow, two stern); six torpedoes; 1 x 37mm
Displacement: Surface: 425 tons; Submerged:	(1.46in) deck gun

Seas Fleet made plans for drawing the British Grand Fleet within range of its submarine squadrons, the only major naval battle of the war, in the North Sea off Jutland in May 1916, did not involve submarines on either side.

In the last year of the war there were fierce struggles between German destroyers and British submarines in the North Sea, with merchant convoys between Britain and Scandinavia as the target or protectee. L-class submarines played a large part. *L-10* sank the German destroyer *S-33* on 3 October 1918 just before being sunk by other German vessels.

Mediterranean

By a pre-war agreement with the British, the French fleet operated largely in the Mediterranean, where French submarines had relatively few opportunities to show their prowess. Small numbers of kills were scored in the Adriatic by the Italian submarines against the Austrians, though Austrian and German U-boats scored kills of their own in return.

Balilla, built in Italy for the German Navy and intended as *U-42*, was taken over by the Italians in 1915, but sunk in the Adriatic on 14 July 1916 after attack by Austrian torpedo boats. It was in the

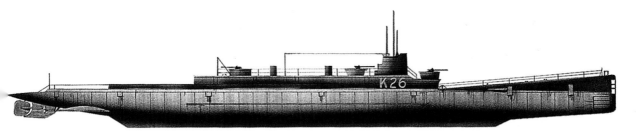

▲ K-Class

Royal Navy, fleet submarine, 1919

The product of the British Admiralty's desire to have a submarine that could keep up with battle-cruisers, the K-class was undoubtedly fast but had few other positive features. They were deployed in two fleet flotillas from 1917, intended to get between an enemy fleet and its base, but they were never engaged in combat.

Specifications

Crew: 40	Displacement: Surfaced: 2174 tonnes (2140
Powerplant: Twin screw; steam turbines; electric	tons); Submerged: 2814 tonnes (2770 tons)
motors	Dimensions (length/beam/draught): 100.6m x
Max Speed: Surfaced: 23 knots; Submerged:	8.1m x 5.2m (330ft x 26ft 7in x 17ft)
9 knots	Commissioned: 1916
Surface Range: 5556km (3000nm) at 13.5 knots	Armament: 10 533mm (21in) torpedo tubes;
	three 102mm (4in) guns

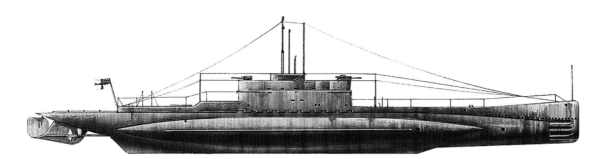

Specifications

Crew: 36	Submerged: 1097 tonnes (1080 tons)
Powerplant: Twin screw diesel; electric motors	Dimensions (length/beam/draught): 72.7m x
Max Speed: Surfaced: 17.5 knots; Submerged:	7.2m x 3.4m (238ft 6in x 23ft 8in x 11ft 2in)
10.5 knots	Commissioned: 1918
Surface Range: 7038km (3800nm) at 10 knots	Armament: Four 533mm (21in) torpedo tubes;
Displacement: Surfaced: 904 tonnes (890 tons);	one 102mm (4in) gun

▲ L-Class

Royal Navy, patrol submarine, 1918

The first L-class boats had 457mm (18in) torpedo tubes but later ones had 533mm (21in) tubes. These were the Royal Navy's largest patrol submarines, though still of relatively modest size. Introduced late in the war, most served on through the 1920s, and three survived as training boats to 1946.

Austrian-Italian submarine war that aerial spotting of submerged boats first became a regular practice. One of the most effective Italian submarine classes of the war was the F-class of 1916, which was well equipped, with two periscopes and with Fessenden signalling apparatus (like some British submarines, including the K-class), which was capable of sending Morse code messages from under the surface. The F-class was a small submarine with two 450mm (17.7in) torpedo tubes and a 76mm (3in) deck gun, and some actually remained in service into the 1930s.

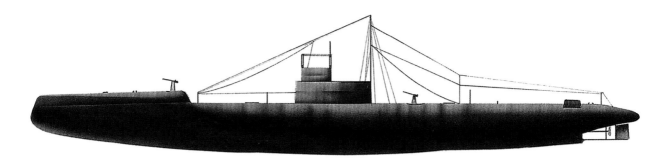

▲ Balilla

Italian Navy, patrol submarine, Adriatic, World War I

The influence of the designer Cesare Laurenti was notable on *Balilla*. Its prominent raised bow casing was unique in its three-strong class; the two sister boats had a flush deck and an additional bow tube. The design was sold to Japan and became the basis of the Japanese Navy's F1- and F2-classes in 1919–21.

Specifications

Crew: 38	Submerged: 890 tonnes (876 tons)
Powerplant: Two-shafts; diesel/electric motors	Dimensions (length/beam/draught): 65m x 6m x
Max Speed: Surfaced: 14 knots; Submerged:	4m (213ft 3in x 19ft 8in x 13ft 1in)
9 knots	Commissioned: August 1913
Surface Range: 7041km (3800nm) at 10 knots	Armament: Four 450mm (17.7in) torpedo tubes;
Displacement: Surfaced: 740 tonnes (728 tons);	two 76mm (3in) guns

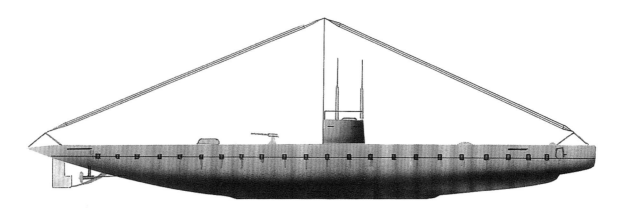

Specifications

Crew: 54	Submerged: 324 tonnes (319 tons)
Powerplant: Twin screw diesel engines; electric	Dimensions (length/beam/draught): 45.6m x
motors	4.2m x 3m (149ft 7in x 13ft 9in x 10ft)
Max Speed: Surfaced: 12.5 knots; Submerged:	Commissioned: April 1916
8.2 knots	Armament: Two 450mm (17.7in) torpedo tubes;
Surface Range: 2963km (1600nm) at 8.5 knots	one 76mm (3in) gun
Displacement: Surfaced: 226 tonnes (262 tons);	

▲ F-1

Italian Navy, patrol submarine, coastal service, World War I

Improved versions of the preceding Medusa class, the 21 F-class boats were built by Fiat-San Giorgio at La Spezia, to a design of Cesare Laurenti, whose consortium with Fiat built submarines for several nations. The 76mm (3in) gun is mounted in an unusual stern-facing position. The F-class served all round the Italian coast.

Operations in the Atlantic
1915–17

By far the most crucial of World War I submarine activities was the long campaign in the Atlantic Ocean by German U-boats against British and Allied merchant ships.

ALTHOUGH HARDLY ANTICIPATED by the German High Command in 1914, the Atlantic campaign was seen by 1917 as a means of achieving victory. The long-range U-boats of 1914 and 1915 were few in number, with only five likely to be on station at any given time. Slow on the surface, with low-calibre guns, they were not well suited to the task of commerce raids on the high seas. Their prime asset was the surprise attack with torpedoes, which was forbidden by international convention.

In February 1915, the German Navy announced a policy of partially unrestricted submarine warfare, claiming it as retaliation for the British blockade of German ports. Rescinded later in the year, the policy was renewed in the spring of 1916 and finally became an unrestricted campaign from 1 February 1917 until the end of the war, involving all shipping in the 'war zone' surrounding the British Isles.

By February 1917, over 110 U-boats could be deployed, 46 of them in the Atlantic, and between then and April 1917, U-boats sank 1,889,847 tonnes (1,860,000 tons) of merchant shipping, for the loss of nine of their own number. British wheat supplies were down to six weeks' worth, and in May and June a further 1,320,860 tonnes (1,300,000 tons) of shipping were sunk. The huge scale of this relentless attrition forced the British to try all sorts of countermeasures, with relatively little success, until the convoy system was adopted from May 1917.

By the autumn of 1917, Germany was losing between six and 10 U-boats a month. In that year, 6,235,878 tons (6,335,944 tonnes) of British, Allied and neutral shipping were sunk by U-boats, almost half the total for the whole war. But in April, the United States had declared war on Germany, and though the U-boats sank another 2,709,738 tonnes (2,666,942 tons) in 1918, the chance of starving Britain into submission had passed by May 1917.

Long-Range Subs

The success of the U-boats in the Atlantic encouraged the German Navy to build large, long-range submarines with powerful guns as well as torpedoes. To avoid British supremacy on the surface, the German Deutschland class of merchant U-boats was also introduced, each 96m (315ft) long with two

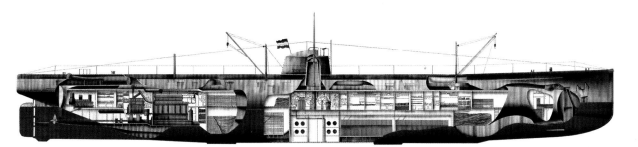

▲ **Deutschland (U-155)**

Imperial German Navy, cargo submarine, Atlantic 1916

The profile shows the boat in its original unarmed mercantile form. Three were built like this and four were converted to combat boats while under construction. An addition of two 148mm (5.9in) deck guns changed the appearance. As *U-155*, this submarine sank 43 ships, with a gross register tonnage of 120,434.

Specifications

Crew: 56

Powerplant: Twin screw diesel engines; electric motors

Max Speed: Surfaced: 12.4 knots; Submerged: 5.2 knots

Surface Range: 20,909km (11,284nm)

Displacement: Surfaced: 1536 tonnes (1512 tons); Submerged: 1905 tonnes (1875 tons)

Dimensions (length/beam/draught): 65m x 8.9m x 5.3m (213ft 3in x 29ft 2in x 17ft 5in)

Commissioned: March 1916

Armament: None

GERMAN SUBMARINE CLASSES 1914–18, WARTIME BUILD			
Class	Number	Launched	Note
U43	8	1914–15	Diesel; ocean-going
UB I	17	1915	Coastal patrol
UC I	15	1915	Coastal minelayer
UB II	30	1915–16	Coastal patrol
U51	6	1915–16	Diesel; ocean-going
UC II	64	1915–17	Coastal minelayer
U57	12	1916	Diesel; ocean-going
U63	3	1916	Diesel; ocean-going
U135	4	1916–18	Diesel; ocean-going
U81	6	1916	Diesel; ocean-going
UE I	10	1916	Ocean minelayer
U87	6	1916–17	Diesel; ocean-going
U151	7	1916–17	'Merchant cruiser'
U139	3	1916–18	'Merchant cruiser'
U93	22	1916–18	Diesel; ocean-going
UC III	16	1916–18	Coastal minelayer
UE II	9	1916–18	Ocean minelayer
UB III	96	1916–19	Coastal patrol
U142	1	1918	'Merchant cruiser'

large cargo compartments. These submarines could carry 700 tonnes (690 tons) of cargo at 12- to 13-knot speeds on the surface and at 7 knots submerged. In June 1916, *Deutschland* made a voyage to the still-neutral United States to load with nickel, tin and rubber.

Deutschland itself became *U-155* when fitted with torpedo tubes and deck guns, and, with seven similar submarines, it served in a combat role during the latter stages of the war. A few made long voyages south to the Azores and the African coast, where they operated generally unmolested against shipping operating in the area, though *U-154* was torpedoed by the British submarine *E-35* off the coast of Portugal in May 1918.

Late in the war, the German High Command decided to take the war to US shores. This required submarines with very long range, which was feasible for the Deutschland class. A purpose-built, long-range naval 'cruiser' design was developed as well,

▼ Deutschland (U-155)

Deutschland's conning tower was quite small and low-set compared with the great bulk of its hull, giving it a low profile on the surface. This was important in its task of evading the British blockade of Germany.

armed with six torpedo tubes and 22 torpedoes, and at least two 150mm (5.9in) deck guns.

One of the most remarkable voyages by a cruiser U-boat began on 14 April 1918, when *U-151* left Kiel to attack shipping along the American Atlantic coast and lay mines off major coastal outlets. The Americans were not expecting trouble off their own shores and had taken no precautions. *U-151* carried on without interference, seizing and sinking three

schooners and laying its remaining mines across Delaware Bay.

It spent three days trawling the sea bottom off New York with a cable-cutter, severing two telegraph lines. On 2 June, *U-151* sank the liner *Carolina*, on its way from Puerto Rico to New York. By this time, there was a degree of panic along the US Eastern Seaboard, but *U-151* safely returned to Kiel on 20 July 1918, after having covered 17,570km (10,915 miles) and

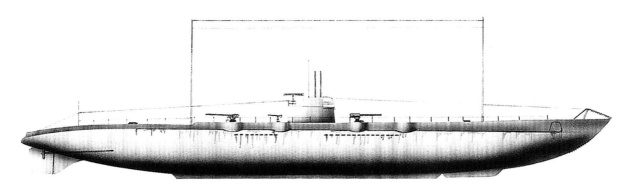

▲ U-139

Imperial German Navy, commerce-raider, Atlantic, 1917

Purpose-built as a cruiser-killer, *U-139* had six torpedo tubes compared to *U-155*'s two, and carried 18 reloads. The deck guns were on barbette-type mountings extending from a central fairing. The command centre in the conning tower was armour-plated, reflecting the expectation of surface gunfights with armed merchantmen.

Specifications

Crew: 62	tons); Submerged: 2523 tonnes (2483 tons)
Powerplant: Twin shafts; diesel/electric motors	Dimensions (length/beam/draught):94.8m x 9m x
Max Speed: Surfaced: 15.8 knots; Submerged:	5.2m (311ft x 29ft 9in x 17ft 3in)
7.6 knots	Commissioned: December 1917
Surface Range: 23,390km (12,630nm) at 8 knots	Armament: Six 508mm (20in) torpedo tubes; two
Displacement: Surfaced: 1961 tonnes (1930	150mm (5.9in) guns

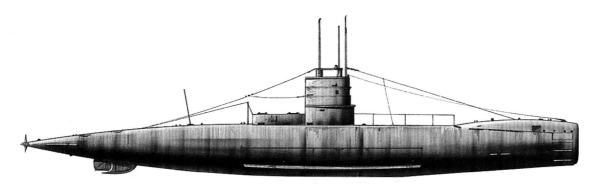

Specifications

Crew: 36	Displacement: Surfaced: 416 tonnes (410 tons);
Powerplant: Single screw, diesel/electric 1200 hp	Submerged: 511 tonnes (503 tons)
motors	Dimensions (length/beam/draught): 49.9m x
Max Speed: Surfaced: 15 knots; Submerged:	4.6m x 3.5m (163ft 9in x 15ft x 11ft 6in)
9.5 knots	Commissioned: April 1918
Surface Range: 3800km (2048nm) at 8 knots	Armament: Six 457mm (18in) torpedo tubes

▲ R-Class

Royal Navy, patrol submarine, North Sea and Western Approaches, 1918

The bulbous bow section contained the most up-to-date hydrophone instruments. Two electric motors each delivered 1200hp (895kW) for high submerged speed while the 8-cylinder diesel was rated at only 210hp (157kW). In November 1918, two R-class were based at Blyth and four at Killybegs on the northwest coast of Ireland.

sent 27 ships to the bottom, including four that were sunk by mines.

Encouraged by this success, *U-140*, *U-156* and *U-117* were sent over as well, but the Americans were now on the alert and there were fewer easy pickings. *U-156* was lost with all hands on the return voyage when it struck a mine off Bergen, Norway, on 25 September 1918. Another trio of long-range submarines, *U-155*, *U-152* and *U-139*, were on their way across the Atlantic when the war ended.

Naval historians have generally discounted the value of their role, with the view that if the German Navy had built more of the medium-sized 'Mittel U-boot' typified by the U-81 and U-87 classes, armed with 16 torpedoes and with a range of 18,000km (11,220 miles), of which 46 were built between 1915 and 1918, the impact on Allied shipping would have been much greater. The cruisers sank less than 2 per cent of total tonnage sent to the bottom by U-boats.

Countermeasures

One result of the U-boat onslaught was to force the British into intensive work on countermeasures. Explosive sweeps towed by trawlers were not very effective. The first effective depth-charge was produced in January 1916, and the first submarine lost to a depth-charge was *U-68* on 22 March. On 6 July, *UC-7* was detected by hydrophones and sunk by depth charges. A submerged submarine was no longer beyond attack.

The Q-ships, or disguised merchantmen, sank nine U-boats. Also noteworthy was the development, during the war, of the concept of an anti-submarine submarine. British submarines sank 18 German U-boats during the conflict, 13 in 1917–18. These were very largely surface encounters, dependent on

US SUBMARINE CLASSES 1914–18			
Class	Number	Launched	Note
A	7	1901–03	Stationed in Philippines
B	3	1906–07	Stationed in Philippines
C	5	1906–09	
D	3	1909–10	
E	2	1911	
F	4	1911–12	
G	4	1911–13	
H	9	1913–16	H4–7 and 8–9 originally for Russia
K	8	1913–14	
L	11	1915–17	7 based Ireland as Class AL, 1918
M	1	1915	
N	7	1916–17	
O	16	1917–18	
R	27	1917–19	6 launched by Nov 1918

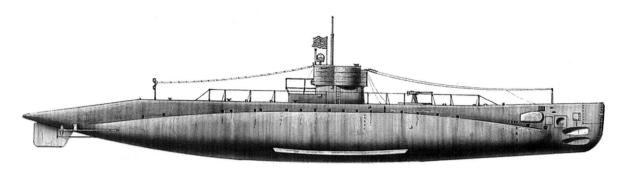

Specifications

Crew: 29

Powerplant: Two shafts; diesel/electric motors

Max Speed: Surfaced: 14 knots; Submerged: 10.5 knots

Surface Range: 10,191km (5500nm) at 11.5 knots

Displacement: Surfaced: 529 tonnes (521 tons); Submerged: 639 tonnes (629 tons)

Dimensions (length/beam/draught): 52.5m x 5.5m x 4.4m (172ft 3in x 18ft 1in x 14ft 5in)

Commissioned: July 1918

Armament: Four 457mm (18in) torpedo tubes; one 76mm (3in) gun

▲ O-Class

US Navy, patrol submarine, 1918

The quickly built O-class's 457mm (18in) torpedo tubes, limited range and diving depth of 61m (200ft) would have hampered their value as combat boats. US submarine design had some catching-up to do in 1918. *O-12*, renamed *Nautilus*, was used in an unsuccessful attempt to reach the North Pole in 1930.

▲ HMS *R7*

The 10 R-class were the first submarines designed to hunt down and attack other submarines. Five hydrophones with bearing instruments were mounted in the bow.

keen look-out work, and might develop into duels in which, on two occasions, the British boat was sunk.

This led to British development of the R-class submarine, which was intended specifically for the hunting role. They were relatively small craft, 49.7m (163ft) long and displacing 416.5 tonnes (410 tons) on the surface, with only one propeller (most contemporary submarines had two). Diesel engines could drive them at 9 knots on the surface but, once submerged, large batteries permitted their electric motors to drive them underwater at the high speed of 15 knots for two hours (8–10 knots was the common speed for submerged submarines until after World War II).

These prototypes of the later 'hunter-killer' were also equipped with hydrophones as underwater listening equipment. Six forward torpedo tubes made them potent weapons, but the R-class submarines appeared too late to have any actual effect on the war. Britain's long-delayed introduction of the convoy system in mid-1917 was the single most effective check on submarine attacks.

United States

At the outbreak of the war the United States was lagging behind the great powers of Europe in submarine development. During the war years, the US Navy built the H-, K-, L-, N-, O- and finally R-class submarines, but failed to keep pace with European improvements.

Nevertheless, when the United States declared war on Germany in April 1917, the US Navy wanted to get its submarines involved. K-class boats were really not meant for blue-water operations, but the Navy decided to tow the eight *K-1* to *K-8* boats to the Mediterranean. This proved to be a disaster, with *K-3, K-4, K-6* and *K-7* lost in a storm, while the survivors were kept in the Azores for the rest of the war. The Navy also tried to tow a number of L-class boats across the Atlantic. Caught in a storm, they were cast off, and remarkably all made it to Ireland, from where they conducted uneventful coastal patrols. A further eight boats of the new O-class were on their way across the Atlantic when the war ended. Only one O-class boat was used on active patrol, from July 1918; the other 16 were completed after the Armistice of 11 November, though seven remained on the Navy list through World War II, and were used for training.

Specifications

Crew: 31

Powerplant: Twin screw diesel; electric motors

Max Speed: Surfaced: 14 knots; Submerged:

10.5 knots

Surface Range: 8334km (4500nm) at 10 knots

Displacement: Surfaced: 398 tonnes (392 tons);

Submerged: 530 tonnes (521 tons)

Dimensions (length/beam/draught): 47m x 5m x

4m (153ft 10in x 16ft 9in x 13ft 2in)

Commissioned: October 1914

Armament: Four 457mm (18in) torpedo tubes

▲ **Walrus (K-4)**

US Navy, patrol submarine, Azores, 1917

K-4 never carried the proposed name *Walrus*. The K-class class of eight boats were of relatively small size compared to post-war American submarines. The hull form is still reminiscent of earlier American types. Their 950hp (708kW) Nelseco diesel engines gave a lot of trouble. *K-4* was based first at Hawaii, then at Key West Florida.

Forces at the end of the war
1917–18

More submarines were lost in the course of the war through accidents, grounding, scuttling by their own crews and capture than by outright sinking in combat. This also reflects the relatively late development of effective anti-submarine weapons.

IN THE YEARS BETWEEN 1914 and 1918, Germany built over 300 submarines, far more than any other country, and amounting to almost half of the world's stock. Out of a total of 373 it had lost 178, but they had sunk 5708 ships, around 15 vessels for each submarine, or 32 ships for each U-boat lost. Although the U-boats failed to win the war, it has been pointed out that they were more thwarted than actually defeated, and were never driven from the seas despite the intensive efforts made by the Royal Navy in 1917–18 to pen them in at their home bases.

In terms of manpower the whole U-boat force numbered less than a single army division, and while the pace and volume of U-boat construction cost the German economy dearly, it was clear that the submarine was unchallenged for economy of force. It was also plain that the whole basis of naval planning and strategy must be changed.

Quite apart from maintaining an effective submarine force, it became clear that any viable navy

SUBMARINE FLEETS, 1914 AND 1918 COMPARED			
Country	1914	1918	War Losses
Austria-Hungary	6	19	8
France	55	60	14
Germany	24	134	173
Great Britain	74	168	56
Italy	22	78	8
Japan	12	15	0
Sweden	9	12	0
Russia	29	44	17
United States	27	79	1

would have to vastly increase its stock of anti-submarine craft and weapons to combat enemy submarines in a future war. Every country, therefore, had to look at its resources and decide on future policy, even while reducing its submarine numbers from wartime levels.

France

France ended the war with a varied collection of submarines. Fourteen had been lost, including the Brumaire class boat *Foucault*, the first submarine to be sunk by air attack (by two seaplanes, on 15 September 1916), and around 19 had been put into commission, making the fleet five stronger than it had been in 1914.

The steam-powered *Dupuy de Lôme*, launched in September 1915, was refitted with cannibalized German diesels after the war. Other wartime classes were the Amphitrite class (eight boats, built 1914–16), of which one was lost; Bellone class (three boats, 1914–17); Diane class (two boats, 1915–17), of which one was lost; Armide class (three boats, 1915–16); Joessel-Fulton class (two boats, 1917–19);

and the Lagrange class (four boats, 1917–24), of which only two saw war service.

After a succession of medium-sized submarine classes, these were bigger, at 920–1320 tonnes (905–1299 tons) surfaced and submerged; and more heavily armed, with eight 457mm (18in) torpedo tubes and two 7.5cm (3in) deck guns. Not the least important addition, however, was *Roland Morillot*, the captured *UB-18*, commissioned into the French Navy in 1917; this boat, with others acquired as war reparations, would influence French post-war designs. One class that did not long survive the war was the 16-strong one that included *Euler* (launched 1912), with only a single integral torpedo tube, plus four carried in drop collars and two in external cradles, and no gun.

Specifications

Crew: 54	Displacement: Surfaced: 846 tonnes (833 tons);
Powerplant: Twin screw, three cylinder	Submerged: 1307 tonnes (1287 tons)
reciprocating steam engine; electric motors	Dimensions (length/beam/draught): 75m x 6.4m
Max Speed: Surfaced: 15 knots; Submerged:	x 3.6m (246ft x 21ft x 11ft 10in)
8.5 knots	Commissioned: September 1915
Surface Range: 10,469km (5650nm) at 10 knots	Armament: Eight 450mm (17.7in) torpedo tubes

▲ Dupuy de Lôme

French Navy, patrol submarine, Mediterranean, World War I

Provided with a minimal tower, and a closable steam funnel, *Dupuy* was commissioned in July 1916 and attached to the Morocco flotilla from 1917 to the the end of the war. It was used to bombard the scene of a local uprising in 1917, and was mistakenly attacked by a British vessel in the same year. It was scrapped in 1935.

▲ Euler

French Navy, patrol submarine, Mediterranean/Adriatic, World War I

One of the Brumaire class, powered by two German MAN diesels of 840hp (626kW) built under licence, *Euler* had a 75mm (3in) deck gun added in 1916. Four of the same design were built in England as the Royal Navy's W-class, but sold to Italy in 1915. All saw service in the Mediterranean and Adriatic Seas.

Specifications

Crew: 35	Submerged: 560 tonnes (551 tons)
Powerplant: Twin screw diesel engines; electric	Dimensions (length/beam/draught): 52m x 5.4m
motors	x 3m (171ft x 17ft 9in x 10ft 3in)
Max Speed: Surfaced: 14 knots; Submerged:	Commissioned: October 1912
7 knots	Armament: One - mm (17.7in) torpedo tube;
Surface Range: 3230km (1741nm) at 10 knots	four drop collars; two external cradles
Displacement: Surfaced: 403 tonnes (397 tons);	

Germany

In November 1918, all remaining German U-boats were surrendered or scuttled. By the end of the war, 134 were in service out of 373 commissioned, and a total of 176, including boats under repair or not yet in commission, were handed over. Among them was *U-60*, launched on 5 July 1916, which sank over 40 Allied ships in the course of its wartime career, and was grounded on 21 November 1918 and later broken up.

In the final months of the war a new class of fast submarines was under construction at Kiel. Class leader was *U-160*, and eight out of 13 were completed. With six 509mm (20in) torpedo tubes and two 104mm (4.1in) guns, and a surface speed of 16.2 knots, they would have been a powerful commerce raiding force, but came too late to have any influence on events.

Under the terms of the Treaty of Versailles, Germany was banned from possessing submarines. All the U-boats that had passed into the possession of the Allies were eventually scrapped or sunk in target practice. But no treaty clause could nullify the fact that among German technicians there was at least as great a degree of expertise in submarine design and construction as in any other country.

Great Britain

Losses in the Royal Navy were high, with 56 submarines lost by the end of the war through a variety of causes including 'friendly fire' or 'friendly ramming'. Among the wartime classes of British submarines were the M-class of 1917–18, with diesel and electric propulsion, mounting a massive 305mm (12in) battleship gun in front of the conning tower. This weapon was in principle capable of giving the M-class ships the firepower and hitting range that torpedoes of the time lacked. The gun could be fired underwater from periscope depth, but had to be loaded on the surface. Only three were built; the first two were completed near the end of the war and never used in action. Although it now appears cumbersome and impracticable, a 30.5cm (12in) M-class shell struck the battle-cruiser HMS *Hood* during a naval exercise in 1922, and this ship was declared disabled.

The British G-class of 14 boats was built primarily to counter the threat of ocean-going U-boats. To reach the Atlantic, German vessels had to pass through the English Channel or make a long detour round the Shetland Islands, and the G-class were intended as interceptors for both submarines and surface craft. Four torpedo tubes of 457mm (18 in) were fitted, with a fifth of 533mm (21in), whose torpedoes were intended for armour piercing.

The G-class submarines were quite fast on the surface, for their time, able to make 14.25 knots, but reports that new German U-boats could reach 22 knots led to the building of seven J-class submarines in 1915, capable of maintaining 17 knots. *J-1* inflicted severe damage on the German battleships *Grosser Kürfurst* and *Kronprinz* on 5 November 1916.

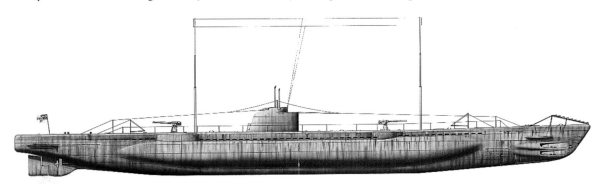

Specifications

Crew: 39	Submerged: 1016 tonnes (1000 tons)
Powerplant: Two shafts; diesel; electric motors	Dimensions (length/beam/draught): 71.8m x
Max Speed: Surfaced: 16.2 knots; Submerged:	6.2m x 4.1m (235ft 6in x 20ft 6in x 13ft 6in)
8.2 knots	Commissioned: February 1918
Surface Range: 15,372km (8300nm) at 8 knots	Armament: Six 509mm (20in) torpedo tubes; two
Displacement: Surfaced: 834 tonnes (821 tons);	104mm (4.1in) guns

▲ **U-160**

Imperial German Navy, commerce raider, World war I

Good seagoing boats and well armed, the U-160 boats were intended to carry out attacks on the surface whenever possible. Based on the design of *U-93*, these were among the 46 submarines known as 'Mittel-U' – a middle size between the smaller U-boats and the large cruisers.

Although many petrol-engined submarines were still in use in 1914, World War I submarines were generally driven by diesels on the surface and by electric motors when submerged. But the British Admiralty's preoccupation with surface speed led to the building of the K-class in 1915–19. These large submarines, intended to operate with battle fleets as scouts for surface warships, were powered by steam turbines, which had to be shut down on diving, with movable lids to cover the two funnels. The K-boats steamed at 23.5 knots on the surface, while electric motors gave them a 10-knot submerged speed, and 10 533mm (21in) torpedo tubes plus three 102mm (4in) guns made them formidable on paper, but five were lost in accidents. Seventeen boats of this class, unsuccessful and deeply disliked (by their crews), were built. Most of the big ships they were intended to engage were now sufficiently armoured to absorb hits from torpedoes and survive, and were also protected at anchor by torpedo nets. All but one of the K-class boats were scrapped in 1926. The most effective British submarines built during the war years were the E-, H- and L-classes.

By the end of the war, the number of submarines in the British Navy had risen to 137 in service, with a further 78 under construction. A programme of scrapping and cancellation was rapidly introduced to bring the numbers down to a peacetime level that would nevertheless ensure the Royal Navy's continued superiority.

Italy

Italy's submarine fleet in 1918 included several boats passed on from the British Navy, including four of

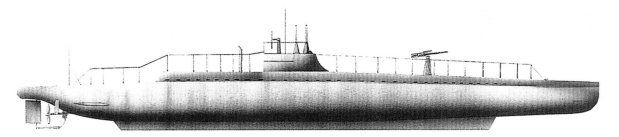

▲ **W-2**

Royal Navy, then Italian, coastal submarine, Adriatic, 1915–18

Ordered after an official visit to the Schneider yard at Toulon, this small British-built class used the design of the French Brumaire boats, with external torpedoes mounted in six Drzewiecki drop collars. Unsuitable for British conditions, the W-class was sold on to the Italian Navy in 1915, and saw service in the Adriatic Sea.

Specifications

Crew: 19	Displacement: Surfaced: 336 tonnes (331 tons);
Powerplant: Twin screw diesel; electric motors	Submerged: 507 tonnes (499 tons)
Max Speed: Surfaced: 13 knots; Submerged:	Dimensions (length/beam/draught): 52.4m x
8.5 knots	4.7m x 2.7m (172ft x 15ft 5in x 8ft 10in)
Surface Range: 4630km (2500nm) at 9 knots	Commissioned: February 1915
	Armament: Two 457mm (18in) torpedo tubes

Specifications

Crew: 60	tons); Submerged: 1977 tonnes (1946 tons)
Powerplant: Twin screw diesel; electric motors	Dimensions (length/beam/draught): 90m x 7.5m
Max Speed: Surfaced: 15 knots; Submerged:	x 4.9m (295ft 7in x 24ft 7in x 16ft)
9 knots	Commissioned: September 1917
Surface Range: 7112km (3840nm) at 10 knots	Armament: Four 533mm (21in) torpedo tubes;
Displacement: Surfaced: 1619 tonnes (1594	one 305mm (12in) gun

▲ **M-1**

Royal Navy, submarine gunboat, 1917

The M-class submarines were adapted from the hulls of four K-class boats then under construction. The big guns were designed for the Formidable-class battleship, and 50 shells could be carried. *M-1* and *M-2* had 457mm (18in) torpedo tubes; *M-3* had 533mm (21in) tubes. *M-1* sank in November 1925 after colliding with a Swedish cargo steamer.

Class W2, built to Italian–French design with two integral 457mm (18in) torpedo tubes and two externally mounted drop-collar torpedoes. They were transferred in 1916 and broken up in 1919. Also transferred in the previous year were three Class S1 boats, also of Italian design, and perhaps considered more suitable for Mediterranean service. Eight British H-class boats were transferred in 1916–17.

But Italy had been actively building on its own account. Wartime classes were the two Pacinotti boats (1916), of which one was sunk in 1917; the F-class – most numerous Italian class with 21 boats – of small submarines, 262 tonnes (258 tons) surfaced, 319 tonnes (314 tons) submerged, with two 457mm (18in) torpedo tubes. Designed and built by Fiat-San Giorgio at La Spezia, it had begun in 1913 as an

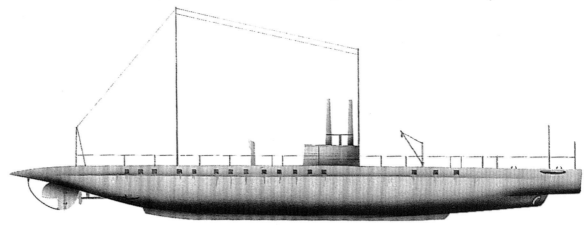

Specifications

Crew: 31	Submerged: 330 tonnes (324 tons)
Powerplant: Twin screw diesel; electric motors	Dimensions (length/beam/draught): 45m x 4.4m
Max Speed: Surfaced: 13 knots; Submerged:	x 3.2m (148ft x 14ft 5in x 10ft 6in)
8.5 knots	Commissioned: 1914
Surface Range: 2963km (1600nm) at 8.5 knots	Armament: Two 457mm (18in) torpedo tubes,
Displacement: Surfaced: 270 tonnes (265 tons);	one 12-pounder gun

▲ S-1

Royal Navy, then Italian, coastal submarine, Adriatic, 1915–18

Like the W-class, the S-class was a British borrowing of a European design, in this case an Italian Laurenti boat, with a partial double hull, and 10 watertight compartments – a more ambitious design than British boats of the period. Only three were built, and after a short time based at Yarmouth, they were transferred to the Italian Navy in 1915.

Specifications

Crew: 35	Submerged: 938 tonnes (923 tons)
Powerplant: Twin shafts; diesel/electric motors	Dimensions (length/beam/draught): 67m x 6m x
Max Speed: Surfaced: 16 knots; Submerged:	3.8m (220ft x 19ft 8in x 12ft 6in)
9.8 knots	Commissioned: November 1917
Surface Range: 3218km (1734nm) at 11 knots	Armament: Six 450mm (17.7in) torpedo tubes;
Displacement: Surfaced: 774 tonnes (762 tons);	two 76mm (3in) guns

▲ Agostino Barbarigo

Italian Navy, coastal submarine, 1918

This was one of the Provana class boats, completed too late for combat work. Novel features included separation of the batteries in four watertight compartments, as a safety measure. Fore and aft 76mm (3in) guns were mounted. Even for a coastal boat, the diving depth of 50ms (155ft) was a limiting factor on operations.

export class, with three supplied to each of Brazil, Portugal and Spain. The N-class of six boats followed in 1917–18, then the X2 coastal minelayer, a class of two boats in 1917; the Pietro Micca class of six boats built 1917–19 (three after the end of hostilities); and four boats of the Provana-class in 1917–19.

In addition, Italy built six A-class midget submarines in 1915–16. At the end of the war, Italy emerged with an enhanced submarine fleet while its foremost rival, the defeated Austria-Hungary, could boast none.

Neutral Nations

Among some of the non-belligerent nations, submarine-building did not stop during the war years. Rather, extension of submarine capability was seen as necessary to maintain the integrity of territorial waters against intrusion from the vessels of warring powers.

Spain preserved neutrality during World War I, and in 1918 had a modest submarine fleet, the American-built Holland-type boat *Isaac Peral*, launched in July 1916, and three A-class boats completed in 1917.

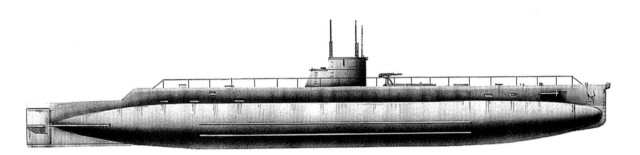

Specifications

Crew: 35

Powerplant: Twin screw diesel; electric motors

Max Speed: Surfaced: 15 knots; Submerged: 8 knots

Surface Range: 5386km (2903nm) at 11 knots

Displacement: Surfaced: 499 tonnes (491 tons);

Submerged: 762 tonnes (750 tons)

Dimensions (length/beam/draught): 60m x 5.8m x 3.4m (196ft 10in x 19ft x 11ft 2in)

Commissioned: July 1916

Armament: Four 457mm (18in) torpedo tubes; one 76mm (3in) gun

▲ Isaac Peral

Spanish Navy, patrol submarine, 1916

Built by the Fore River Co., this was Spain's first and, for several years, its only substantial submarine. The 76mm (3in) gun was fixed to a collapsible mount. Based at Cartagena, the boat was hulked in the 1930s and played no part in the Civil War combat.

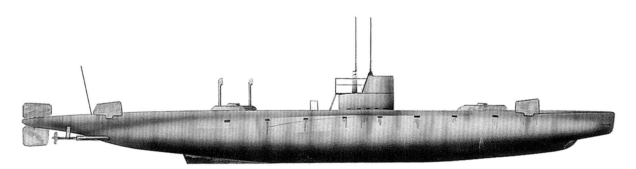

Specifications

Crew: 30

Powerplant: Single screw petrol engines; electric motors

Max Speed: Surfaced: 14.8 knots; Submerged: 6.3 knots

Surface Range: 8338km (4500nm) at 10 knots

Displacement: Surfaced: 189 tonnes (186 tons); Submerged: 233 tonnes (230 tons)

Dimensions (length/beam/draught): 42.4m x 4.3m x 2.1m (139ft x 14ft x 6ft 11in)

Commissioned: 1909

Armament: Two 457mm (18in) torpedo tubes

▲ Hvalen

Swedish Navy, test boat, Baltic Sea, 1915

Hvalen was a small boat, with a single screw and two torpedo tubes, apparently bought so that Swedish naval architects could study an up-to-date submarine from a major builder. On patrol in late 1915, *Hvalen* was shelled by a German gunboat, *Meteor*, in Swedish territorial waters, causing a diplomatic incident.

Sweden in 1918 had 13 submarines, of which 12 had been completed during the war years. All were home built, except for *Hvalen*, bought in 1909 from Fiat-San Giorgio, and which made one of the earliest long voyages (on the surface) by a submarine, from La Spezia to Sweden. It was stricken in 1919 and sunk as a target in 1924.

Japan

Japan's contribution to the Allied victory had been comparatively small, and its submarine force had played no part. During the war Japan built only three submarines. Japanese naval planners, however, followed the events of the war at sea with great attention, and, with a vast ocean at their east side, perceived the advantages of the long-range submarine. At the end of the war, Japan was handed nine U-boats as part of German war reparations, and these would be subjected to intensive study.

Russia

In the war years the Russian Empire had built 32 submarines, of which the Bars class accounted for 24. Built between 1914 and 1917, these were an enlarged version of the pre-war Morzh class: a single-hulled boat with four 457mm (18in) torpedo tubes but also mounting a further eight in drop-collar release mechanisms. Most carried a 37mm (1.5in) AA gun. A serious defect was their lack of interior bulkheads;

RUSSIAN SUBMARINE CLASSES 1914–18, PRE-WAR BUILD			
Class	Number	Launched	Note
Delfin	1	1903	Sunk 1904; salvaged
Kasatka	6	1904–05	Baltic and Black Sea
Som	7	1904–07	Baltic and Black Sea
Karp	3	1907	Black Sea
Akula	1	1908	Diesel motor; Baltic
Minoga	1	1908	Diesel, Black and Caspian Seas
Kaiman	4	1910–11	Baltic
Morzh/Nerpa	3	1911–13	Black Sea
Narval	3	1914	Black Sea

RUSSIAN SUBMARINE CLASSES 1914–18, WARTIME BUILD			
Class	Number	Launched	Note
Bars	24	1915–17	Baltic
Krab	1	1915	Minelayer; Black Sea
Sviatoi Georgi	1	1916	Italian built
AG 'Holland'	6	1916–17	7 built after 1918; US reclaimed 6

another was their short range, only 740km (460 miles). They were active both with the Baltic and Black Sea fleets, six of them with the former. Fifteen survived the war, nine having been sunk in action or scuttled. Russia, between 1918 and 1921, was caught

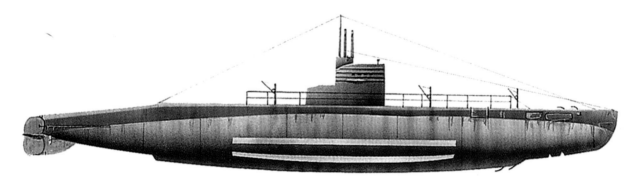

▲ H-4

Imperial Russian Navy, coastal submarine, 1917

The Russian Holland boats (Class AG, 'American Golland') were ordered in three batches. Two were delivered between June 1916 and early 1917, but only the first five were commissioned. The second batch remained unassembled when the Revolution came. Batch three was not despatched, and was eventually bought by the US Navy (*H-4* to *H-9*).

Specifications

Crew: 27

Powerplant: Twin screw; diesel/electric motors

Max Speed: Surfaced: 12.5 knots; Submerged: 8.5 knots

Surface Range: 1750nm (3240km; 2010 miles) at 7 knots

Displacement: Surfaced: 370 tonnes (365 tons); Submerged: 481 tonnes (474 tons)

Dimensions (length/beam/draught): 45.8m x 4.6m x 3.7m (150ft 3in x 15ft 4in x 12ft 5in)

Commissioned: October 1916

Armament: Four 450mm (17in)torpedo tubes

up in revolution and civil warfare. While only seven submarines are known to have been lost in action, many more were scuttled to prevent them falling into the hands of the Germans or the Bolsheviks.

This was the fate of the Karp class, two boats scuttled at Sebastopol on 26 April 1919; also of the Narval class (Holland 31A) of three boats, a superior design to the Bars, with watertight bulkheads and a crash-diving tank; and of the one-off *Krab*, the first submarine designed specifically as a minelayer, ordered in 1908 but commissioned only in 1915, later than the first German UC-boats. Unlike these, its mines were laid in horizontal stern-discharging galleries.

In 1915, 17 H-class (Holland-602 type) submarines had been ordered from the Electric Boat Co. in America and, in 1917, 11 were assembled in British Columbia, shipped to Vladivostok in kit form and brought over the Trans-Siberian Railway for assembly. *H-4*, however, was cancelled as a Russian order and bought by the US Navy in 1918, renumbered in 1920 as *SS147*, and served until 1930.

The Holland-602 was built for several navies: the United States and British Navies already had 'H' boats of essentially the same design. It was considered an effective class within the limitations of its size, 398 tonnes (392 tons) surfaced, 529 tonnes (521 tons) submerged, and range, 3800km (2361 miles). The Baltic boats were scuttled in 1918; the Black Sea boats passed to the Ukrainian, then the Soviet, Navy.

United States

In 1918, the US Navy had a total of 79 submarines. None had been lost to enemy action; *F-4* had foundered and *H-1* had been wrecked in the Gulf of Mexico. The L-class boats based at Berehaven in Ireland returned home, as did the K-class from the Azores. Two further divisions of four L- and four O-class arrived on the European coast too late to join in hostilities. For war service the L-boats had been classed AL to distinguish them from the British L-class. They were the first American submarines to be fitted with a deck gun, which was partially retractable into the deckhouse.

The N-class was a smaller, lower-powered version of the L-class; it was without a deck gun but with the same number of torpedo tubes, four 457mm (18in). Unlike the L-class, however, it was used exclusively on coastal defence patrols. At the end of 1918, *R-15* to *R-20* were deployed to Hawaii to form the first squadron at the new submarine base of Pearl Harbor.

Although the United States' boats had made no 'kills' in the war, their crews had learned a great deal about the tactics of submarine warfare – and its hazards. All Berehaven boats were attacked at least twice by Allied ships or planes. As the war ended, 59 submarines were being built in the United States, but most of the older boats were plainly obsolete or in a worn-out condition.

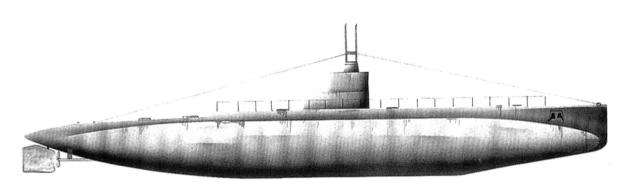

Specifications

Crew: 35

Powerplant: Twin screw; diesel/electric motors

Max Speed: Surfaced: 13 knots; Submerged:

11 knots

Surface Range: 6485km (3500nm) at 5 knots

Displacement: Surfaced: 353 tonnes (348 tons);

Submerged: 420 tonnes (414 tons)

Dimensions (length/beam/draught): 45m x 4.8m

x 3.8m (147ft 4in x 15ft 9in x 12ft 6in)

Commissioned: December 1916

Armament: Four 457mm (18in) torpedo tubes

▲ N-1

US Navy, patrol submarine, World War I

Seven boats formed the N-class, the first US submarines to have metal rather than canvas-protected bridges. The lower-powered diesels, 300hp (224kW), were much more reliable and the same policy was used on subsequent types. *N-2* was used to try out an air-independent propulsion system, but it was not developed further.

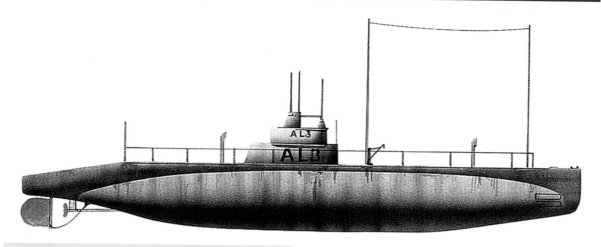

Specifications

Crew: 35	Submerged: 556 tonnes (548 tons)
Powerplant: Twin screw diesel; electric motors	Dimensions (length/beam/draught): 51m x 5.3m
Max Speed: Surfaced: 14 knots; Submerged:	x 4m (167ft 4in x 17ft 4in x 13ft 1in)
8 knots	Commissioned: February 1915
Surface Range: 6270km (3380nm) at 11 knots	Armament: Four 457mm (18in) torpedo tubes;
Displacement: Surfaced: 457 tonnes (450 tons);	one 76mm (3in) gun

▲ **L3**

US Navy, patrol submarine, Atlantic 1917–18

Eleven boats formed the L-class. Although the United States' first 'ocean-going' submarines, they were really intended for coastal defence. To the crews they were 'pig-boats', partly because of their shape, partly because of their typical submarine living conditions. In action they made 21 U-boat sightings and four attacks, but without success.

The Submarines of 1918

The submarines of 1918, apart from those most recently delivered, had seen hard service and were often in poor condition. Even the newest were largely based on pre-1914 designs, and though more up-to-date equipment and instruments had been fitted, their packed and narrow hulls were not easily adaptable for the installation of new equipment. They were slow, often also slow to dive, and in order to communicate required the rigging of tall radio masts. There had been little progress in engine development during the war. Also, they were vulnerable to the anti-submarine warfare (ASW) techniques that, though still crude, had been brought to a high pitch of intensity, especially by the British navy. Now that the war was over, few would survive in the major navies for more than a couple of years.

But though its importance in naval warfare was beyond doubt, the future of the submarine was ringed by question marks. The basic question was not 'Do we need submarines?' but 'What more can submarines do?' The notion of the submarine as essentially a coastal defence and anti-warship vessel had been discredited. The role of submarines in long-front coastal defence had not been particularly

distinguished, though more effective at 'choke points' like the entrances to the English Channel and the Straits of Otranto. What they excelled at was exactly what made the high naval authorities most nervous – commerce raids, stealth and surprise attacks.

Technical Issues

A raft of technical questions demanded answers. Submarines could be single-hulled or double-hulled, or single-hulled with external saddle-tanks. But which was best? Also, surfaced, submerged and in-between (diving/surfacing) characteristics had to be balanced. Wartime experience had shown that rapid diving was extremely desirable, but so too was surface speed, and a submarine designed for the first was not likely to be so good at the second. A central issue was reserve buoyancy, the volume and placing of the tanks, which were flooded for the boat to submerge, or emptied for the boat to operate on the surface; this had a direct impact on the boat's surface performance.

The single-hull submarine had to have all its tanks inside the pressure hull, reducing the space available for everything else. But it was cheaper and faster to build, and offered less resistance than a double hull in submerged performance because of its smaller area.

The double hull, with its greater area, also had a higher freeboard when surfaced and was capable of higher surface speeds because more of the surface was in contact with the water. The space between the hulls could be used not only for flooding/voiding tankage, but for fuel storage and even for weapon stowage, in pressure-proof containers. More space was made available inside the pressure hull. But a double-hull boat took longer to dive.

The British Navy attempted to square the circle with the saddle tank, fixing external tanks around a single hull (beginning with the D-class in 1906) and despite experiments with double hulls, remained faithful to this solution. The Imperial German Navy favoured the double hull, partly in the interest of good sea-keeping on the surface, though it too had single-hulled boats, normally smaller types like the UB-coastal and UC-minelayer classes. The United States Navy opted for the double hull with its World War I designs and did not abandon it until the nuclear era.

It was generally accepted, and would be for another 25 years, that externally mounted guns were an essential part of the combat submarine's armoury. Here again questions arose. In the war, the gun had been a supplement to the limited stock of torpedoes, used for attack rather than for defence. But the development of ASW tactics, using escort ships and aircraft, made defence, especially anti-aircraft defence, important. What kind of gun or guns should a submarine have? To this and many other issues, there was no simple answer. Periscope location was also debated.

At this time, though the control room was located within the hull, submarines had a bridge, or command and navigating post, mounted on the conning tower, reflecting the fact that most of its time would be spent on the surface. A periscope with eyepiece mounted in the conning tower could be extended further beyond the boat than one that descended to the control room inside the pressure hull. In the engine-room there was no practical alternative to dual power, but there was clearly room for improvement in the diesel engines. The form of drive was also a matter of choice, with the diesels either driving electrical generators or turning the drive shafts directly, in which case they had to be de-clutched from the drive shafts when it was necessary to recharge the batteries. All in all, the technical challenges were enormous.

▲ **U-boats surrender**
Crews line up on the decks as three U-boats prepare to surrender at an unidentified British base, November 1918. Most were scrapped or sunk in target practice over the next few years.

Chapter 2

The Interwar Years: 1919–38

Submarine development followed some
strange courses, as strategists and designers struggled
to define the role of the submarine and to build boats to
fulfil it. Important technical challenges were also being
tackled, notably in engine efficiency and in underwater
detection. By 1930, the lines of development were becoming
clear, and substantial numbers of submarines were built in
the following decade. The majority were intended for
relatively short-range work, but the concept of the
long-distance cruising submarine was also elaborated,
especially by Japan. All nations agreed not to engage in
commerce-raiding. By the late 1930s, Germany was
emerging once again as a formidable naval power,
and at the end of the decade, with war looming,
submarine construction began to accelerate.

◀ O-class
The Royal Navy's nine O-class submarines were designed for long-range operations, and were intended for
service anywhere from Portsmouth to Hong Kong after their launch in 1926.

Introduction

The 1920s were a decade of experiment for designers and builders, as, in conjunction with the various navies, they explored the operational potential of the submarine.

TECHNIQUES CONTINUED to move forward with greater use of welding. A welded hull was much more resistant to vibration and less prone to tiny leaks than a riveted one, and stronger steels were also introduced, to facilitate deeper diving. Bow diving planes were introduced and crews were trained to operate a more sophisticated arrangement of tanks to allow for working in a variety of conditions, with greater or less salinity or temperatures.

The MAN works in Germany, Vickers in England, and Nelson Engine Co. in the Unites States had all provided engines for the combat submarines and in the 1920s and 1930s international competition intensified to develop a compact and lightweight diesel engine that could produce enough power for a meaningful increase in speed. New names began to appear in the United States, with Winton and Fairbanks-Morse producing submarine diesels. Various drive systems were used. Some engines were reversible and could be used for manoeuvring. Others were not and the commander had to change over to the battery-driven electric motors. Drive by diesels through generator sets emerged as the best compromise, providing maximum flexibility for directing power for any combination of battery charging, propulsion and manoeuvring operations.

Alongside these developments, important improvements were under way in underwater detection and communication. The primitive hydrophone listening devices of World War I were elaborated into steadily more complex and bulky detection equipment. Simple hydrophones were a passive mode of detection, but from late in the war, active systems were made possible by the French development of the transducer, based on the piezolelectric effect of passing an alternating current through a quartz crystal, causing it to vibrate and send out 'waves' whose impact on a solid object could

▲ **Cruiser submarine**

Carrying four 132mm (5.2in) deck guns, the one-off British *X-1* was an attempt by the Royal Navy to combine the stealth of a submersible with the surface fighting ability of a cruiser.

▲ **Krupp workshops**
German Type II and Type VII U-boats undergo service checks in the docks at Krupp's Germania shipyard in Kiel, 1939. Krupp were Nazi Germany's largest steelmaker, and were consequently involved in the production of many of the *Kriegsmarine*'s U-boats.

be traced. From the late 1920s, most new French and British submarines carried early forms of this sonar array. But submariners found that active sonar was better at finding submarines from surface ships than vice versa. Submarine-to-shore communication by radio was assisted by the development of a worldwide network of transmitting/receiving stations, though a boat could use high-frequency radio only when surfaced, and masts were needed. But development of VLF radio, which could reach a submerged submarine if it was within range of a transmitter, meant that British submarines, for example, could keep in touch while in the Mediterranean or the North Atlantic: this was a considerable boost to their value as scouts.

New Fleets

By the 1930s, most navies had come to the view that the submarine's prime importance and value in warfare lay in its ability to operate on its own, or with

a tactical group, in patrol and reconnaissance. Improved communication and undersea detection systems played a considerable part in this. Although the economic depression of the early 1930s caused cancellation and cut-backs of building orders, technical development continued.

Italy and France followed a dynamic policy of submarine design and construction, with a variety of types, though no class was built in large numbers. Soviet Russia also began the construction of a substantial submarine fleet. At opposite sides of the Pacific Ocean, the Japanese Empire and the United States were drawing up plans for a future war. Surreptitiously at first, then openly under Hitler's Reich, the German Navy re-entered the submarine domain with a new generation of U-boats and a powerful vision of how to use them. In the late 1930s, Italian and German submarine crews went on active service in support of the Nationalist side in the Spanish Civil War.

The war legacy
1919–29

After 1918, the navies of the world faced vital issues: among them were the reduction of submarine fleets, the post-war role of the submarine and even whether it should be abolished.

WHEN THE FIRST International Conference on Limitation of Naval Armaments began in Washington in October 1921, the British tried to ban submarines altogether. The reason was simple: although Britain had a large fleet of submarines itself, it also still had the world's largest merchant fleet. The Washington Treaty that resulted from the 1921 conference did manage to impose restrictions on the numbers of major surface warships, but not on submarines. Like it or not, submarines were here to stay.

Despite the horrendous loss of Allied shipping to a relatively small number of U-boats, navies in the 1920s seemed to shy away from full acceptance of the submarine. Germany itself was forbidden to build them, though very soon the embargo was being bypassed. In Britain and France the submarine was still seen mainly as an adjunct to the surface fleet, and design focused on building larger submarines that could travel fast on the surface.

One lesson well learned from the war years was that submarines had more effective uses than coastal defence work, and this was one reason for the increase in size. France received 10 U-boats in 1919, and after inspection of these, nine boats of the Requin class were built in 1923–26, of 990 tonnes (974 tons) surfaced and 1464 tonnes (1441 tons) submerged, with 10 550mm (21.7in) torpedo tubes and a 76mm (3in) deck gun. Part of their role was protection of outlying colonial territories and islands. Modernized in 1935–37, they served in World War II. Requin is seen with full radio gear fixed to dismountable masts; *Espadon*, of the same class, is in submersible configuration. A medium-size and range boat, *Galathée*, was one of three completed between 1923 and 1927; they too had the larger-size 533mm (21in) torpedo tubes (seven). From 1925, 31 submarines of the Redoutable class were built up to 1930, in three sets, of increasing power and speed. Displacing 1595 tonnes (1570 tons) surfaced and 2117 tonnes

FRENCH SUBMARINE CLASSES 1920–38			
Class	Number	Launched	Note
O'Byrne	3	1919–20	Stricken by 1935
Joessel	2	1920	Stricken 1935
Maurice Callot	1	1921	Stricken 1936
Pierre Chailley	1	1921	Stricken 1936
Requin	9	1924–27	Last survivor scrapped 1946
Sirène	4	1925–26	Last survivor sunk 1944
Ariane	4	1925–27	Last survivor sunk 1942
Circe	4	1925–27	Last survivor sunk 1943
Redoutable	31	1928–37	Last 4 broken up 1952
Saphir	6	1928–35	Last one stricken 1949
Argonaute	4	1929–32	All broken up 1946
Diane	9	1930–32	Last 3 broken up 1946
Orion	2	1931	Broken up 1943
Surcouf	1	1934	Sunk 1942
Minerve	6	1934–38	Last one broken up 1954

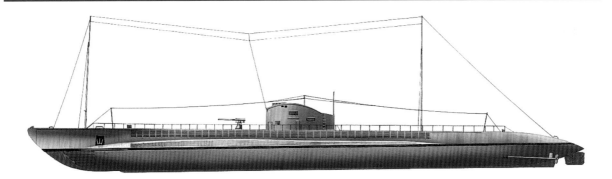

▲ Requin

French Navy, patrol submarine, Mediterranean, 1942

Requin was seized by the Germans at Bizerta in December 1942 and passed to the Italians as *FR113*. It was scuttled on 9 September 1943. Another, *Souffleur*, was sunk by the British submarine *Parthian* on 29 June 1941. *Marsouin* and *Narval* evaded German capture at Toulon, but *Narval* was sunk by a mine en route for Malta in December 1940.

Specifications

Crew: 54

Powerplant: Twin screw diesel; electric motors

Max Speed: Surfaced: 15 knots; Submerged: 9 knots

Surface Range: 10,469km (5650nm) at 10 knots

Displacement: Surfaced: 974 tonnes (990 tons); Submerged: 1464 tonnes (1441 tons)

Dimensions (length/beam/draught): 78.25m x 6.84m x 5.10m (256ft 7in x 22ft 6in x 16ft 9in)

Commissioned: July 1924

Armament: 10 550mm (21.7in) torpedo tubes

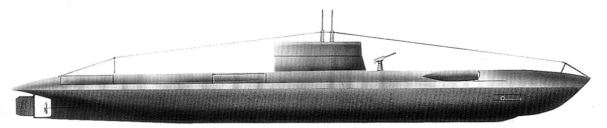

▲ Galathée

French Navy, patrol submarine, 1940

Galathée formed part of the Vichy French fleet at Toulon from June 1940, but these boats saw little or no action. When the Germans occupied Toulon on 27 November 1942, it was scuttled. Refloated in 1945, it was not recommissioned and was eventually sold as a derelict hulk in 1955.

Specifications

Crew: 41

Powerplant: Twin screw diesel; electric motors

Max Speed: Surfaced: 13.5 knots; Submerged: 7.5 knots

Surface Range: 6485km (3500nm) at 7.5 knots

Displacement: Surfaced: 619 tonnes (609 tons);

Submerged: 769 tonnes (757 tons)

Dimensions (length/beam/draught): 64m x 5.2m x 4.3m (210ft x 17ft x 14ft)

Commissioned: December 1925

Armament: Seven 551mm (21.7in) torpedo tubes; one 76mm (3in) gun

▲ Espadon

French Navy, then Italian transport submarine, Mediterranean, 1943

Captured at Bizerta with *Requin* and *Phoque* of the same class, and commissioned into the *Regia Marina* as *FR114*, *Espadon* was undergoing conversion to a transport boat at Castellamare di Stabia, but with the fall of Italy in September 1943, it was scuttled. Though raised by the Germans, it was not recommissioned.

Specifications

Crew: 54

Powerplant: Twin screw diesel engines; electric motors

Max Speed: Surfaced: 15 knots; Submerged: 9 knots

Surface Range: 10,469km (5650nm) at 10 knots

Displacement: Surfaced: 1168 tonnes (1150 tons); Submerged: 1464 tonnes (1441 tons)

Dimensions (length/beam/draught):78.2m x 6.8m x 5m (256ft 9in x 22ft 5in x 16ft 9in)

Commissioned: May 1926

Armament: 10 533mm (21in) torpedo tubes; one 100mm (3.9in) gun

(2084 tons) submerged, the original armament was nine 21.7in (551mm) and two 15.7in (399mm) torpedo tubes, one 100mm (3.9in) deck gun and two 13.2mm (0.5in) AA machine guns.

Prohibitions

Germany was prohibited from building submarines, but a hint of what might have been is the design of *U-112*, projected in the last months of the war as a large, heavily armed submarine with eight 533mm (21in) torpedo tubes, four 127mm (5in) guns and two 20mm (0.8in) AA guns. Though a keel was never laid, this concept of the submarine cruiser, which was also intended to carry a spotter aircraft, was highly influential, not least on the Imperial Japanese Navy. Meanwhile, by 1922, the Germans were

circumventing the ban on submarine-building by using a front-company as a submarine design office in The Netherlands. This was at first not so much a political as an industrial move: several large German companies had acquired great expertise in submarine construction and were determined to capitalize on it. But soon the German Navy was discreetly involved. Confidential negotiations with several governments, including Estonia, Finland and Turkey, would ultimately lead to construction orders. From mid-decade, Germany and Russia co-operated in clandestine development of new submarine types.

British Developments

After the war Great Britain scrapped 90 submarines and cancelled orders for 31 under construction,

▲ U-boat Cruiser

Imperial German Navy, projected cruiser design

A German submarine that might have been. Drawings showed a boat with twin gun turrets and heavy AA armament. With a projected surface speed of 23 knots, they were intended to sink other ships while surfaced, reserving torpedoes for large targets. Many elements of the design went into the Type XI U-boats of World War II.

Specifications

Crew: 110	tons); Submerged: 3688 tonnes (3630 tons)
Powerplant: Two shafts, diesel; electric motors	Dimensions (length/beam/draught): 115m x
Max Speed: Surfaced: 23 knots; Submerged:	9.5m x 6m (377ft x 31ft x 20ft)
7 knots	Commissioned: N/A
Surface Range: 25,266km (13,635nm) at	Armament: Eight 533mm (21in) torpedo tubes;
12 knots	four 127mm (5in) guns; two 30mm (1.18in)
Displacement: Surfaced: 3190 tonnes (3140	and two 20mm (0.8in) AA guns

Specifications

Crew: 75	tons); Submerged: 3657 tonnes (3600 tons)
Powerplant: Twin screw diesel; electric motors	Dimensions (length/beam/draught): 110.8m x
Max Speed: Surfaced: 19.5 knots (36.1km/h;	9m x 4.8m (363ft 6in x 29ft 10in x 15ft 9in)
22.4mph)	Commissioned: December 1925
Surface Range: 23,000km (12,400 nm)	Armament: Six 533mm (21in) torpedo tubes; four
Displacement: Surfaced: 3098 tonnes (3050	132mm (5.2in) guns

▲ X-1

Royal Navy, experimental submarine

Britain's final attempt to produce a ship that combined the qualities of a submersible and a surface-combat vessel. Double-hulled, *X-1* carried ASDIC and range-finding instruments. The fire-control platform could be raised 0.6m (2ft) in action. Though it handled well and its mechanical problems might have been resolved, it remained a one-off.

though a further 24 were completed. The British 'submarine monitor' *M-1* was lost with all hands in a collision with a surface vessel in 1925, and the Admiralty used the remaining two of the class for experiments. *M-2* was fitted with a watertight seaplane hangar in place of the big gun, as well as a catapult ramp for launching the seaplane. It sank off Portland, England, in 1932, and was found on the bottom with the hangar doors and the hatch to the hangar flooded. *M-3* was converted to a minelayer, and survived to be sold off in 1932.

The Royal Navy launched the one-off X-1 type in 1925, with four 5.2in (132mm) guns in twin turrets set fore and aft of the tower and six 21in (533mm) torpedo tubes. Powered by two Admiralty diesels with two ex-U-boat MAN diesels for battery-

charging, and two electric motors, it had a theoretical power output of 8000hp (6000kW) and was intended for long-range cruising to and between foreign stations, but although it had good handling qualities, a potential surface speed of 20 knots, and could travel halfway around the world without refuelling, its engines were chronically unreliable, and it was scrapped in 1936.

Italian Navy

In 1927, the Italian Navy received its first large submarines, the four Balilla class boats of which *Domenico Millelire* was one, built by Ansaldo-San Giorgio. An emergency auxiliary motor was provided in addition to two diesels and two electric motors. All made long ocean cruises in the 1930s to boost the

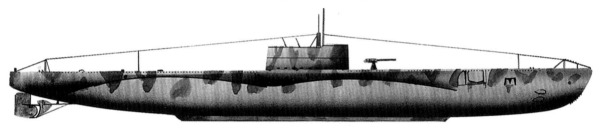

Specifications

Crew: 76	Submerged: 2275 tonnes (2240 tons)
Powerplant: Twin screw diesels; one auxiliary	Dimensions (length/beam/draught): 97m x 8.5m
motor; two electric motors	x 4m (319ft 3in x 27ft 9in x 13ft 1in)
Max Speed: Surfaced: 17.5 knots; Submerged:	Commissioned: September 1927
8.9 knots	Armament: Six 533mm (21in) torpedo tubes; one
Surface Range: 7401km (3800nm) at 10 knots	102mm (4in) gun
Displacement: Surfaced: 1585 tonnes (1560 tons);	

▲ Domenico Millelire

Italian Navy, Balilla class submarine, 1941

In order to get under anti-submarine nets and avoid entanglement, submarines involved in inshore attacks, or having to pass through narrow protected straits, had a pair of heavy wires rigged from bow to tower and stern. These were intended to lift the base of the net without the hull being touched.

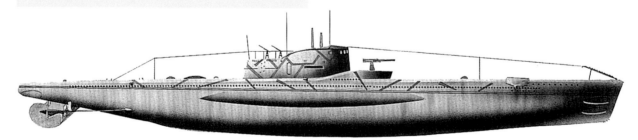

▲ Giovanni Bausan

Italian Navy, Pisani class patrol submarine

The Pisani class suffered from instability problems, which were partly rectified by fitting bulges to the bows, but this, and their obsolescent design, meant that little use was made of them as combat boats in World War II. *Des Genys* was used as a battery-charging hulk and *Marcantonio Colonna* was broken up in 1943. Only *Vettor Pisani* survived the war.

Specifications

Crew: 48	Submerged: 1075 tonnes (1058 tons)
Powerplant: Twin screw diesel; electric motors	Dimensions (length/beam/draught): 68.2m x 6m
Max Speed: Surfaced: 15 knots; Submerged:	x 4.9m (223ft 9in x 20ft x 16ft 2in)
8.2 knots	Commissioned: March 1928
Surface Range: 9260km (5000nm) at 8 knots	Armament: Six 533mm (21in) torpedo tubes; one
Displacement: Surfaced: 894 tonnes (880 tons);	120mm (4in) gun

prestige of Mussolini's Fascist state, and were involved on the Nationalist side in the Spanish Civil War. Also among the considerable range of Italian submarines of the 1920s were the Pisano class, medium-to-large boats of 894 tonnes (880 tons) surfaced and 1075 tonnes (1058 tons) submerged, but with a relatively short range of 9260km (5754 miles) at 8 knots.

Giovanni Bausan, one of the four, launched March 1928, was used as a training ship in 1940–42, when it was converted to an oil hulk. In April 1929, *Ettore Fieramosca* was launched, a one-off design which incorporated a seaplane hangar as an extension of the conning tower, though a plane was never installed.

The unwieldy craft was laid up in June 1941. A more serviceable design was that of the Fratelli Bandiera class, also of 1929; four boats that survived through World War II (engaged on training and transport duties) to be discarded in 1948.

Japan

In accordance with a new naval strategy, Japan's ocean-going boats began to appear from 1919, with *I-21* as the first. It was based on Italian drawings of the Fiat-Laurenti F1-type. In 1924, its number was altered to *RO-2* and a new *I-21* was built, based on the design of the German *UB-125*, which Japan had

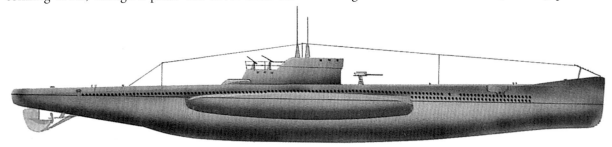

Specifications

Crew: 52	Displacement: Surfaced: 880 tonnes (866 tons);
Powerplant: two diesel engines; two electric	Submerged: 1114 tonnes (1096 tons)
motors	Dimensions (length/beam/draught): 69.8m x
Max Speed: Surfaced: 15.1 knots; Submerged:	7.2m x 5.2m (229ft x 23ft 8in x 17ft)
8.2 knots	Commissioned: August 1929
Surface Range: 8797km (4750nm) at 8.5 knots	Armament: Eight 533mm (21in) torpedo tubes

▲ Fratelli Bandiera

Italian Navy, patrol, then transport submarine

Like the Pisani class, the four Bandiera boats had to be modified to obviate stability problems in heavy seas, which slowed them down. They were used for training and transport in World War II; one, *Santorre Santarosa*, was torpedoed and scuttled in January 1943; the others were stricken in 1948.

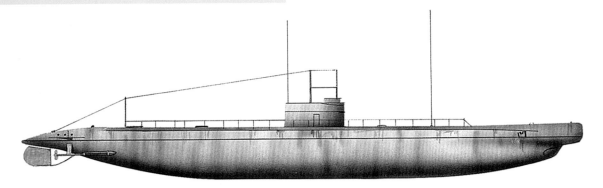

▲ I-21

Imperial Japanese Navy, patrol submarine, 1930

Marking the start of the Japanese Navy's interest in ocean-going submarines, built at the Kawasaki Yard in Kobe, *I-21* was a large boat for 1920, but was later reclassified as a second-class RO type. Its career was relatively brief, being stricken in 1930, by which time Japanese submarine design had made considerable strides.

Specifications

Crew: 45	Displacement: Surfaced: 728 tonnes (717 tons);
Powerplant: Twin screw diesel; electric motors	Submerged: 1063 tonnes (1047 tons)
Max Speed: Surfaced: 13 knots; Submerged:	Dimensions (length/beam/draught): 65.6m x 6m
8 knots	x 4.2m (215ft 3in x 19ft 8in x 13ft 9in)
Surface Range: 19,456km (10,500nm) at	Commissioned: November 1919
8 knots	Armament: Five 457mm (18in) torpedo tubes

acquired at the end of the war. The original *I-21* was stricken in 1930. By then, Japanese submarine technology was well embarked on its own unique course. Designers were instructed to work on boats with a high surface speed, able to keep up with a battle-fleet or a fast cruiser squadron, and the concept of the 'submarine cruiser' was pursued with maximum enthusiasm at the new Submarine School that had been set up at Kure in 1920.

Japan also played host to several hundred German technicians and ex-naval officers. The *KD-1* submarine, completed in 1924, was said to be partly based on the British L-class, but had a double hull, displacing 1525 tonnes (1500 tons) surfaced and 2469 tonnes (2430 tons) submerged. Its range was a remarkable 37,000km (23,000 miles) but its engines were inadequate. More successful was *KD-2*, completed in 1925 and based on *U-139*. Its range was half that of *KD-1*. It was armed with eight 533mm (21in) torpedo tubes, 16 torpedoes and a 120mm (4.8in) deck gun. From 1924, the Imperial Japanese Navy reclassified its submarines under the rubrics I (first-class submarine), RO (medium or coastal submarine), and HA (small or midget type).

US Navy

The US Navy obtained six U-boats as war prizes in 1919, including *U-140*, and US Navy officers quickly found the German vessels superior to US submarines in almost every respect. This discovery came too late to change the S-class currently under construction, of which no fewer than 51 were launched between 1919 and 1925. Following a basic order for an 813-tonne (800-ton) patrol boat, three prototypes were built, of which *S1*, from the Electric Boat Co., and *S3*, designed by the USN Bureau of Construction and Repair and built at the Portsmouth Navy Yard, were accepted. *S1* was a single-hull design and 25 were built on this models. The others, based on *S3*, were double-hulled, with the conning tower set distinctly behind the mid-point.

S1 was one of the first submarines to have retractable bow planes. All the S-class had four forward 533mm (21in) torpedo tubes, and some had a stern tube. Various deck guns were fitted at different times. In 1923, *S1* was experimentally fitted with a cylindrical hangar to hold a partially dismantled Martin *MS-1* floatplane. Despite their shortcomings, even more apparent by 1941, 42 of the S-boats were

JAPANESE SUBMARINE CLASSES, 1920–38			
Class	Number	Launched	Note
L4	10	1922–26	Patrol/training. Based on GB 'L-class'
KD1	1	1924	Fleet boat
KD2	1	1925	Training boat
J1	4	1926–29	Long-range cruiser
KR5	4	1927–28	Minelayer
KD3	9	1927–30	Training boats
KD4	3	1929–30	Patrol boats
KD5	3	1932	Patrol boats
KD6	8	1934–38	Patrol boats
J1 (modified)	1	1932	Seaplane carrier
J2	1	1935	Seaplane carrier
J3	2	1937–38	Seaplane carrier/command boat

still in service in December 1941, in both the Atlantic and Pacific fleets. Six were transferred to Britain's Royal Navy as the P-class in 1942 (one later passed on to the Polish navy and lost through friendly fire) and seven were lost through wreck or enemy action. S-class boats sank 14 Japanese ships in the Pacific, but by mid-1943 they were relegated to the training role. Wartime alterations included modification of the tower to allow for installation of AA guns, and new shear structure to accommodate periscope and masts.

Cruiser submarines form only part of a pattern of design and construction that by the mid-1920s also embraced the more modest objective of improving the small-to-medium size patrol submarine, primarily for work in coastal waters but also as an ocean-going attack boat. Design work was going ahead in several countries, including the Netherlands and the recently formed Soviet Russia. A secret German–Soviet co-operation agreement was made in 1926, and the drawings for four types, *U-105*, *UB-48*, *U-122* (minelayer) and *U-139* (cruiser) were passed on. A six-year programme for 12 submarines was initiated. By 1928, this had been enlarged to 18 large and five small submarines, and Soviet Russia's first two classes, Dekabrist and Leninets, resulted from this. In 1930, the sunken and salvaged British *L-55* was recommissioned and became an additional test-bed for Soviet engineers, who also had their own submarine tradition to draw on.

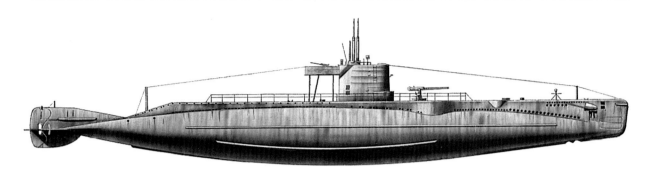

Specifications

Crew: 42	Submerged: 1107 tonnes (1090 tons)
Powerplant: Twin shaft diesels	Dimensions (length/beam/draught): 64.3m x
Max Speed: Surfaced: 14.5 knots; Submerged:	6.25m x 4.6m (211ft x 20ft 6in x 15ft 3in)
11 knots	Commissioned: September 1922
Surface Range: 6333km (3420nm) at 6.5 knots	Armament: Four 533mm (21in) torpedo tubes;
Displacement: Surfaced: 864 tonnes (850 tons);	one 102mm (4in) gun

▲ **S-28**

US Navy, patrol submarine

The S-class formed the backbone of America's inter-war submarine fleet, and marked a real advance on the wartime classes. They were the first USN boats to have 533mm (21in) tubes. These proved unsuitable for the Mark 14 torpedo developed prior to World War II and they fired the older (and more reliable) Mark 10.

Technical developments
1920s–30s

From modest beginnings with simple externally mounted hydrophones, the quest is on to enable submarines to track their targets and communicate with land, while submerged.

THE USE OF PULSED SOUND waves to detect the distance and course of an underwater vessel had been experimented with since at least 1914, and the principle of the hydrophone was well known. Originally, this was simply a microphone extended into the water that could pick up sound waves, such as those of a turning propeller, though soon it was elaborated into a pair of directional microphones fixed on a revolvable mount.

But it was 1920 before the ASDIC system was given sea trials by the Royal Navy, and the JP submarine hydrophone by the US Navy. ASDIC combined hydrophones with a sound emitter whose pulses would reflect off any solid body they met. Range could be calculated by the length of time the echo took to return. The first submarine with an operational ASDIC system was HMS *H-32* (commissioned April 1919) in 1922, followed by some of the L-class boats.

The sets were placed on the deck of the hull. But only seven were installed on submarines by 1926. As

an 'Anti-Submarine Detection' device it was relatively primitive, confined to low speeds and short range, and was hard to interpret. Effective depth finding would not be achieved until the summer of 1944.

Although British naval planners would place great reliance on ASDIC, it was far from dependable. The Italian submarine *Iride* fired a torpedo at the British destroyer HMS *Havock*, on anti-belligerent patrol off Spain, on 31 August 1937; the destroyer had picked up Iride's ASDIC signal but failed to hold it (the torpedo missed).

In 1938, the Type 129 ASDIC set was designed, as an attack set, and would be the standard British system in World War II. It was the first to be located inside a streamlined keel dome set at the fore-end of the ballast-keel, and could be used for echo-detection ranging, hydrophone-listening and underwater communication.

As with radar, there is a myth that only the British possessed underwater detection systems, but this is not the case. In the 1930s, the Germans too were working on underwater listening devices, of several kinds. One was the TAG (*Torpedoalarmgerät* or torpedo alarm), which listened for approaching torpedoes; another was the NHG (L), which was intended to tell an ASW vessel which side a submarine was approaching from; and then there was the multiple-receiver GHG (*Gruppehörgerät*), using a minimum of 24 microphones distributed along the sides of a Type II U-boat to 48 on a Type VIIC. The US Navy, too, was experimenting with echo-ranging gear, though in a rather lethargic manner. By 1933, only five boats had been fitted.

One of the submarine designers' prime tasks was to come up with a diesel engine that was compact, reliable and sufficiently powerful to drive the boat at a speed better than 10 knots, which was as much as most pre-1920s submarines could achieve. There were other demands, including the improvement of communications systems and diving mechanisms, and improving manoeuvrability when submerged.

The new larger submarines were often slow to dive, a potentially fatal shortcoming now that aerial detection was a regular feature of life for submariners. Amidst the various concerns for improvement of the vessel, most countries, with the exception of Japan, paid little attention to its armament, and the technology of torpedoes remained at a World War I stage.

▲ Argonaute

French Navy, coastal submarine for Mediterranean service

This Schneider-Laubeuf design for a 'second-class' (i.e. smaller, not ocean-going) boat was a successful and effective one, with good handling qualities and a fast diving time. They served in the Mediterranean, for which they were designed. Completed in 1932, *Argonaute* also provided better crew accommodation than its predecessors.

Specifications

Crew: 89	tons); Submerged: 4145 tonnes (4080 tons)
Powerplant: Twin shaft diesels; electric motors	Dimensions (length/beam/draught): 116m x
Max Speed: Surfaced: 15 knots; Submerged:	10.4m x 4.6m (381ft x 34ft x 15ft 6in)
8 knots	Commissioned: November 1927
Surface Range: 10,747km (5800nm) at 10 knots	Armament: Four 533mm (21in) torpedo tubes;
Displacement: Surfaced: 2753 tonnes (2710	two 152mm (6in) guns; 60 mines

▲ Surcouf

French Navy, submarine gunboat, Atlantic 1942

Described as a 'corsair-submarine', *Surcouf* was intended as a commerce raider, equipped with a Besson MB411 floatplane and a 4.5m (15ft) motorboat, and with room to hold around 40 prisoners. Its cruising endurance was a maximum 90 days. Its designers did not anticipate attacks from the air, as it took two minutes to dive.

Specifications

Crew: 118	tons); Submerged: 4373 tonnes (4304 tons)
Powerplant: Twin screw diesel; electric motors	Dimensions (length/beam/draught): 110m x
Max Speed: Surfaced: 18 knots; Submerged:	9.1m x 9.07m (360ft 10in x 29ft 9in x 29ft 9in)
8.5 knots	Commissioned: October 1929
Surface Range: 18,530km (10,000nm) at	Armament: Two 203mm (8in) guns; eight 551mm
10 knots	(21.7in) and four 400mm (15.75in) torpedo
Displacement: Surfaced: 3302 tonnes (3250	tubes

BRITISH SUBMARINE CLASSES, 1920–38			
Class	Number	Launched	Note
X1	1	1925	'Commerce raider'; 4 13cm (5.2in) guns
O	9	1926–29	First with ASDIC; 3 built for Chile, 1929
P	6	1929	Far East service; scrapped 1946
R	4	1930	Far East service; scrapped 1946
S	12	1930–37	
River	3	1932–35	Final effort at a 'fleet' submarine
Porpoise	6	1932–38	Minelayers; scrapped 1946
T	15	1935–38	More built 1940–42
U	3	1938	More built 1939–40

French Developments

In France, the submarine *Fulton* had been laid down as early as 1913, intended to be driven by 4000hp (2983kW) turbines, but these were displaced by diesel motors. The original machinery was responsible for the rearwards elongation of the conning tower. Between 1929 and 1932, five boats of the Argonaute class were completed for service in the Mediterranean, armed with six 550mm (21.7in) torpedo tubes and a 75mm (3in) gun. *Argonaute*, manned by a Vichy French crew, was sunk by the

British ships *Achates* and *Westcott* in 1942 when trying to oppose Operation Torch, along with a sister boat, *Actéon*. They serve as a reminder that practical, medium-size boats were also being built at this time, though the headlines were grabbed by the end-product of the drive for size, the huge *Surcouf*. Launched on 18 October 1929, this was the largest submarine in the world until the introduction of the Japanese 400 class, displacing 3302 tonnes (3250 tons) surfaced, and 4373 tonnes (4304 tons) submerged. *Surcouf* carried two 203mm (8in) guns and a seaplane hangar as well as 12 torpedo tubes, eight of 550mm (21.7in) and four of 400mm (15.75in). It proved to be a clumsy vessel with an embarrassing history of mishaps, but in June 1940 it escaped from Brest and was taken over by the Royal Navy at Plymouth. Later crewed by Free French sailors, it was lost in collision with a freighter in the Gulf of Mexico, on 18 February 1942.

Royal Navy

In 1926, Britain launched HMS *Oberon*, first of the nine O-class submarines. With a surface displacement of 1513 tonnes (1490 tons) and 1922 tonnes (1892 tons) submerged, eight 533mm (21in) torpedo tubes, and a 102mm (4in) gun, they were intended for long-distance patrol, with a range of up to 15,550km (9660 miles). Britain still maintained fleets across the globe, and the O-class were intended to serve anywhere from Portsmouth to Hong Kong (*Otway* and *Oxley*, at first sent to the Royal Australian Navy, were returned to

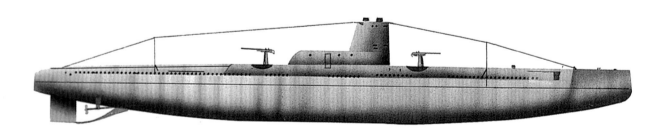

▲ **Fulton**

French Navy, fast submarine

With its sister-boat *Joessel*, *Fulton* was meant to make 20 knots with steam turbines, but the diesels actually fitted gave 16.5 knots, still above average. Two integral bow tubes were fitted, with four hull-mounted tubes and two external cradles. The conning towers were rebuilt in the 1920s. Both boats were stricken in 1935.

Specifications

Crew: 45

Powerplant: Twin screw diesel engines; electric motors

Max Speed: 16.5 knots

Surface Range: 7964km (4300nm) at 10 knots

Displacement: Surfaced: 884 tonnes (870 tons);

Submerged: 1267 tonnes (1247 tons)

Dimensions (length/beam/draught): 74m x 6.4m x 3.6m (242ft 9in x 21ft x 11ft 10in)

Commissioned: April 1919

Armament: Eight 450mm (17.7in) torpedo tubes; two 75mm (3in) guns

Britain in 1931). These were boats of traditional configuration and size, in line from World War I classes, though they incorporated many improvements, such as a longer periscope to allow them to cruise at periscope depth without danger of being rammed. Maximum diving depth was 152m (500ft).

The Oberons were easily identifiable with their long tower and high-mounted gun. These were the first British boats equipped with VLF radio, operable at periscope depth, also with Type 116 ASDIC. This system was installed in a large vertical tube that

passed through the pressure hull; it was soon replaced by Type 118/9, which was fitted close to the hull. The slightly larger Parthian class were completed in 1930–31 and stationed at first with the China Squadron. In World War II they were adapted to lay 18 M2 mines from the torpedo tubes, and sent to the Mediterranean. *Parthian* was lost in the Adriatic on 11 August 1943; only one of the class survived the war.

Of similar size to the O-class, but with six 533mm (21in) torpedo tubes and one 102mm (4in) gun, the

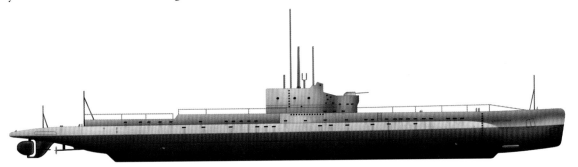

▲ HMS Oberon

Royal Navy, patrol submarine, China Squadron

Completed in 1927, *Oberon* was of an advanced design for the period, and with up-to-date instrumentation. One defect was the riveted saddle tanks, which contained additional fuel but tended to leave a trail of leakage. Placed in reserve between 1937 and 1939, it was used in World War II primarily for training and decommissioned in July 1944.

Specifications

Crew: 54

Powerplant: Twin screw diesel; electric motors

Max Speed: Surfaced: 13.7 knots; Submerged: 7.5 knots

Surface Range: 9500km (5633nm) at 10 knots

Displacement: Surfaced: 1513 tonnes (1490 tons); Submerged: 1922 tonnes (1892 tons)

Dimensions (length/beam/draught): 83.4m x 8.3m x 4.6m (273ft 8in x 27ft 3in x 15ft)

Commissioned: 1927

Armament: Eight 533mm (21in) torpedo tubes

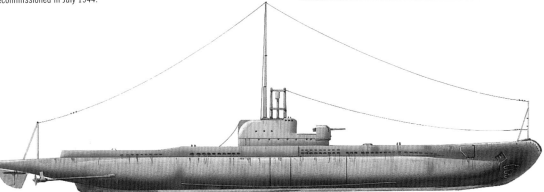

Specifications

Crew: 53

Powerplant: Twin shaft diesel; electric motors

Max Speed: Surfaced: 17.5 knots; Submerged: 8.6 knots

Surface Range: 9500km (5633nm) at 10 knots

Displacement: Surfaced: 1788 tonnes (1760

tons); Submerged: 2072 tonnes (2040 tons)

Dimensions (length/beam/draught): 88.14m x 9.12m x 4.85m (289ft 2in x 29ft 11in x 16ft)

Commissioned: June 1929

Armament: Eight 533mm (21in) torpedo tubes; one 102mm (4in) gun

▲ HMS Parthian

Royal Navy, patrol submarine/minelayer, Mediterranean, 1940–41

New higher-capacity batteries gave the Parthian class greater underwater endurance. If not carrying mines, they took 14 torpedoes of the standard British Mark VIII type. *Parthian* sank the Italian submarine *Diamante* on 20 June 1940 and the Vichy French *Souffleur* on 25 June 1941, as well as numerous Axis merchant vessels.

six-strong Porpoise class entered service between 1932 and 1938. Sometimes known as the Grampus class, it was the only British submarine designed specifically for minelaying, though six each of the E- and L-classes had been converted for the purpose during the war.

Drawing on experience with the converted *M-3* in 1927, the class carried 50 mines stored on racks between the pressure hull and the floodable deck casing. Mines were laid while running on the surface. *Porpoise's* range of 16,400km (10,190 miles) was slightly greater than that of *Oberon* or *Parthian*.

Italian Types

Italy in the 1930s continued to expand an impressive range of submarine types. Minelaying was seen as a key aspect of submarine work, and many boats were converted for this purpose. *Filippo Corridoni*, launched 1930, was designed as a minelayer, capable of carrying up to 24 mines, and also armed with four 533mm (21in) torpedo tubes and a 102mm (4in) gun. Surprisingly, its speeds were undistinguished: 11.5 knots on the surface, 7 knots submerged.

With its sister boat *Bragadin* it survived until the dispersal of the Italian fleet in 1948. In 1933, the *Sirena* class was introduced, classed as a coastal submarine, capable of diving to 100m (330ft). Two 13mm (0.5in) AA guns were added to the 100mm (3.9in) deck gun during World War II. *Galatea* was the sole member of the class to survive the war.

Long-range cruising was the purpose of the *Calvi* class, one of which was *Enrico Tazzoli*, launched in October 1935. Like many Italian submarines, it was semi-secretly involved in the Spanish Civil war. Refitted as a transport boat in 1942, it was sunk by aircraft in the Bay of Biscay in May 1943 while on a voyage to Japan, along with the transport submarine *Barbarigo*.

Yet another large Italian type was *Pietro Micca*, launched at Taranto as a prototype in March 1935, and though no others followed, it was a reliable and useful boat, storing 20 mines in vertical trunks and also fitted with six 533mm (21in) torpedo tubes and two 120mm (4.7in) guns. In late 1940 it was converted for transporting ammunition and fuel, but its career was terminated by the British submarine HMS *Trooper* in the Otranto Straits on 29 July 1943.

Japanese Subs

More rigorously and successfully than any other Navy, the Japanese worked on the concept of the large cruising, aircraft-carrying, fleet-escorting submarine. This was not a random decision but a carefully worked-out policy, anticipating trans-Pacific war with the United States and how it should be waged. The boats *I-7* and *I-8*, launched in July 1935, had a range of 26,600km (16,530 miles) at a speed of 16 knots. The diesel motors could produce a maximum speed of 23 knots. Diving depth was

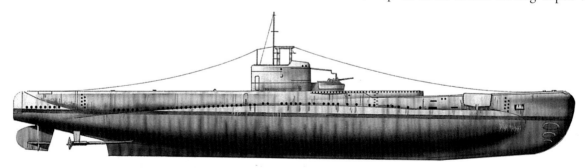

Specifications

Crew: 61	tons); Submerged: 2086 tonnes (2053 tons)
Powerplant: Twin screw diesels; electric motors	Dimensions (length/beam/draught): 81.5m x 9m
Max Speed: Surfaced: 15 knots; Submerged:	x 3.75m (267ft x 29ft 9in x 13ft 9in)
8.75 knots	Commissioned: August 1932
Surface Range: 10,191km (5500nm) at 10 knots	Armament: Six 533mm (21in) torpedo tubes; one
Displacement: Surfaced: 1524 tonnes (1500	102mm (4in) gun

▲ HMS Porpoise

Royal Navy, Grampus class minelayer, Malacca Straits, January 1945

Porpoise was recognizable from the others in its class by the external fuel tanks terminating about 18m (60ft) short of the bow structure. They served at various times in the West Indies, the Mediterranean and the China Station. Five were lost in World War II, including *Porpoise* itself, sunk by Japanese aircraft in the Malacca Straits on 19 January 1945.

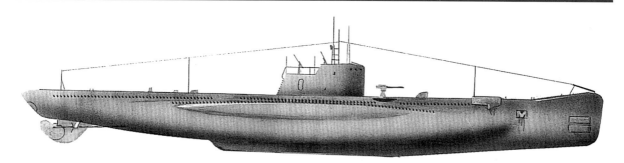

Specifications

Crew: 55

Powerplant: Twin screw diesels; electric motors

Max Speed: Surfaced: 11.5 knots; Submerged:
7 knots

Surface Range: 16,668km (9000nm) at 8 knots

Displacement: Surfaced: 996 tonnes (981 tons);

Submerged: 1185 tonnes (1167 tons)

Dimensions (length/beam/draught): 71.5m x 6m
x 4.8m (234ft 7in x 20ft 2in x 15ft 9in)

Commissioned: March 1950

Armament: Four 533mm (21in) torpedo tubes;
one 102mm (4in) gun; up to 24 mines

▲ Filippo Corridoni

Italian Navy, minelayer, Mediterranean, 1942

Mines were carried in two tubes. Seventeen different mine types were used by Italy, plus German versions. Some 54,457 were laid, mostly of moored types, accounting for 32 vessels, including 11 submarines. *Corridoni* was also used as a transport boat between Italy and North Africa. It was stricken in 1948.

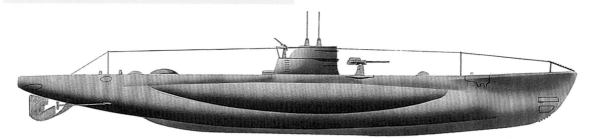

▲ Galatea

Italian Navy, coastal submarine, Mediterranean, 1941

International agreements limited the size of coastal submarines to 610 tonnes (600 tons) and the Italians and French both had several '600' designs, though size tended to creep up with successive variants. Most of the Sirena class saw intensive action in the Mediterranean in 1940–43, and all except *Galatea* were lost. It was stricken in 1948.

Specifications

Crew: 45

Powerplant: Twin screw diesel; electric motors

Max Speed: Surfaced: 14 knots; Submerged:
7.7 knots

Surface Range: 9260km (5000nm) at 8 knots

Displacement: Surfaced: 690 tonnes (679 tons);

Submerged: 775 tonnes (701 tons)

Dimensions (length/beam/draught): 60.2m x
6.5m x 4.6m (197ft 5in x 21ft 2in x 15ft)

Commissioned: October 1933

Armament: Six 533mm (21in) torpedo tubes;
one 100mm (3.9in) gun

Specifications

Crew: 76

Powerplant: Twin screw diesels; electric motors

Max Speed: Surfaced: 17.5 knots; Submerged:
9 knots

Surface Range: 7041km (3800nm) at 10 knots

Displacement: Surfaced: 1473 tonnes (1450

tons); Submerged: 1934 tonnes (1904 tons)

Dimensions (length/beam/draught): 87.7m x
7.8m x 4.7m (288ft x 25ft 7in x 15ft 5in)

Commissioned: April 1928

Armament: Six 533mm (21in) torpedo tubes;
one 120mm (4.7in) gun

▲ Enrico Tazzoli

Italian Navy, attack submarine then transport, 1943

Like the Balilla class, which it resembled, the Calvi class was designed by the civilian Ansaldo team. With a full double hull, and improved crew facilities, it was meant for long-range work. Prior to conversion as a transport, *Tazzoli* had sunk 96,553 GRT of Allied shipping in the Atlantic and Mediterranean.

99m (325ft) and they could cruise independently for up to 60 days.

When war came, *I-7* and *I-8* sank seven merchant ships before *I-7* was sunk by the USS *Monaghan* on 22 June 1943. *I-8*'s seaplane was removed and the hangar adapted to carry four Kaiten 'human torpedoes' or suicide submarines. It was sunk on 30 March 1945 in the Okinawa landings. In 1939, the *I-15* or *B-1* type was introduced, a slightly larger, more streamlined version of the aircraft-fitted scouting submarine, of which 20 were completed. One of these, *I-19*, sank the US carrier *Wasp* on 15 September 1942. Two were modified, like *I-8*, to carry Kaiten manned torpedoes.

Not all Japan's first-class submarines were giants. The legacy of *U-139* lived on in the 33 successive Kaidai or KD-class boats, culminating in *KD7*, designed in 1939. Displacing 1656 tonnes (1630 tons) surfaced and 2644 tonnes (2602 tons) submerged, with a range of 15,000km (9320 miles), they carried six 533mm (21in) torpedo tubes and a stock of 12 Type 95 torpedoes.

I-176 is the only Japanese submarine of this class to have sunk a US one, USS *Corvina*, in November 1943. It also severely damaged the cruiser USS *Chester* in October 1942. Later converted to a transport role, *I-176* was blown up in May 1944 by depth charges from US destroyers.

US Navy V-boats

The US Navy also felt the lure of the big cruising submarine. The ability of the *U-151* and similar classes to strike at the American coast had made a deep impression. Drawing on the U-boat designs, nine boats, known as the V-boats, were built between 1919 and 1934. In fact, they formed five separate types. Originally designated only by the V and a number, they received names in 1931. The basic aim was to find an acceptable 'fleet boat' design, on the lines of the German cruisers. *V-1* to *V-3*, later named *Barracuda*, *Bass* and *Bonita*, were not considered successes, partly because of unreliable and underpowered motors, and because they failed to make the required surface and submerged speeds of 21 knots and 9 knots.

ITALIAN SUBMARINE CLASSES, 1920–38			
Class	Number	Launched	Note
Mameli	4	1926–28	Ocean-going; last one stricken 1948
Pisani	4	1927–28	Ocean-going; last one stricken 1947
Balilla	4	1927–28	Ocean-going; all out of action 1943
Bandiera	4	1929	Ocean-going; last one stricken 1948
Ettore Fieramosco	1	1930	Intended as seaplane carrier
Bragadin	2	1929–30	Minelayers; stricken 1948
Settembrini	2	1930–31	Ocean-going; last one stricken 1947
Squalo	4	1930	Ocean-going; last one stricken 1948
Argonauta	7	1931–32	Coastal; last one stricken 1948
Sirena	12	1933	Coastal; last one stricken 1948
Archimede	4	1933–34	Two transferred to Spain, 1937
Glauco	2	1935	Originally for Portugal; stricken 1948
Calvi	3	1935	None survived WWII
Micca	1	1935	Minelayer; sunk 1943
Argo	2	1936	Originally for Portugal; lost WWII
Perla	10	1936	Coastal; two passed to Spain, 1937
Adua	17	1936–38	Another 2 sold to Brazil, 1937
Brin	5	1938–39	Ocean-going; last one stricken 1948
Marcello	11	1937–39	Two converted for cargo work, 1943
Foca	3	1937–38	Minelayers; last 2 stricken 1948

Decommissioned in 1937, they were re-entered and overhauled in 1942–43, converted to cargo carrying, but never used in this role. *Bass* was scuttled as a sonar target in 1945. *V-4*, commissioned in April 1928 and later named *Argonaut*, was the United States' only purpose-built minelaying submarine. It was also the largest US submarine until the nuclear generation; at 116m (382ft) it was longer than its own diving depth of 91m (300ft). In a sense it was a mirror-image of Japan's long-range boats, fulfilling the US side of the same war-plan scenario. Sixty Mark XI moored mines were carried. Despite its size,

lack of engine-space meant it was under-powered, its diesels producing only 15 knots. In World War II *Argonaut* was re-engined and converted to a troop carrier. It was lost off the Solomon Islands on 10 January 1943.

V-5 and *V-6*, *Narwhal* and *Nautilus*, were commissioned in 1930. Displacing 2770 tonnes (2730 tons) surfaced and 3962 tonnes (3900 tons) submerged, they carried two 150mm (6in) guns, as did *Argonaut*. Plans for accommodating a seaplane were dropped and the boats never undertook the scouting missions, but both served usefully. *Nautilus*

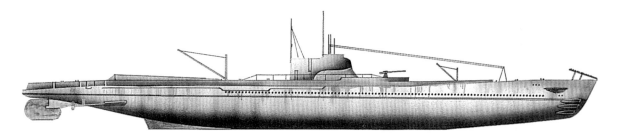

▲ **I-7**

Imperial Japanese Navy, Type Junsen 3 large patrol submarine, 1942

This was an expanded version of the KD-6 patrol submarine design. The intended scouting role of *I-7* and *I-8* was heavily curtailed by American use of carrier-borne attack planes, though both were refitted with extra AA guns in 1942. They were not well adapted to attack mode despite being fast on the surface. Destroyers were faster.

Specifications

Crew: 100

Powerplant: Twin screw diesel; electric motors

Max Speed: Surfaced: 23 knots; Submerged: 8 knots

Surface Range: 26,600km (14,337nm) at 16 knots

Displacement: Surfaced: 2565 tonnes (2525 tons); Submerged: 3640 tonnes (3583 tons)

Dimensions (length/beam/draught): 109.3m x 9m x 5.2m (358ft 7in x 29ft 6in x 17ft)

Commissioned: July 1935

Armament: Six 533mm (21in) torpedo tubes; one 140mm (5.5in) gun

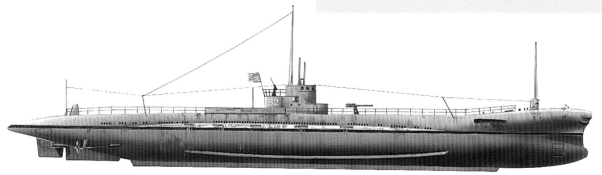

▲ **USS Bass**

US Navy, V-boat, Atlantic, 1942

Originally *V-2*, *Bass* was twice the size of the S-boats, with only two more torpedo tubes. It served with Submarine Division 20 in the Caribbean and Pacific. Put on reserve in 1937, recommissioned in 1940, it was part of Submarine Squadron 3, Submarine Division 31, Atlantic Fleet. A fire on 17 August 1942 killed 25 crewmen.

Specifications

Crew: 85

Powerplant: Twin shaft diesel engines; electric motors

Max Speed: Surfaced: 18 knots; Submerged: 11 knots

Surface Range: 11,118km (6000nm) at 11 knots

Displacement: Surfaced: 2032 tonnes (2000 tons); Submerged: 2662 tonnes (2620 tons)

Dimensions (length/beam/draught): 99.4m x 8.3m x 4.5m (326ft x 27ft 3in x 14ft 9in)

Commissioned: December 1924

Armament: Six 533mm (21in) torpedo tubes; one 76mm (3in) gun was adapted as a seaplane refueller and in World War II both were used as troop carriers on secret missions of both invasion and troop retrieval. They were withdrawn and broken up in 1945. *V-7, Dolphin*, commissioned in 1932, was only half the size of the previous two and was not considered a success though its dimensions are close to those of the wartime Gato and Balao classes.

V-8 and *V-9, Cachalot* and *Cuttlefish*, were the smallest of the V-boats and though they incorporated numerous innovations, from air conditioning (*Cuttlefish*) to partially welded hulls and sophisticated fire-control, they were not effective in wartime conditions and were relegated to training activities

from late 1942. The air conditioning was an immediate success, though other navies were slow to follow the Americans in this. Given the environment they operated in, damp and humidity had always been features of submarine life, but a drier atmosphere was now needed as more sophisticated electrical equipment came into use. Crew comfort was a secondary consideration.

The V- boats have come in for some criticism, with the skipper of one heard to say: 'They were too large for easy handling, too slow in submerging, and too easily seen as targets.' They were, however, perhaps necessary milestones in the search for the 'fleet boat' that the Navy needed.

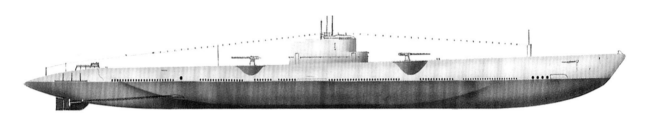

▲ USS Argonaut

US Navy, V-boat, Pacific 1942

On 1 December 1941, *Argonaut* was stationed off Midway on a reconnaissance patrol. Soon after Pearl Harbor it was converted to a transport and special operations role. In June 1942, along with USS *Nautilus*, it landed 211 US Marines to raid Makin Island, by far the biggest submarine landing yet attempted.

Specifications

Crew: 89

Powerplant: Twin shaft diesels; electric motors

Max Speed: Surfaced: 15 knots; Submerged: 8 knots

Surface Range: 10,747km (5800nm) at 10 knots

Displacement: Surfaced: 2753 tonnes (2710 tons); Submerged: 4145 tonnes (4080 tons)

Dimensions (length/beam/draught): 116m x 10.4m x 4.6m (381ft x 34ft x 15ft 6in)

Commissioned: November 1927

Armament: Four 533mm (21in) torpedo tubes; two 152mm (6in) guns, 60 mines

Specifications

Crew: 60

Powerplant: Twin screw diesel engines; electric motors

Max Speed: Surfaced: 17 knots; Submerged: 8 knots

Surface Range: 11,112km (6000nm) at 10 knots

Displacement: Surfaced: 1585 tonnes (1560 tons); Submerged: 2275 tonnes (2240 tons)

Dimensions (length/beam/draught): 97m x 8.5m x 4m (319ft 3in x 27ft 9in x 13ft 3in)

Commissioned: March 1932

Armament: Six 533mm (21in) torpedo tubes; one 102mm (4in) gun

▲ USS Dolphin

US Navy, V-boat

Originally *V-7*, it was smaller than the previous V-boats, and represented an attempt to pack their features and technology into a structure that offered more destructive power per ton of displacement. This problem was resolved more effectively by later designs. *Dolphin* was used through World War II as a training boat, and was broken up in 1946.

Submarine deployment
1930s

The building of very large submarines was given up by most countries, but the numbers of operative boats were growing steadily, despite international conferences aimed at limiting them.

A T THE TALKS preceding the London Naval Treaty in 1930–31, Great Britain again sought the abolition of submarines as combat craft. At that time, the Royal Navy had just over 50, all capable of firing 533mm (21in) torpedoes, and 27 of them had six front tubes for firing salvoes.

Of the other powers, the United States had the largest fleet, 81 boats, though the majority were of the not very satisfactory S-class. France had 66 submarines, Japan had 72 and Italy had 46, but the two latter countries also had substantial building programmes. The Treaty itself limited the size of new submarines to 2032 tonnes (2000 tons) and gun calibre to 130mm (5.1in).

This was no great restriction, since most navies, except Japan's, had abandoned the concept of the very large submarine and wanted to build more medium-sized boats, which were cheaper to build and easier to deploy in a variety of situations.

Great Britain, the United States and Japan agreed not to exceed a total submarine tonnage of 53,545 tonnes (52,700 tons), which was the current British total; France and Italy refused to be bound by this. Neither the Soviet Union nor Germany were represented at these talks.

France

French submarine policy continued to be dictated by the French Navy's relative lack of major surface ships. Of its 66 boats, more than two-thirds were capable of long-range sea-going. Organized in flotillas, squadrons and divisions, submarines were based at Dunkirk and Cherbourg on the Channel coast, Brest and Lorient on the Atlantic, and Toulon on the Mediterranean. On the North African coast there were squadrons or divisions based at Casablanca and Oran with a flotilla HQ at Bizerta. Divisions were also based at Beirut (Libya), Djibouti on the Red Sea and Saigon in French Indo-China (Vietnam).

Henri Poincaré, launched at Lorient in April 1929, was one of the first series of Redoutable class boats, double-hulled and classified as first class or ocean-going, and commissioned in December 1931. Thirty-one of the class were built, in three groups, with 19 in 1924–28, six in 1929–30, and six in 1930–31. Up to 11 torpedo tubes were carried, including six or seven externally mounted. Diving depth was 80m (262ft). Group I's diesel engines produced 6000hp (4474kW); later series were higher powered. They were effective boats whose main defect was a relatively slow dive-time (45–50 seconds), which in

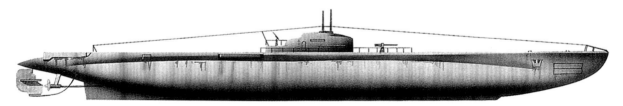

▲ **Henri Poincaré**

French Navy, surface raider

The double-hulled Redoutable class was designed as an advance on the Requin boats and were heavily armed with torpedoes. Their function was that of surface raiders and defenders of the maritime supply line between France and its colonies. In World War II they did very little of either before most were scuttled.

Specifications

Crew: 61	tons); Submerged: 2117 tonnes (2084 tons)
Powerplant: Twin screw diesel; electric motors	Dimensions (length/beam/draught): 92.3m x
Max Speed: Surfaced: 17–20 knots; Submerged:	8.2m x 4.7m (302ft 10in x 27ft x 15ft 5in)
10 knots	Commissioned: April 1929
Surface Range: 18,530km (10,000nm) at	Armament: Nine 550mm (21.7in) and two
10 knots	400mm (15.7in) torpedo tubes; one 82mm
Displacement: Surfaced: 1595 tonnes (1570	(3.2in) gun

World War II conditions was potentially fatal. *Henri Poincaré* was scuttled with six others of the class at Toulon on 27 November 1942; it was salvaged by the Italians and recommissioned, but was sunk in September 1943.

British Subs

In Great Britain, 17 further L-class submarines were commissioned after the end of World War I. With their high-mounted 102mm (4in) gun and raised bridge on a long conning tower, they had a distinctive appearance. By the 1930s they were obsolescent and

most were scrapped during the decade. Two remained in service in World War II, L-23 and L-27, both as training boats. Stricken in 1946, L-23 foundered off Nova Scotia while on tow to a breaker's yard. The successor to the L-class was the O-class, intended to to have greater sea endurance, for service in the Far East.

HMS *Odin*, built at Chatham Naval Dockyard, was lead ship of a second batch of six, launched in 1928–29. Compared to *Oberon* it was slightly longer and wider, with a differently shaped 'ram' bow and retractable bow hydroplanes mounted quite high on the pressure hull. Like the L-class, the gun was

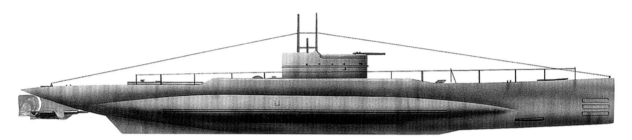

▲ **L-23**

Royal Navy, patrol submarine, North Sea, 1940

Laid down at Vickers, Barrow in Furness, and completed at Chatham RN Dockyard, *L-23* was commissioned on 5 August 1924. By 1929, 30 boats of the class remained, of which 10 were in reserve. By 1939, only a handful remained. In February 1940, *L-23* had a narrow escape from a depth-charge attack from German destroyers.

Specifications

Crew: 36	Submerged: 1097 tonnes (1080 tons)
Powerplant: Twin screw diesel; electric motors	Dimensions (length/beam/draught): 72.7m x
Max Speed: Surfaced: 17.5 knots; Submerged:	7.2m x 3.4m (238ft 6in x 23ft 8in x 11ft 2in)
10.5 knots	Commissioned: July 1919
Surface Range: 8338km (4500nm)	Armament: Four 533mm (21in) torpedo tubes;
Displacement: Surfaced: 904 tonnes (890 tons);	one 102mm (4in) gun

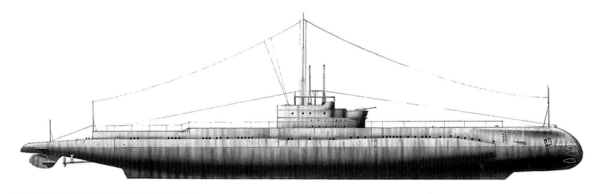

Specifications

Crew: 54	Displacement: Surfaced: 1513 tonnes (1490
Powerplant: Twin screw diesel; electric motors	tons); Submerged: 1922 tonnes (1892 tons)
Max Speed: Surfaced: 17.5 knots; Submerged:	Dimensions (length/beam/draught): 83.4m x
8 knots	8.3m x 4.6m (273ft 8in x 27ft 3in x 15ft)
Surface Range: 9500km (5633nm) at 10 knots	Commissioned: May 1928
	Armament: Eight 533mm (21in) torpedo tubes

▲ **HMS Odin**

Royal Navy, O-class long-range patrol submarine, Mediterranean, 1940

The O-class is more properly named after HMS *Odin* than *Oberon*, which was shorter, lighter and less powerful than the subsequent boats. Apart from *Odin*, *Orpheus* and *Oswald* were also sunk by Italian destroyers, and *Olympus* struck a mine off Malta. *Osiris* and *Otus* were scrapped at Durban, South Africa, in September 1946.

mounted on the forepart of the tower, but the bridge was stepped up in order to provide a wider view. *Odin* had a surface speed of 17.5 knots as against *Oberon's* 15.5, but in most respects there were no significant differences. *Odin* was sunk on 14 June 1940, off Taranto, by the Italian destroyer *Strale*. Only one of the six survived World War II. Three boats of the O-class were built for Chile in 1929, to form the Capitan O'Brien class. They long outlived the British boats, being decommissioned in 1957–58.

Italian Torpedoes

Italian submarines of the 1930s have been criticized for a low ratio of destructive power to weight, and for being too big and bulky to escape detection in clear Mediterranean waters. But they also had positive aspects in combat, among which were very effective torpedoes, produced by the Whitehead plant at Fiume and the naval ordnance factory at Naples. Fiume produced a torpedo that could travel up to 4000m (4400yds) at 50 knots, or 12,000m (13,100 yds) at 30 knots, with a 250kg (551lb) warhead. Italy also produced the magnetically activated torpedo, which exploded underneath a ship's keel, usually breaking its back. (The inventor, Carlo Calosi, was taken to the United States in 1944 after Italy's surrender and passed on details of how to disrupt the torpedo's magnetic field and render it harmless.)

The Squalo class of medium submarines numbered four, completed at Monfalcone in 1930–31, the single-hull design being based on Curio Bernardis' for Fratelli Bandiera. Stability problems

▲ **Delfino**

Italian Navy patrol submarine/transport, Mediterranean, 1942

In an active career *Delfino* was first with the 2nd Submarine Squadron at La Spezia. Then, after a Black Sea cruise, it was based at Naples, before deploying to the Red Sea. In 1940 it was attached to the 51st Squadron, 5th Submarine Division, on the island of Leros. From 1942 it operated as a transport boat from Taranto.

Specifications

Crew: 52

Powerplant: Two diesel engines, two electric motors

Max Speed: Surfaced: 15 knots; Submerged: 8 knots

Surface Range: 7412km (4000nm) at 10 knots

Displacement: Surfaced: 948 tonnes (933 tons); Submerged: 1160 tonnes (1142 tons)

Dimensions (length/beam/draught): 70m x 7m x 7m (229ft x 23ft x 23ft)

Commissioned: April 1930

Armament: Eight 533mm (21in) torpedo tubes, one 102mm (4in) gun

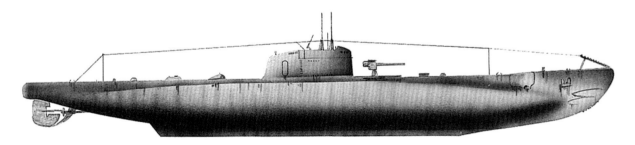

Specifications

Crew: 46

Powerplant: Twin screws, diesel/electric motors

Max Speed: Surfaced: 14 knots; Submerged: 8 knots

Surface Range: 9260km (5000nm) at 8 knots

Displacement: Surfaced: 807 tonnes (794 tons);

Submerged: 1034 tonnes (1018 tons)

Dimensions (length/beam/draught): 63m x 6.9m x 4.5m (207ft x 22ft 9in x 14ft 8in)

Commissioned: December 1936

Armament: Six 533mm (21in) torpedo tubes, one 100mm (3.9in) gun

▲ **Velella**

Italian Navy, surface raider, Atlantic 1940–41

A good sea-boat, *Velella* also saw much action. Though classed as coastal, it was among the submarines sent to Bordeaux for Atlantic service, making four patrols between November 1940 and August 1941. Its sinking in September 1943, while opposing Allied landings at Salerno, was on the day before the Armistice (already signed) was announced.

SOVIET SUBMARINE CLASSES, 1920–38			
Class	Number	Launched	Note
AG	6	1920–21	Two reclaimed by United States; last one sunk 1943
Series I 'Dekabrist'	6	1928–29	Last one stricken c.1958
Series II 'Leninets'	6	1931	Last one broken up 1959
Series III 'Shchuka'	4	1930–31	Last one broken up 1958
Series IV 'Pravda'	3	1934	Last one broken up 1956
Series V 'Losos'	19	1933–35	Last one broken up 1958
Series Vb 'Strelad'	12	1934	Stricken 1950
Series Vbii 'Sayda'	9	1935	Last one broken up 1958
Series VI 'M1'	30	1933–34	Small boats; last ones broken up 1950s
Series VIb 'M53'	20	1934–35	Small boats; last ones broken up 1950s
Series XI 'Voroshilovets'	6	1935–36	Stricken 1950
Series IX 'Nalim'	3	1935–36	All lost in WWII
Series X 'Shch126'	33	1935–37	Last ones broken up 1958
Series XII 'M87'	4	1936–37	Last ones broken up in 1950s
Series IXb 'S4'	4	1936–38	More built from 1939
Series XIII 'L13'	7	1937–38	Stricken 1950
Series XIV 'K1'	5	1937–38	Minelayer; more built from 1939
Series XV 'Mest'	4	1937	More built from 1939

when diving and surfacing were resolved by an enlarged bow design. Operational diving depth was 90m (297ft) . The Squalo boats were assigned first to the 2nd Squadron at La Spezia, then to the 4th Squadron at Naples; in 1936, they were involved in Spanish Civil War operations. In 1937, all four were transferred to the Red Sea. Back in the Mediterranean during World War II, *Delfino* sank the Greek cruiser *Helli* in harbour on 15 August 1940, although Italy and Greece were not yet at war. On 1 August 1941, it shot down an attacking Sunderland flying boat. After 29 missions and 67 training sorties, it sank on 23 March 1942 after colliding with a pilot boat off Taranto.

The economic slump of the 1930s caused Portugal to cancel a 1931 order for two submarines from Italy. The boats, *Argo* and *Velella*, were finally completed for Italy's *Regia Marina* in August 1937. Portugal's Atlantic-facing coast is very different to Italy's, but the boats were of relatively standard type. *Velella* was first attached to the 42nd squadron of the 4th Submarine Group at Taranto, then saw service in the Red Sea with the Submarine Flotilla of Italian East Africa before returning to the Mediterranean. From

US SUBMARINE CLASSES, 1918–39			
Class	Number	Launched	Note
O	7	1918	
R	18	1918–19	1 lost 1942
S	51	1920–25	7 lost
V1-3	3	1925–27	*Barracuda, Bass* and *Bonita* from 1931
V4 Argonaut	1	1928	Minelayer; lost 1943
V5-6 Narwhal	2	1930	Intended seaplane carriers; 66mm (2.6in) guns
V7 Dolphin	1	1932	Carried a motor boat
V8-9 Cachalot	2	1933–34	Submarine cruisers
Porpoise	10	1935–37	4 lost
Salmon	6	1937–38	
Sargo	10	1939	4 lost

December 1940 it was part of the Italian squadron at Bordeaux for a few months, making four Atlantic patrols. Once again in the Mediterranean, it was sunk in the Gulf of Salerno by the British submarine HMS *Shakespeare* on 7 September 1943.

The Soviet Union

Soviet Russia's submarine fleet was greatly expanded in the 1930s, to become numerically the world's largest, though most of the boats were small. The most numerous class, the M- ('Baby') boats, from 1933, totalled 111, with a surfaced displacement ranging from 160 tonnes (158 tons) to 285 tonnes (281 tons). Submarines had to be distributed among the four sea fleets. The S- or Shch-class (from *Shchuka*, 'Pike'), intended to be 200-strong, numbered 88 submarines, all designated as coastal. With a range of 11,100km (6900 miles), they operated with the Baltic, Black Sea, Northern and Pacific fleets. *Shch 303*, *Ersh*, was part of the Baltic fleet. Thirty-two of the class were lost in World War

II, but *Shch 303* was one of the survivors, and was not finally broken up until 1958.

United States

USS *V-6* was launched on 15 March 1930 and commissioned on 1 July that year, as one of the few large American submarines of the period. The name *Nautilus* was given in February 1931. At Pearl Harbor it was flagship of Submarine Division 12, then relocated to San Diego as flagship of Submarine Division 13 from 1935 to 1938 before returning to Pearl Harbor. The rest of its career was spent in the Pacific, where it saw much action during World War II, in 14 patrols that encompassed sea battles, troop landings and reconnaissance missions. *Nautilus* was

▲ **Shch 303**

Soviet Navy, patrol submarine, Baltic Sea, 1941

The Baltic was a difficult sea from every point of view. For most of World War II it was a German pond (with Finnish help), with the Soviet fleet hemmed in at Kronstadt and Leningrad, where Submarine Brigades 1 and 2 were based. Only submarines could slip by, and 26 were lost in 1941 alone. It was very late in the war before the Soviet Union gained control.

Specifications

Crew: 45	Displacement: Surfaced: 595 tonnes (586 tons);
Powerplant: Twin screw diesel engines; electric	Submerged: 713 tonnes (702 tons)
motors	Dimensions (length/beam/draught): 58.5m x
Max Speed: Surfaced: 12.5 knots; Submerged:	6.2m x 4.2m (192ft x 20ft 4in x 13ft 9in)
8.5 knots	Commissioned: November 1931
Surface Range: 11,112km (6000nm) at 8 knots	Armament: Six 533mm (21in) torpedo tubes, two
	45mm (1.8in) guns

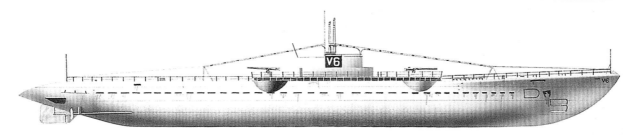

Specifications

Crew: 90	Displacement: Surfaced: 2773 tonnes (2730
Powerplant: Twin screw diesel engines; electric	tons); Submerged: 3962 tonnes (3900 tons)
motors	Dimensions (length/beam/draught): 113m x 10m
Max Speed: Surfaced: 17 knots; Submerged:	x 4.8m (370ft x 33ft 3in x 15ft 9in)
8 knots	Commissioned: March 1930
Surface Range: 33,336km (18,000nm) at	Armament: Six 533mm torpedo tubes; two
10 knots	152mm (6in) guns

▲ **USS Nautilus (V-6)**

US Navy, V-boat, later transport, Pacific, World War II

Commissioned as V-6, *Nautilus* was to be a heavily armed ocean-going boat with trans-Pacific range. However, the US Navy made the strategic decision to opt for more compact fleet boats. In 1940, *Nautilus* was modified to carry 19,320 gal (73,134 litres) of aviation fuel, but retained its tubes and sank three freighters in the course of the war. It was scrapped in 1945.

decommissioned at Philadelphia on 30 June 1945 and scrapped in 1946.

Yugoslavia

The Kingdom of Yugoslavia had four submarines to patrol its Adriatic coast, two of British L-type (intended as *L-67* and *L-68*, but cancelled in 1919), completed for Yugoslavia by Vickers-Armstrong in 1927–28; and two built in France, all based at Kotor. When the Italians captured Kotor, three were seized and one escaped to link up with the British Navy to make it to Britain. *Osvetnik*, built at Nantes, France in 1929, became the Italian *Francesco Rismondo* and, after the Italian surrender, sailed for Corsica but was seized and scuttled by the Germans on 18 September 1943. *Osvetnik* was a medium-size boat, of 630 tonnes (620 tons) surfaced and 809 tonnes (796 tons) submerged, and with an operational depth of 80m (262ft). Another of the Yugoslav boats, *Nebojsa*, escaped to Alexandria and was later used by the British. It was last heard of at Malta in August 1945.

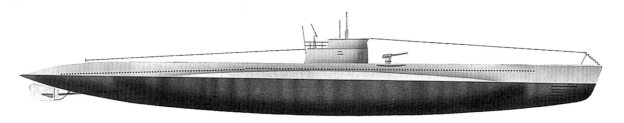

Specifications

Crew: 45	Submerged: 835 tonnes (822 tons)
Powerplant: Two diesel engines; two electric	Dimensions (length/beam/draught): 66.5m x
motors	5.4m x 3.8m (218ft 2in x17ft 9in x 12ft 4in)
Max Speed: Surfaced: 14.5 knots; Submerged:	Commissioned: 929
9.2 knots	Armament: Six 551mm (21.7in) torpedo tubes;
Surface Range: 5003km (2700nm) at 10 knots	one 100mm (3.9in) gun
Displacement: Surfaced: 676 tonnes (665 tons);	

▲ **Ostvenik (N1)**

Yugoslav Navy, patrol submarine, Adriatic

Built at the Ateliers de le Loire, Nantes, *Osvetnik* and its sister boat *Smeli* were designed by the French architect Simonot on the lines of French '600' type boats and had many French features, including the 551mm (21.7in) torpedo tubes. The diesel engines were by MAN, and the electric motors from CGE, Nancy. After capture, modifications were made to the conning tower structure.

Return of the U-boats
1935–39

Renewal of Germany's U-boat programme began from 1935. But the British response was surprisingly mild, and U-boat chief Karl Dönitz did not succeed in getting the number of submarines that he needed.

ADOLF HITLER came to power in Germany in 1933. In March 1935, he repudiated the Versailles Treaty. In the same year Germany signed a naval arms limitation treaty with Britain, the terms allowing Germany to have 45 per cent of the naval strength of the British, and a 100 per cent match in submarines. Considering British memories of 1914–18, this was a remarkable concession, usually explained by excessive confidence in the London Submarine Agreement, signed by Germany in 1936, that submarines in war would respect international law and rescue the crews of sunken ships; and also in the detection capabilities of ASDIC.

The building of new German submarines began immediately: the plans already existed and Command of the *Reich*'s First Submarine Flotilla was given to *Kapitän-sur-See* Karl Dönitz, a submarine veteran of World War I. From 1935, he began to develop ideas that had long been discussed among ex-U-boat officers, on how to make the submarine a really effective weapon. Allied convoys from 1917 had proved able to fend off lurking U-boats. However, if a group of U-boats, a 'wolfpack', concentrated their attacks on a convoy, they might be able to overwhelm the escorts and inflict major damage. Dönitz had many other ideas, including scepticism about the effectiveness of ASDIC. Looking ahead, he felt he needed 300 ocean-going submarines if the task should be to cut British supply lines in the event of war. This would take several years to achieve, and Dönitz found that submarines were not the top priority of the Nazi High Command.

Design of Type 1A (*U-25* and *U-26*) went back to the pre-Hitler period, and construction began in in 1934. It was not an effective craft: handling was tricky, it was difficult to keep level at periscope depth, and it rolled violently. Type IIA, comprising *U-1* to *U-9*, were completed in 1935. The design was newly tested and proved by a submarine launched at Turku, Finland, as a supposedly commercial venture backed by the German front-company in The Hague. This boat, known first as *CV-707*, was launched in May 1933 and later sold to the Finnish Government as *Vesikko*. *U-2*, like most other early U-boats, was used for training. Its small size limited it to coastal patrols and forays into the the North and Baltic Seas. *U-2* was lost in a collision in the Baltic Sea in April 1944 while on a training run as part of the 22nd (training) flotilla. The first active group was Dönitz's *U-Flotille Weddigen,* formed of *U-7* to *U-9*.

U-3 made five combat patrols and sank two ships of neutral nations, one Danish and one Swedish, and

▲ **Type VIIA *U-30***

U-30 is seen here along with other *Flottille Salzwedel* boats at Hamburg in December 1937, en route to their new base at Wilhelmshaven.

with the other training boats was part of the fleet supporting the German invasion of Norway in April 1940. It was then transferred to a training flotilla, the 21st. Captured by the British in May 1945, it was scrapped that year.

Training boats were essential to produce a new generation of U-boat crews, but there was a sense of urgency about producing submarines that would fulfil the ocean-going, commerce-raiding role. These would have to be substantially bigger than the Type II, and the need was filled by the Type VII design, tested in the Finnish Vetehinen class (launched 1930) under the same auspices as the *CV-707*, though the Type VII, intended for the Atlantic, was larger.

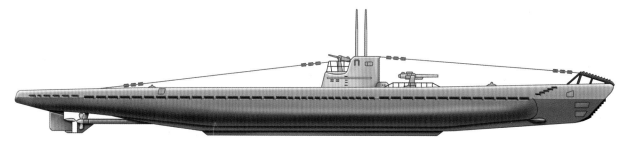

Specifications

Crew: 43	Dimensions (length/beam/draught): 72.4 x 6.2
Powerplant: Diesel engine; electric motors	x 4.3m (237.5 x 20.34 x 14.11ft)
Max Speed: 33/15.4km/hr (17.8/8.3kt) s/d	Commissioned: 6 April 1936
Surface Range: 12,410km (6700nm)	Armament: 14 torpedoes (4 bow/2 stern tubes);
Displacement: 876/999 tonnes (862/983 tons) s/d	1 x 10.5cm (4.1in) and 1 x 2cm (0.8in) guns

▲ U-25

German Navy, Type IA patrol submarine, North Sea

Laid down at Deschimag, Bremen, in June 1935, *U25* was completed less than a year later, in April 1936. Of saddle-tank design, it could carry 28 TMA or 42 TMB mines as an alternative to torpedoes. *U25* was lost on 3 August 1940 when it ran into a British minefield off Terschelling on the North Sea coast.

▲ **U-32**

This grainy photograph shows *U-32* moving through friendly waters, probably off northern Germany. The stripes painted on the conning tower are the distinguishing marks used by warships of the 'Non-Interventionist Committee', patrolling shipping lanes off the Spanish coast during 1938–39.

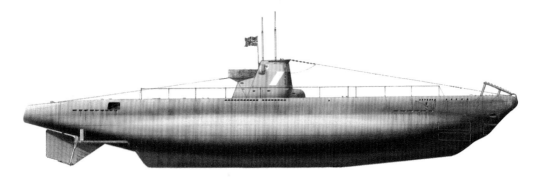

▲ **U-2**

German Navy, Type IIA coastal submarine

Though not a large boat, *U2* was built in a very short time: laid down in February 1935 and commissioned on 25 July of the same year, at the Deutsche Werke, Kiel. Its entire career was spent as a training boat, under 10 successive commanders. It sank on 8 April 1944 after colliding with a trawler. Though raised the next day, it was stricken from the active list.

Specifications

Crew: 25

Powerplant: Diesel engine; electric motor

Max Speed: 33/15.4km/hr (17.8/8.3kt) s/d

Surface Range: 1945km (1050nm)

Displacement: 258/308t (254/303 tons) s/d

Dimensions (length/beam/draught): 40.9 x 4.1 x 3.8m (1134.2 x 13.5 x 12.5ft)

Commissioned: 6 August 1935

Armament: Six torpedoes (three bow tubes); 1 x 2cm (0.8in) gun

Specifications

Crew: 44

Powerplant: Diesel engine; electric motors

Max Speed: 29.6/14.8km/hr (16/8kt) s/d

Surface Range: 7964km (4300nm)

Displacement: 636/757t (626/745 tons) s/d

Dimensions (length/beam/draught): 64.5 x 5.8 x 4.4m (211.6 x 19 x 14.4ft)

Commissioned: 8 October 1936

Armament: 11 torpedoes (4 bow/1 stern tubes); one 8.8cm (3.5in) and one 2cm (0.8in) gun

▲ **U-32**

German Navy, Type VIIA patrol submarine

U32 was one of the first Type VIIA boats, laid down at Germaniawerft, Kiel, in March 1936 and commissioned on 15 April 1937. Ten VIIA were built, and the class was immediately popular with crews, who realized that they had a submarine superior to any other. Payload was 11 torpedoes, or 22 TMA/33 TMB mines. *U32* made nine combat patrols and sank a total tonnage of 116,836GRT.

U-32 was an early Type VIIA, launched in 1937, and one of the few ready for ocean combat in 1939. Although the Type VII would go through several stages of improvement, it could already dive in under 30 seconds and reach a depth of 100m (330ft) and go even deeper to 200m (660ft) in emergency. It could travel submerged at 7.6 knots for two hours, or at 2 knots for 130 hours. Perhaps its main defect was its limited range: 10,000km (6200 miles).

Great Britain

The official British view in the late 1930s, expressed even by Winston Churchill, was that 'the sub had been mastered'. Confidence in the combination of ASDIC detectors with depth charge throwers fitted on destroyers and sloops meant that they thought that a submarine threat could be readily dealt with, and the role of submarines in the Royal Navy was not seen as a priority.

Contemporary with the German developments, a new class of ocean-going submarine, the Triton or T-class was developed from 1935, and 15 had been built by September 1939. The smaller Undine or U-class was under construction at the same time, with 15 completed by the outbreak of war. Both classes would be extended, with 53 of the T-class ultimately built, and 49 of the Undines. The first three U-class were seen as training vessels, but their operational value was soon perceived.

Most served in the North Sea and Mediterranean, in the latter with the 10th Submarine Flotilla based at Malta. The first three had two external bow torpedo tubes in addition to the four integral tubes, but these were not applied to the rest of the class. *Undine* itself had a short career, being scuttled off Heligoland when immobilized by anti-submarine warfare surface craft in January 1940.

Italy

Commissioned just before World War II were three Italian minelayers of the Foca class, built by Tosi at Taranto. The 100mm (6in) gun was originally installed in the after part of the conning tower but was later placed more conventionally on the deck facing forward. Mines were carried in both vertical and horizontal tubes, a total of 28. The class had an operational depth of 100m (330ft). *Zoea* was seized by the Allies after the fall of Italy and used in late 1943 to run supplies to the garrisons on the islands of Samos and Leros. It was discarded in 1947.

Another class completed by CRDA, *Monfalcone*, just before hostilities began, was the 11-strong *Marcello*, built 1938–39, large and well-armed ocean-going boats, considered by some experts to be the best of the large Italian submarines, whose number included *Barbarigo* and *Dandolo*. In 1939–40 they were stationed in the Mediterranean, but 10 were transferred to Bordeaux in August 1940.

◀ **U-4** and **U-6**

Type IIA training boats *U-6* (centre) and *U-4* (right) are shown in the docks at Kiel, 1937. Both submarines served with the *U-Bootschulflottille* until being transferred to the 21st Training Flotilla in July 1940. Although too lacking in range to be truly combat effective, the Type IIA boats briefly became operational at the outbreak of war in 1939. *U-4* made four patrols, sinking three ships and the British submarine HMS *Thistle*. *U-6* made two patrols, but had no success. Both were back in their training role when the 21st Flotilla was established in July 1940.

As Atlantic raiders, they never achieved the success rate of the U-boats, and four were sunk. In early 1941, *Dandolo* returned to the Mediterranean, where it torpedoed the cruiser HMS *Cleopatra* in July 1943. Ultimately, the only member of the class to survive the war, *Dandolo*, was scrapped in 1947. Two of the class were converted to cargo-carrying; one of them, *Comandante Cappellini*, was commissioned (at Singapore) in the *Reichsmarine* as *UIT-24*, and later in the Japanese Navy as *I-503*, one of only two boats to serve in all three Axis navies.

Poland

The German invasion of Poland in September 1939 was the action that finally triggered World War II. Poland, with a short Baltic coast, had five submarines in 1939, three French-built minelayers of the Wilk class (1931), and *Orzel* and *Sep*, built in the Netherlands and commissioned in 1939. On 14 September 1939, all were ordered to head for British ports, but only *Orzel* and *Wilk* succeeded. *Orzel* sank two German troop transports on 8 April 1940 while opposing the invasion of Norway but was sunk by a mine on 8 June.

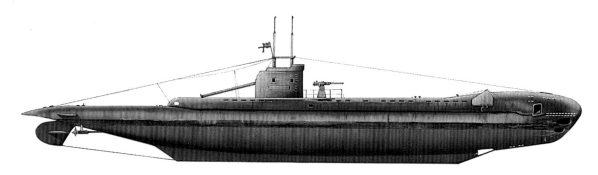

Specifications

Crew: 31	Submerged: 752 tonnes (740 tons)
Powerplant: Twin screw diesel; electric motors	Dimensions (length/beam/draught): 54.9m x
Max Speed: Surfaced: 11.2 knot; Submerged:	4.8m x 3.8m (180ft x 16ft x 12ft 9in)
10 knots	Commissioned: October 1937
Surface Range: 7041km (3800nm) at 10 knots	Armament: Four 533mm (21in) torpedo tubes;
Displacement: Surfaced: 554 tonnes (545 tons);	one 76mm (3in) gun

▲ HMS Undine

Royal Navy, U-class patrol submarine, Mediterranean, World War II

Unlike most submarines, the U-class did not have a separate hatch for the gun crew. HMS *Unity* was the first British submarine to have a propeller for optimum submerged performance: on this class the electric motors developed more power than the diesels. Most were attached to the 10th flotilla at Malta, and 16 were lost in the Mediterranean.

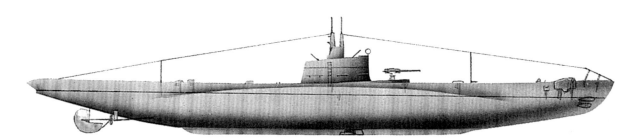

▲ Zoea

Italian Navy, coastal minelayer

Described as coastal boats despite their size, the class was also heavily armed for minelayers. One photo of *Atropo* shows the gun mounted on the conning tower, perhaps a temporary arrangement. *Foca* was lost off Palestine in October 1940; *Atropo* was used by the Allies in the same way as *Zoea*.

Specifications

Crew: 60	tons); Submerged: 1685 tonnes (1659 tons)
Powerplant: Twin screw diesel engines; electric	Dimensions (length/beam/draught): 82.8m x
motors	7.2m x 5.3m (271ft 8in x 23ft 6in x 17ft 5in)
Max Speed: Surfaced: 15.2 knots; Submerged:	Commissioned: February 1936
7.4 knots	Armament: Six 533mm (21in) torpedo tubes; one
Surface Range: 15,742km (8500nm) at 8 knots	100mm (3.9in) gun
Displacement: Surfaced: 1354 tonnes (1333	

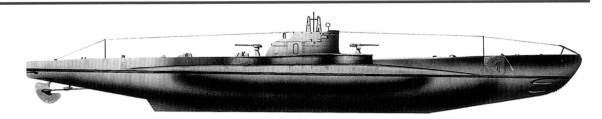

Specifications

Crew: 57

Powerplant: Twin screw diesel engines; electric
motors

Max Speed: Surfaced: 17.4 knots; Submerged:
8 knots

Surface Range: 4750km (2560nm) at 17 knots

Displacement: Surfaced: 1080 tonnes (1063

tons); Submerged: 1338 tonnes (1317 tons)

Dimensions (length/beam/draught): 73m x 7.2m
x 5m (239ft 6in x 23ft 8in x 16ft 5in)

Commissioned: November 1937

Armament: Eight 533mm (21in) torpedo tubes;
two 100mm (3.9in) guns

▲ Dandolo

Italian Navy, patrol submarine

As with numerous other Italian classes, 'stability bulges' were added to the
single hull to improve performance on diving and surfacing, but the Marcello
class handled well both on the surface and submerged. All were built by CRDA
at Monfalcone.

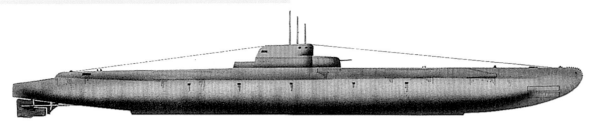

Specifications

Crew: 56

Powerplant: Twin screw diesel; electric motors

Max Speed: Surfaced: 15 knots; Submerged:
8 knots

Surface Range: 13,300km (7169nm) at 10 knots

Displacement: Surfaced: 1117 tonnes (1100

tons); Submerged: 1496 tonnes (1473 tons)

Dimensions (length/beam/draught): 84m x 6.7m
x 4m (275ft 7in x 22ft x 13ft 1in)

Commissioned: 1938

Armament: 12 550mm (21.7in) torpedo tubes;
one 105mm (4in) gun

▲ Orzel

Polish Navy, patrol submarine

Poland had a five-strong submarine squadron in 1939, three Wilk class
minelayers and two patrol boats. *Orzel*'s sister boat *Sep* escaped to Sweden and
was interned. Similar to the Dutch O19 class, they were excellent boats, of welded
construction with double hulls and powered by two Sulzer 6QD42 six-cylinder
diesels and two Brown-Boveri electric motors.

Spanish Civil War
1936–39

**The conflict in Spain between Nationalist and Republican forces provided Italy and Germany
with opportunities to test their new submarines in action.**

WHEN CIVIL WAR BEGAN in July 1936, the
Spanish Navy had 12 submarines, 6 B-class
dating from from 1921–23 and six more modern C-
class, commissioned in 1936. All were in the
Republic's hands, though little effective use was
made of them. Help was sought by the Nationalists
from the sympathetic governments of Italy and
Germany. German aid came in late 1936 with
Operation Ursula. Two new submarines, *U-33* and

U-34, were sent to Spain. On 12 December, *U-34*
sank the Spanish *C-3*, but soon afterwards both U-
boats were recalled. Four Italian submarines, *Iride*
and *Onice* of the *Perla* class (temporarily given
Spanish names, *Gonsales Lopes* and *Aquilar Tablada*),
and *Galileo Galilei* and *Galileo Ferraris* of the
Archimede class, were hired out to the Nationalists.
In addition, two other Archimede class boats,
Archimede and *Evangelista Torricelli*, were sold to the

Nationalists and renamed *General Sanjurjo* and *General Mola*.

Evangelista Torricelli was commissioned in 1934 and secretly sold to the Nationalist forces in Spain in 1937. While still under Italian colours, *Torricelli* disabled the Spanish cruiser *Miguel de Cervantes* in 1937; as *General Mola* it sank the merchant ship *Ciudad de Barcelona* in May 1937 and the British *Endymion* in January 1938. Spanish neutrality in World War II helped extend their longevity and *General Mola* was not decommissioned until 1958.

Many other Italian submarines served on short deployments. Among them was *Enrico Toti* of the

Balilla class, launched in 1928, a sister-ship of *Domenico Millelire*. *Toti* and the others were too large to be effective in off-shore patrolling, being designed for long-range transit to Italy's colonies in northeast Africa. During World War II it sank a British submarine in a surface gun battle, on 15 October 1940, now thought to be HMS *Triad*, though often said to be HMS *Rainbow*, which was more probably lost through collision at the same time. Laid up in April 1943, *Toti* saw no further service.

Also involved off Spain were all four boats of the Mameli class, including *Giovanni da Procida*. Medium-sized, they were better suited to the task, although their

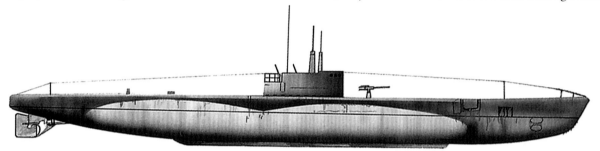

▲ **Enrico Toti**

Italian Navy, patrol submarine, Mediterranean, 1940

The only Italian submarine to sink a Royal Navy submarine in World War II, *Toti* was already quite elderly on 15 October 1940. It was attached to the 40th Squadron of the 4th Submarine Group at Taranto, making patrols into the Ionian Sea. After its exploit, it was used as a training boat.

Specifications

Crew: 76

Powerplant: Twin screw diesels; electric motors

Max Speed: Surfaced: 17.5 knots; Submerged: 9 knots

Surface Range: 7041km (3800nm) at 10 knots

Displacement: Surfaced: 1473 tonnes (1450 tons); Submerged: 1934 tonnes (1904 tons)

Dimensions (length/beam/draught): 87.7m x 7.8m x 4.7m (288ft x 25ft 7in x 15ft 5in)

Commissioned: April 1928

Armament: Six 533mm (21in) torpedo tubes; one 120mm (4.7in) gun

SUBMARINES OF THE SPANISH CIVIL WAR: NATIONALIST FORCES		
Class	**Name**	**Note**
Archimede (Italian)	*General Mola* (ex *Archimede*)	Purchased 1937
	General Sanjurjo (ex *Evangelista Torricelli*)	Purchased 1937
	General Mola II (ex *Galileo Galilei*)	Hired 1937–38
	General Sanjurjo II (ex *Galileo Torricelli*)	Hired 1937–38
Perla (Italian)	*Gonsalez Lopez* (ex-*Iride*)	Hired 1937–38
	Aguilar Tablada (ex-*Onice*)	Hired 1937–38
Type VII (German)	*U-33*	Operation Ursula, 1936
	U-34	Operation Ursula, 1936

SUBMARINES OF THE SPANISH CIVIL WAR: REPUBLICAN FORCES			
Class	**Built**	**Name**	**Note**
B	1921–23	1	Scuttled April 1939
		2	Survived war
		3	Scuttled April 1939
		4	Scuttled April 1939
		5	Sunk 12 October 1936
		6	Sunk 19 September 1936
C	1927–29	1	Sunk 9 November 1936
		2	Not involved in war
		3	Sunk 21 December 1936
		4	Not involved in war
		5	Lost December 1936
		6	Scuttled November 1937

design, based on World War I U-boats, was showing its age. After its Spanish deployment, *Giovanni da Procida* next saw active service in June 1940, in the unsuccessful effort to stop the transfer of French war materiel and personnel to North Africa in June 1940, after the French surrender. It was deployed in the eastern Mediterranean from August 1940 and, after the armistice with Italy, it was eventually brought into in a US anti-submarine warfare training programme in 1943–44 along with eight other Italian submarines.

The Italian submarines sank a number of ships of other nations as well as Spanish vessels, causing an international outcry. Other naval powers, especially Britain and France, instituted coastal surface patrols, and there were a number of close encounters

between surface ships and submerged submarines. Germany joined in this, sending U-boats again, though with 'peacekeeping' intention. Around 15 U-boats made 47 patrols.

By the end of the war on 1 April 1939, the Republican submarine fleet was reduced to eight, through combat or scuttling. Only one B-class remained, and three C-class.

The Spanish Civil War was yet another demonstration of the power of submarines as commerce raiders. It also showed up the limitations of ASDIC in the failure of British patrol vessels to locate, identify or stop the activities of the Italian submarines. But this was a very small-scale rehearsal for things soon to come.

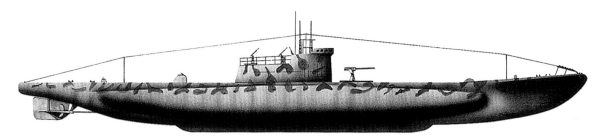

▲ Giovanni da Procida

Italian Navy, patrol submarine

The Mameli class, based partly on World War I U-boats, was designed by the Cavallini Bureau, with a cylindrical hull that could reach greater depths than previous Italian types. Its saddle-tank design was a model for the Archimede and Brin classes, though there was much experimentation with bow and stern shapes.

Specifications

Crew: 49	Submerged: 1026 tonnes (1010 tons)
Powerplant: Twin shaft diesel engines; electric	Dimensions (length/beam/draught): 64.6m x
motors	6.5m x 4.3m (212ft x 21ft 4in x 14ft)
Max Speed: Surfaced: 17 knots ; Submerged: 7 knots	Commissioned: April 1928
Surface Range: 5930km (3200nm) at 10 knots	Armament: Six 533mm (21in) torpedo tubes; one
Displacement: Surfaced: 843 tonnes (830 tons);	102mm (4in) gun

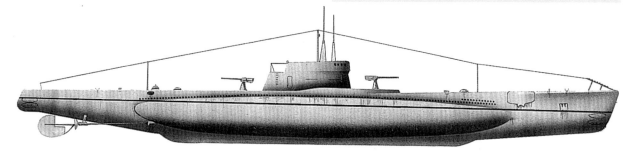

Specifications

Crew: 55	Submerged: 1026 tonnes (1010 tons)
Powerplant: Twin shaft diesel engines; electric	Dimensions (length/beam/draught): 64.6m x
motors	6.5m x 4.3m (212ft x 21ft 4in x 14ft)
Max Speed: Surfaced: 17 knots; Submerged: 7 knots	Commissioned: April 1934
Surface Range: 5930km (3200nm) at 10 knots	Armament: Six 533mm (21in) torpedo tubes;
Displacement: Surfaced: 843 tonnes (830 tons);	one 102mm (4in) gun

▲ General Mola

Spanish Navy (ex-Italian), patrol submarine

General Mola and *General Sanjurjo* outlasted all their Italian sister boats, which, if they survived world War II, were stricken with other Italian naval units in 1948. The two ex-Archimede class boats made patrols in Spanish waters during World War II, with large neutrality symbols on the conning towers. They remained on the active list until September 1959, when both were decommissioned.

Chapter 3

World War II:
1939–45

The submarines of 1939 were not very different
in the essentials to their predecessors of 20 years before.
Indeed, many of them were still of World War I design. All
that was to change swiftly, however, as a deadly struggle
was waged in and below the world's seas. Would Hitler's
wolfpacks succeed where the Kaiser's raiders had failed? In
Germany, construction of submarines reached unprecedented
levels, but could not match the ever-increasing losses. Yet
even as the Battle of the Atlantic was won by the Allies,
Germany was developing new submarines far superior to any
yet built, and another submarine war was being fought in the
vastness of the Pacific, as the Japanese were gradually
forced back from their early conquests.

◀ *U-47*

The close-up shot of *U-47*'s conning tower shows many details, including the port-side navigation light,
the hardwood deck planking, the free-flooding holes, and the casing of the airtrunk feeding air to the
diesel engines.

Introduction

Twenty-six navies possessed a total of 777 submarines in September 1939. Those with more than 10 were Denmark (11), France (77), Germany (65), Great Britain (69), Italy (107), The Netherlands (29), Sweden (24), the Soviet Union (about 150), United States (100), Japan (65).

THE OTHER SUBMARINE-OWNING nations were Argentina (3), Brazil (4), Estonia (2), Finland (5), Greece (6), Latvia (2), Norway (9), Peru (5), Poland (5), Portugal (4), Romania (1), Siam (Thailand) (4), Spain (9), Turkey (9), Yugoslavia (4). Some of these countries would preserve neutrality, but the great majority of existing submarines, plus many yet unbuilt, would be caught up in the global battles to come.

In the larger navies, the submarine arm was established as a separately run command under a flag officer. Submarine strength was grouped in flotillas, each with its own senior officer. Flotilla size was usually from eight to 10 boats. Submarines required a range of facilities and were normally based only at large naval depots. Even before World War I, the submarine tender or depot ship had been introduced,

at first a converted merchant vessel, which could carry submarine stores and supplies and provide accommodation and messing-space for crews – it was impossible for a submarine crew to inhabit their boat in dock, as there were not enough bunks when the watch system was not in use.

The British HMS *Maidstone*, commissioned in May 1938, was a typical purpose-built depot ship with workshops, auxiliary engines, laundries, medical facilities and salvage equipment, as well as ammunition (100 torpedoes). It could service nine submarines and was intended to accompany a flotilla to remote locations. In World War II, *Maidstone* served in the Mediterranean, the Far East and South Africa. Britain, Japan and the United States all used tenders to support submarine operations.

▲ HMS *United* (P44)

The Royal Navy produced 51 boats of the U-class. Effective combat boats, the U-class suffered heavy losses. Direction-finding and radar antennas are noticeable. Also in the picture are a minesweeper and barrage balloon.

▲ **Kiel harbour**
This 1939 photograph shows in the foreground the 2nd Flotilla boats *U-27*, *U-33* and *U-34* (all Type VIIAs) as well as two Type IIAs (background, left). Kiel was one of the chief bases and production areas for U-boats throughout the war.

By 1939, submarines were in many ways vastly more capable of effective combat than they had been in 1918. After the experiments of the 1920s, it was generally accepted that the medium-sized patrol-attack boat was the most versatile and useful type, and it formed the backbone of the European submarine fleets. They could fire torpedo salvoes with large warheads that could sink any battleship. Radio communication enabled close direction of operations. Mechanical reliability of diesel engines, whether two- or four-stroke, had greatly improved. Stronger construction and design improvements had made crash diving remarkably fast, and new submarines could now operate to depths of around 100m (330ft).

Some form of underwater detection apparatus was in use by all large navies, though this was of course a threat as well as an asset to submarine operation.

The least progress had been made with surface endurance, and speeds both surfaced and submerged remained slow. Manoeuvring and maintaining trim while submerged was still a difficult business, and underwater endurance time, though improved, was still limited. Though the 533mm (21in) torpedo was now standard, the quality of torpedoes varied greatly between the different navies. The United States in particular suffered badly from defective torpedoes in the the first year of the Pacific War. The most effective were those of the Japanese and the Italians. In 1939, all torpedoes were still straight-running, which meant the submarine had to be lined up to fire. The sophistication and lethal power of torpedoes was greatly increased in the course of the war. Mine-design also was worked on to enable detonation at greater depths.

Submarine deployment
1939–40

Events began to move quickly in the course of 1940. Germany established a strong strategic position by overcoming Norway and France, opening the Atlantic to U-boat raids.

GERMANY'S FAST VICTORIES along the Atlantic seaboard quickly neutralized France's naval forces and immediately threatened Britain's supply lines with North America.

France

Twenty-three new submarines were ordered or under construction in France in September 1939. When the German *Blitzkrieg* was launched in June 1940, submarines were based at Cherbourg (2nd, 12th and part of the 16th Submarine Divisions); Brest (6th, 8th, 13th, 16th and 18th Divisions, also the unique *Surcouf*); and Toulon (1st, 15th, 17th, 19th and 21st). The strength of a division varied between two and six boats. In North Africa, *Oran* had the 14th and 18th; at Bizerta were boats from the 1st, also the 3rd, 4th, 7th, 9th and 20th. The 11th was at Sousse, Tunisia; some of the 3rd and all of the 10th were at Beirut. There were also two 1st Submarine Division boats at Dakar in Senegal.

When German forces entered Toulon, France's main submarine base, in November 1942, 12 submarines were undergoing refit. Eleven were scuttled, but *Casabianca* slipped out and joined the Free French forces in North Africa, and had an adventurous wartime career in seven secret missions, bringing agents, weapons and supplies to Corsica and the southern French coast until 1944. *Casabianca* was one of the third series of Redoutable-class submarines, launched at Nantes in February 1935, with a diesel power rating of 8600hp (6413kW) and a surface speed of 20 knots. The only third-series boat to survive the war, it was sent to the United States for a refit in 1944 after being hit in a blue-on-blue air attack, and was finally stricken in 1952.

Germany

By the summer of 1939, the German Navy had 57 U-boats, of which 46 were operational, with the majority being Type II coastal boats, allocated to seven flotillas. An unprecedented building programme was about to begin that sent the numbers rising steadily, but not until between August 1942 and August 1943 would there be 100 U-boats at sea at any one time.

As in 1914, the U-boats announced their presence in an emphatic way. On the first day of the war, *U-30*, one of the first Type VII boats, sank the liner

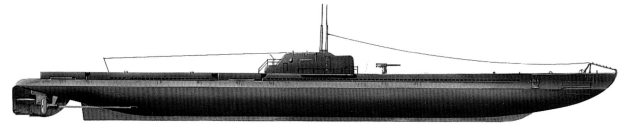

▲ **Casabianca**

French Navy, patrol submarine, Mediterranean 1942

First based at Brest with the 2nd Division, *Casabianca* made two wartime patrols off Norway in 1940, then was deployed to Dakar in Senegal until October 1941. After escaping Toulon, it reached Algiers on 30 November 1942, and operated with the 8th Royal Navy Flotilla from Oran, sinking an Axis ASW patrol vessel.

Specifications

Crew: 61

Powerplant: Two twin-shaft diesel engines; two electric motors

Max Speed: Surfaced: 17–20 knots; Submerged: 10 knots

Surface Range: 18,530km (10,000nm) at 10 knots

Displacement: Surfaced: 1595 tonnes (1570 tons);

Submerged: 2117 tonnes (2084 tons)

Dimensions (length/beam/draught): 92.3m x 8.2m x 4.7m (210ft x 18ft 7in x 10ft 9in)

Commissioned: February 1935

Armament: Nine 550mm (21.7in) and two 400mm (15.7in) torpedo tubes; one 100mm (3.9in) gun

BOATS THAT SERVED WITH 5TH FLOTILLA (7 BOATS)

U-Boat	Type	Commissioned	Flotilla(s)	Patrols	Fate
U-56	IIC	26 Nov 38	26 Nov 1938 – 31 Dec 1939 (training and combat)	12 patrols. 3 ships sunk: total 8860GRT; 1 auxiliary warship sunk: total 16,923GRT; 1 ship damaged: total 3829GRT	To 1. Flottille
U-57	IIC	29 Dec 38	29 Dec 1938 – 31 Dec 1939 (training and combat)	11 patrols. 11 ships sunk: total 48,053GRT; 1 auxiliary warship sunk: total 8240GRT; 1 ship damaged beyond repair: total 10,191GRT; 2 ships damaged: total 10,403GRT	To 1. Flottille
U-58	IIC	4 Feb 39	4 Feb – 31 Dec 1939 (training and combat)	12 patrols. 6 ships sunk: total 16,148GRT; 1 auxiliary warship sunk: total 8401GRT	To 1. Flottille
U-59	IIC	4 Mar 39	4 Mar – 31 Dec 1939 (training and combat)	13 patrols. 16 ships sunk: total 29,514GRT; 2 auxiliary warships sunk: total 864GRT; 1 ship damaged beyond repair: total 4943GRT; 1 ship damaged: total 8009GRT	To 1. Flottille
U-60	IIC	22 Jul 39	22 Jul – 31 Dec 1939 (training)	9 patrols. 3 ships sunk: total 7561GRT; 1 ship damaged: total 15,434GRT	To 1. Flottille
U-61	IIC	12 Aug 39	12 Aug – 31 Dec 1939 (training)	10 patrols. 5 ships sunk: total 19,668GRT; 1 ship damaged: total 4434GRT	To 1. Flottille
U-62	IIC	21 Dec 39	21 – 31 Dec 1939 (training)	5 patrols. 1 ship sunk: total 4581GRT; 1 warship sunk: total 1372t/1350 tons	To 1. Flottille

Athenia without warning. Another Type VIIA, *U-29*, sank the British aircraft carrier HMS *Courageous* off Ireland on 17 September 1939, and a Type VIIB, *U-47*, made a daring entry into the Scapa Flow anchorage and sank the battleship HMS *Royal Oak*, on 14 October. From mid-1940, the main operational bases were mostly outside Germany, though Kiel was always the prime base. At the end of 1940, U-boats were operating from major bases at Lorient, St Nazaire, Brest and La Pallice in France, and Bergen, Trondheim and Kristiansand in Norway.

The 16-strong Type IID, introduced from June 1940, was the most advanced version of Type II, with supplementary saddle tanks giving it a range almost double that of the original IIA, enabling it to patrol beyond the British Isles. Like all Type IIs, it was hampered by limited torpedo capacity, carrying only six. As the size of the U-boat fleet grew, the Type IIs

5TH FLOTILLA INSIGNIA

U-boat insignia varied from the overtly military through humorous to personal emblems of the commander. Many had an underwater theme, the rarely seen 5th Flotilla's insignia being a seahorse.

were generally used as training boats. The *Reichsmarine*'s urgent need for more and bigger submarines was met by the Type VII. By 1937, it was already being modified, and Type VIIB had twin rudders, greatly helping manoeuvrability, and with the stern tube placed between them inside the pressure hull, allowing for submerged reloading.

The surrender of France in June 1940 made it possible for Germany to base U-boats on the French Atlantic coast, with no need to pass repeatedly

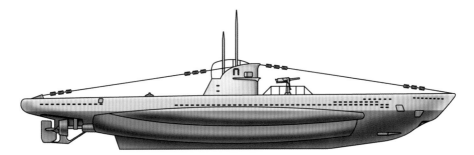

▲ U-139

German Navy, Type IID coastal submarine

Shared features of all Type IIs were the single hull, undivided into watertight compartments; the engines, and the armament, though Type IID, was somewhat larger. *U-139* was commissioned on 24 July 1940 and served as a training boat with the 1st, 21st and 22nd Flotillas. It was scuttled at Wilhelmshaven on 2 May 1945.

Specifications

Crew: 25

Powerplant: Diesel; electric motors

Max Speed: 23.5/13.7km/hr (12.7/7.4kt) surf/sub

Surface Range: 6389km (3450nm)

Displacement: 319/370t (314/364 tons)

surf/sub

Dimensions (length/beam/draught): 44 x 4.9 x 3.9m (144.4 x 16.8 x 12.8ft)

Commissioned: 15 June 1940

Armament: Six torpedoes (three bow tubes); one 2cm (0.8in) gun

7TH FLOTILLA INSIGNIA

The 'Snorting Bull' was originally the emblem of *U-47*, after Gunther Prien's nickname of 'the Bull'. Designed by Engelbert Endrass, it was later selected as the 7th Flotilla's insignia.

through the heavily guarded English Channel or the North Sea. At Brest, Lorient, St Nazaire and La Pallice, massive concrete 'pens' were built to house the three main U-boat combat flotillas.

This inaugurated the 'happy time' – June 1940 to February 1941 – when with little interference, the U-boats raided freely into the Atlantic. From June to October they sank 270 Allied ships. The spoils were shared by Type IX boats, which were bigger and with a greater range, introduced in August 1938 when *U-37* was commissioned.

U-505, commissioned in August 1941, was one of 54 Type IXC boats, with larger fuel tanks giving a range of 12,660 miles (20,370km). Powered by two supercharged nine-cylinder diesels, it made 18.3 knots on the surface. Having sunk eight ships on previous patrols, *U-505* was captured intact on 4 June 1944 in the South Atlantic by destroyers from an American task force using HF/DF (high frequency direction-finding) and supported by air reconnaissance; an indication of how intense the U-boat hunt had become. Its secret cipher code books were retrieved and delivered to the Decryption

▲ **U-boat ace**

He was not the highest-scoring ace, but Prien's feat at Scapa Flow early in the war meant that he became the most famous of all U-boat commanders.

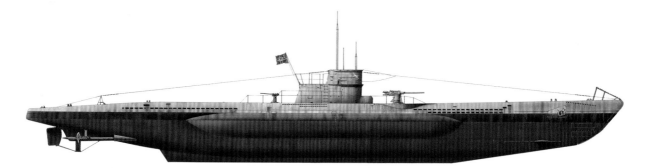

▲ **U-47**

German Navy, Type VIIB attack submarine, Scapa Flow, 1939

With 33.5 tonnes (33 tons) of extra fuel in external saddle tanks, Type VIIB had greater range than VIIA, and carried two extra torpedoes (14 in all). *U-47* sank 30 merchant ships with a GRT of 162,769, in addition to HMS *Royal Oak* (29,618 tonnes/29,150 tons). It was lost on 7 March 1941 in the North Atlantic.

Specifications

Crew: 44	Dimensions (length/beam/draught): 66.5 x 6.2 x
Powerplant: Diesel; electric motors	4.7m (218.1 x 20.34 x 15.4ft)
Max Speed: 31.9/14.8km/hr (17.2/8kt) surf/sub	Commissioned: 17 December 1938
Surface Range: 12,040km (6500nm)	Armament: 14 torpedoes (4 bow/1 stern tubes);
Displacement: 765/871t (753/857 tons) surf/sub	one 8.8cm (3.5in) gun and one 2cm (0.8in) gun

Establishment at Bletchley Park, England. In all, 191 IX-class boats were built, in six sub-classes, of which IXC and IXC40 combined made up 141. IXC40 was virtually identical to IXC, but slightly larger and with an extra 740km (460-mile) range.

Great Britain

The Royal Navy had six operational submarine squadrons in September 1939. The 1st, with nine boats, was at Malta; the 2nd with 10 boats, at Dundee; the 4th, with 16 boats, was with the China fleet at Hong Kong; the 5th, with 11 boats, was at Portsmouth; the 6th, with six boats, at Blyth; and the

▶ **U-boat captured**

U-505 was one of the few German U-boats to be captured on the high seas. Taken off West Africa two days before D-Day, it was towed first to Bermuda.

U-505 TIMETABLE		
Patrol Dates	**Operational Area**	**Ships Sunk**
19 Jan 1942 – 3 Feb 1942	Transit around Britain from Kiel to Lorient	0
11 Feb 1942 – 7 May 1942	Central Atlantic off Freetown	4
7 Jun 1942 – 25 Aug 1942	Central Atlantic/Caribbean	3
4 Oct 1942 – 12 Dec 1942	Central Atlantic/Caribbean	1
1 Jul 1943 – 13 Jul 1943	Mechanical damage forced early return	0
1 Aug 1943 – 2 Aug 1943	Unidentifiable faults forced early return	0
14 Aug 1943 – 15 Aug 1943	Unidentifiable faults forced early return	0
21 Aug 1943 – 22 Aug 1943	Unidentifiable faults forced early return	0
18 Sep 1943 – 30 Sep 1943	Mechanical damage forced early return	0
9 Oct 1943 – 7 Nov 1943	Captain's suicide forced early return	0
25 Dec 1943 – 2 Jan 1944	Biscay, rescuing German warship survivors	0
16 Mar 1944 – 4 Jun 1944	Central Atlantic off Freetown	0

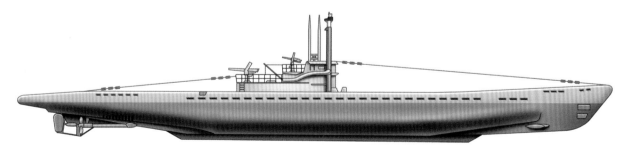

Specifications

Crew: 48–50

Powerplant: Diesel; electric motors

Max Speed: 33.9/13.5km/hr (18.3/7.3kt) surf/sub

Surface Range: 20,370km (11,000nm)

Displacement: 1138/1232t (1120/1232 tons) surf/sub

Dimensions (length/beam/draught): 76.8 x 6.8 x 4.7m (252 x 22.31 x 15.42ft)

Commissioned: 26 August 1941

Armament: 22 torpedoes (four bow/two stern tubes); one 10.5cm (4.1in), one 3.7cm (1.5in) and one 2cm (0.8in) gun

▲ **U-505**

German Navy, Type IXC attack submarine, Bay of Biscay, December 1943

Type IXC had two tower periscopes and snorkel equipment. They carried torpedoes of G7a, G7e and G7s type (the last being an acoustic homing torpedo to hit escort craft), with a total of 18. No deck gun was mounted, to minimize drag when submerged. AA guns were mounted on upper and lower wintergardens.

7th with two boats was at Freetown, Sierra Leone. Sixteen boats were in the North Sea, while the western side of the country had none. This distribution of forces would soon change.

The British T-class was intended to supersede the O-, P- and R-class submarines, and was built strictly within the London Treaty limits. The T-boats were built to operate in all major theatres of action, and eventually did so. Considering their overall size, it was remarkable that they should have incorporated 10 forward-facing torpedo-tubes, six internal and four externally mounted. This enabled them to fire a massive salvo, intended to destroy a large warship. Seventeen torpedoes were carried. Later T-class submarines had the midship tubes reversed to fire astern but, by this time, it was clear that commerce raiding and destruction of small escort vessels was a more regular task than trying to sink battleships.

Fifty-three were built between October 1937 and March 1942, in three groups: 15 in 1935–38, seven in 1939, and 31 in 1940–42. *Thistle* was one of the first group, launched in October 1937, with a riveted hull, divided into six watertight compartments. Like some previous British classes, the 100mm (4in) gun was set on a raised mounting.

Many of the class served in the Mediterranean, where their size was a disadvantage, making them too visible from the air. Sixteen were lost in the war years, and 13 Axis submarines were sunk by T-class boats. The 31 'Group 3' boats, with all-welded hulls, were retained after the war and modernized. Four went to the Royal Netherlands Navy and three to Israel (one, *Totem*, was lost in transit). The last

T-class boats, much modernized and lengthened, were withdrawn in 1977 and 1978.

The Norway Campaign

Thistle was sunk off Norway by *U-4* on 10 April 1940, during the failed effort to prevent German occupation. This was the first major submarine confrontation, with all available U-boats, including training craft, mobilized to support the invasion fleet, and 20 British submarines among the opposing forces. Though the Polish submarine *Orzel* sank a German transport ship on 8 April, and HMS *Sterlet* sank the gunnery training ship *Brummer* on 14 April, the British submarines achieved few successes in this campaign and were gradually forced away from the Norwegian coast by anti-submarine warfare (ASW) planes and trawlers.

Only one Norwegian submarine escaped to join up with the British forces. Nine U British submarines were lost off Norway between April and August 1940, only one to a U-boat, and four U-boats were sunk by air and surface ship attacks.

The Dutch Contribution

Until the commissioning of *O-19* and *O-20* in 1939, submarines of the Royal Netherlands Navy were designated as O, for service in home waters, and K, for service in the Dutch West and East Indies. When German forces overran the Netherlands in June 1940, 12 O-class and five K-class submarines joined the Royal Navy in Portsmouth and Singapore and were immediately deployed in British flotillas. The Dutch were the largest group of 'free' boats from defeated nations, which also included Greek, Norwegian, Free

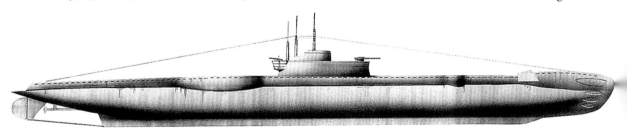

Specifications

Crew: 59	tons); Submerged: 1600 tonnes (1575 tons)
Powerplant: Twin screw diesel; electric motors	Dimensions (length/beam/draught): 80.8m x 8m
Max Speed: Surfaced: 15.25 knots; Submerged:	x 4.5m (265ft x 26ft 6in x 14ft 9in)
9 knots	Commissioned: October 1938
Surface Range: 7041km (3800nm) at 10 knots	Armament: 10 533mm (21in) torpedo tubes; one
Displacement: Surfaced: 1107 tonnes (1090	100mm (4in) gun

▲ **Thistle**

Royal Navy, T-class patrol submarine, North Sea, 1940

Commissioned on 4 July 1939, *Thistle* was patrolling off Stavanger when it fired torpedoes at the Type IIA *U-4*, but without success, and itself fell victim to *U-4*. Many modifications were made to the T-class, providing it with Type 267 and 291 radar for sea and air detection, in addition to the integral Type 129 ASDIC.

French and Polish vessels. *O-19* and *O-20* are of particular interest as the first submarines to be equipped with any form of the snorkel apparatus that enabled the boat to run on its diesel engines while submerged. *O-20*, working from Singapore, was sunk in the South China Sea in December 1941 but *O-19* survived until July 1945, when it grounded on a Pacific reef and had to be destroyed.

Italy

Italian submarine deployment had two main aspects: protection of the long domestic coastline and the islands; and maintaining connection with Italian colonial possessions in North and East Africa. With its existing fleet plus an ongoing building programme, it did not lack boats to fulfil these roles. Around 30 of its submarines were of a size and endurance for oceanic work, and 28 were despatched to the Atlantic from June 1940, to make Atlantic patrols in the latitudes south of Lisbon, from the base of Bordeaux. Eight other boats were in the Red Sea flotilla at Massawa. The remainder of the fleet was spread across Mediterranean bases, La Spezia, Naples, Messina, Taranto, Fiume, Tobruk and Leros.

Convoy attack and commerce raiding was the purpose of the four Ammiraglio Cagni class submarines, laid down in September to October 1939. They mounted 14 torpedo tubes, though of 450mm (17.7in) calibre, considered adequate to deal with merchant vessels. Each boat carried 36 torpedoes, more than twice the capacity of most other submarines. The original high conning tower was designed for Indian Ocean conditions, but for Atlantic operations it was reduced to a lower German-style form.

Cagni, part of the Italian flotilla at Bordeaux in late 1942, sank a tanker and a Greek sloop. These were the *Regia Marina*'s largest attack submarines but were not hugely successful. *Cagni* accounted for less than 10,000 gross register tonnage (GRT) of Allied shipping in two long patrols and, like other large boats, it was converted in 1943 to a transport role. It surrendered at Durban in September 1943. Two Cagni class boats were sunk by British U-class submarines and a third was scuttled. *Cagni* was the only member of the class to survive the war, and was broken up in 1948.

Japan

Still pursuing their decade-long objective of building up a force of long-range

September 1939 to December 1941

— Limit of US merchant responsibility from April

— Extent of air escort cover

- - - Limit of surface escort cover

☐ Major convoy routes

• Allied merchant ships sunk by U-boats

⬩ U-boats sunk

▨ Territory under Allied control

▨ Territory under Axis control

☐ Territory under Vichy government (unoccupied France)

☐ Neutral territory

▶ **September 1939 to May 1940**

In 1939, Admiral Karl Dönitz had only 56 U-boats in service, of which only 22 were ocean-going types. Initially, pickings for the U-boat commanders were rich, as their boats sank merchantmen returning individually to Britain. Even when convoys were established, they could be escorted through only 15 degrees of longitude at either end of the transatlantic route due to a lack of suitable escorts. Even so, the U-boats were little more than a nuisance – until the fall of France.

scouting submarines and fleet supports, the Japanese introduced the B1 Type or I-15 class in 1939. These 20 large boats were of streamlined design, with a rounded seaplane hangar set forward of the conning tower, carrying a Yokosuka E14Y 'Glen' floatplane. Twin diesels produced 12,400hp (9200kW), giving a best surface speed of 23.5 knots, and operating range was 26,000km (16,155 miles). This enabled them to undertake trans-Pacific operations. *I-17* and *I-25* shelled land installations at Santa Barbara, California and Fort Stevens, Oregon, respectively. In August 1942, *I-25's* floatplane dropped two bombs on the Oregon mainland, starting a forest fire.

As the progress of the war increasingly showed the faulty nature of the Japanese submarine strategy,

some members had the hangar removed and replaced by a second 140mm (5.5in) gun to operate as attack submarines; and *I-36* and *I-37* were modified to carry Kaiten manned torpedoes. Only one of the I-15-class survived the war; *I-15* itself was sunk on 14 December 1942. For all its size and firepower, it had failed to sink any Allied vessel.

The Soviet Union

By 1939, the Soviet Union had more submarines than any other country, though more than half were of the small M-class, only useful for inshore work and harbour protection: something the Soviets took seriously. The Soviet Navy had to dispose its forces among the Baltic, Black Sea, Northern and Pacific

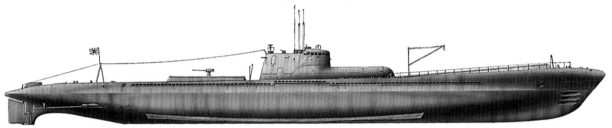

▲ **I-15**

Imperial Japanese Navy, Type B-1 patrol submarine, Pacific, 1942

In the Guadalcanal battles of August 1942, the Japanese deployed the big submarines in a screen in advance of the fleet, with the senior officer in a command boat. Co-ordination was difficult, but either *I-15* or *I-19* hit the battleship North Carolina with a torpedo and *I-15* narrowly missed USS *Washington*.

Specifications

Crew: 100	Submerged: 3713 tonnes (3654 tons)
Powerplant: Twin shaft diesel; electric motors	Dimensions (length/beam/draught): 102.5m x
Max Speed: Surfaced: 23.5 knots; Submerged:	9.3m x 5.1m (336ft x 30ft 6in x 16ft 9in)
8 knots	Commissioned: March 1939
Surface Range: 45,189km (24,400nm) at 10 knots	Armament: Six 533mm (21in) torpedo tubes; one
Displacement: Surfaced: 2625 tonnes (2584 tons);	140mm (5.5in) and two 25mm AA guns

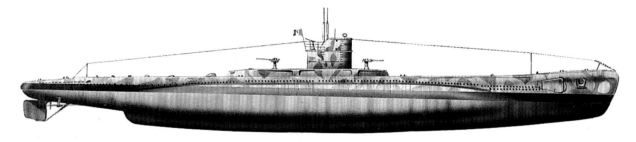

Specifications

Crew: 85	Submerged: 1707 tonnes (1680 tons)
Powerplant: Two diesel engines, two electric	Dimensions (length/beam/draught): 87.9m x
motors	7.76m x 5.72m (200ft 5in x 17ft 7in x 13ft)
Max Speed: Surfaced: 17 knots; Submerged:	Commissioned: July 1940
9 knots	Armament: 14 450mm (17.7in) torpedo tubes; two
Surface Range: 22,236km (12,000nm) at 11 knots	100mm (3.9in) guns
Displacement: Surfaced: 1528 tonnes (1504 tons);	

▲ **Ammiraglio Cagni**

Italian Navy, long-range patrol submarine, South Atlantic, 1943

Built at Monfalcone to a Bernardis design, this boat made some of the longest patrols of any World War II submarine, operating into the South Atlantic for up to 135 days. After surrendering at Durban, it returned to Italy in January 1944 and was used as a training boat by the Allied forces at Palermo.

fleets. These formed a set of very different undersea environments for submarines, in terms of temperature range, salinity, currents and depths, but the planners appear to have allocated vessels to bases and switched them without great regard for these aspects.

The Soviet plans of the later 1920s began to bear fruit with the construction of a substantial fleet, beginning with the Dekabrist class or Series I, of which six were built from 1927. The second design was the L- or Leninets class of minelaying submarine, inaugurated with six boats in 1931–32, followed by six in 1935–36, seven in 1937–38 and five in 1939–40. The first group were shared between the Black Sea and Baltic fleets, the second was all with the Pacific fleet, and the others were distributed between the Baltic, Black Sea, and Northern fleets. Some historians have suggested that some features were copied from the British *L-55*, sunk in the Baltic in 1919, salvaged and reinstated two years later, and certainly the Soviet class, though double-hulled, also had a British-style saddle ballast-tank, unlike the preceding double-hulled *Dekabrist*.

They were among the larger Soviet submarines, and the first group were distinctly underpowered, with German diesels of 2200hp (1600kW), replaced from Group 2 on with engines of 4200hp (3100kW). Groups 3 and 4 also had two stern-mounted torpedo tubes fitted. They carried 20 mines in stern galleries, modelled on the pioneer Krab design of the 1900s. Four L-class boats were lost during World War II; and the survivors were decommissioned between 1956 and 1963.

Class	Number	Launched	Note
S	50	1939–45	Pre-war class, North Sea/coastal
T	38	1940–45	Ocean-going; pre-war design
U	46	1939–	North Sea, Mediterranean
P611	4	1940	Turkish order transferred to RN
V	22	1941–44	Improved U-class
X-craft	20	1942	Midget type
XE	12		Midget type
Amphion	16	1943–45	Only 2 completed by May 1945

BRITISH SUBMARINE CLASSES, 1939–45

Wilhelm Gustloff and Goya

As the Red Army advanced towards the Baltic coast, refugees both civilian and military left German-held ports on commandeered transport ships. One of these, the former cruise-liner *Wilhelm Gustloff*, was sunk on 30 January 1945 by the Shchuka class submarine *S-13*, with a loss of life estimated to exceed 9000.

Another packed vessel, the 5314-tonne (5230-ton) *Goya*, was sunk in the Baltic by torpedoes from *L-3* on 16 April. Estimates of the number on board range from 6100 to 7000: only 183 survived. These sinkings rank as the greatest single events of human destruction yet caused by submarines.

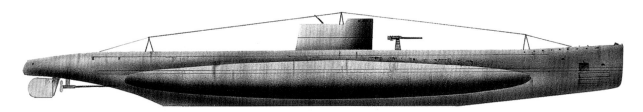

▲ **L-3**

Soviet Navy, patrol submarine/minelayer, Baltic Sea 1944–45

Submarine war in the Baltic Sea was dominated by extensive minefields and massive nets, often many miles long, set by the Germans and Finns, which the Soviet boats had to skirt. Meanwhile, until the end of 1944, the surface was dominated by German ships. *L-3*'s conning tower has been preserved as a memorial.

Specifications

Crew: 50

Powerplant: Twin screw diesel; electric motors

Max Speed: Surfaced: 15 knots; Submerged: 9 knots

Surface Range: 11,112km (6000nm) at 9 knots

Displacement: Surfaced: 1219 tonnes (1200 tons); Submerged: 1574 tonnes (1550 tons)

Dimensions (length/beam/draught): 81m x 7.5m x 4.8m (265ft 9in x 24ft 7in x 15ft 9in)

Commissioned: July 1931

Armament: Six 533mm (21in) torpedo tubes; one 100mm (3.9in) gun

The Battle of the Atlantic
1940–43

A titanic struggle was fought out between Axis submarines and Allied convoy-protection craft. If the U-boats could prevent Allied ships from reaching Britain, the war would be as good as won.

A MASSIVE BUILDING PROGRAMME was launched by Germany from the end of 1939, concentrating primarily on the Type VII and Type IX, but for the first two years of the war the U-boat command remained chronically short of long-range boats. Only from three to five were out at any one time, and though their rate of success was high, it was mid-1940 before new commissionings exceeded losses.

The British began to use convoys immediately, but escorting forces were small. U-boat captains developed the tactic of surface night-attacks in order to avoid ASDIC detection, and for a time this, combined with radio contact and direction, and the wolfpack system, brought excellent results, even with only 10 or 12 U-boats active at any one time. Realizing that they had been overconfident about the effectiveness of ASDIC, the British began to develop

further countermeasures from the spring of 1941, by which time 13 new U-boats were being commissioned each month.

The British were able to gauge the qualities of a Type VIIC when *U-570* was captured with its crew on its first patrol, south of Iceland, on 27 August 1941. It was incorporated into the Royal Navy as HMS *Graph*. Germany's declaration of war against the United States (11 December 1941) made it possible for the U-boats to operate in the former Pan-American Security Zone, and the first half of 1942 was known as a second 'Happy Time' for U-boats in the western Atlantic. By February 1942, they were active off the eastern coastline of Canada and the United States. Type IXC boats could strike as far away as Trinidad. Type VII, with shorter range, were refuelled and resupplied by the 10 submarines of

▲ **Under attack**

A Type IXB boat, probably *U-106*, as seen from one of two attacking Short Sunderland flying boats just before sinking in the Bay of Biscay.

Type XIV, capable of holding 439 tonnes (432 tons) of fuel. A Type XIV could enable 12 Type VII boats to stay operational for four weeks, or five Type IX boats for five weeks. Type XB minelayers were also used as supply boats.

Between January and July 1942, 681 ships, a GTR of around 3.5 million, were sunk for the loss of 11 U-boats. But convoys along the US coast, and ever-more intensive countermeasures, began turning the tide from mid-1942. In August 1942, 140 U-boats were operational, with 50 on patrol and 20 on passage at any time. Even though their numbers were still increasing, the attrition rate climbed faster, until by mid-1943 the destruction rate of U-boats exceeded the number being commissioned.

Until 1942, the depth charge was the only anti-submarine weapon, essentially a drum of high explosive with a hydrostatically set switch, which had been improved since World War I, with a weighted Mark IV version from the end of 1940 to speed up its descent. It could break a pressure hull at 6m (20ft) and force a submarine to surface from a detonation 12m (40ft) away. Later, improved depth charges and other devices were introduced. The 'Hedgehog', which threw a set of charges ahead of the pursuing vessel, was not very effective, as they exploded only on contact. By 1944, the 'Squid', a three-barrelled mortar, with an ASDIC link to explode at the correct depth, was much feared by submariners and contributed to the short service life of the later U-boats.

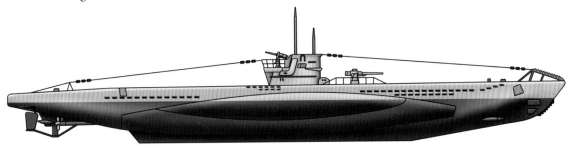

▲ **U-48**

German Navy, Type VIIB attack submarine, Atlantic, 1941

U-48 was commissioned into the 7th U-boat Flotilla on 22 April 1939 and remained with it while on combat operations. From June 1941 to 1945, it was attached to the 26th Training Flotilla (for live torpedo firing practice), then the 27th. From October 1943, it was a non-operational instructional unit.

Specifications

Crew: 44

Powerplant: Diesel; electric motors

Max Speed: 31.9/14.8km/hr (17.2/8kt) surf/sub

Surface Range: 12,040km (6500nm)

Displacement: 765/871t (753/857 tons) surf/sub

Dimensions (length/beam/draught): 66.5 x 6.2 x 4.7m (218.1 x 20.34 x 15.4ft)

Commissioned: 3 December 1940

Armament: 14 torpedoes (4 bow/1 stern tubes); one 8.8cm (3.5in) and one 2cm (0.8in) gun

U-48 TIMETABLE		
Patrol Dates	**Operational Area**	**Ships Sunk**
19 Aug 1939 – 17 Sep 1939	W of Biscay	3
4 Oct 1939 – 25 Oct 1939	W of Finsterre	5
20 Nov 1939 – 20 Dec 1939	Orkneys/Channel approaches	4
24 Jan 1940 – 26 Feb 1940	Channel approaches	4
3 Apr 1940 – 20 Apr 1940	Norway	0
26 May 1940 – 29 June 1940	WNW of Finisterre	7
7 Aug 1940 – 28 Aug 1940	WSW of Rockall	5
8 Sep 1940 – 25 Sep 1940	W of British Isles	8
5 Oct 1940 – 27 Oct 1940	NW of Rockall	7
20 Jan 1941 – 27 Feb 1941	S of Iceland	2
17 Mar 1941 – 8 Apr 1941	S of Iceland	5
22 May 1941 – 21 June 1941	W of St Nazaire (supporting *Bismarck*)/N of the Azores/central Atlantic	0
June 1941 – 1945	Served with 26 and 21 Flotillas as a training boat	
Oct 1943	Decommissioned: used by 3 ULD	
3 May 1945	Scuttled at Neustadt	

Its exploits from August 1939 to April 1941 made the Type VIIB *U-48* the single most successful submarine of World War II. In 12 patrols, between September 1939 and June 1941, it sank a total of 51 Allied ships, with a GRT of 306,875, plus a Royal Navy sloop. From June 1941, it was used as a training boat with the 26th Flotilla, but after heavy wear and tear was decommissioned in October 1943, and finally scuttled on 3 May 1945. Others of the 24 VIIBs had shorter lives. *U-100*, commissioned on 30 May 1940, was a very successful boat, which sank 25 ships on six patrols, with a total GRT of 135,614, plus others damaged. On 17 March 1941, it was sunk after being rammed by the British destroyer HMS *Vanoc*. *U-100* had surfaced in foggy conditions but

was caught by *Vanoc*'s Type 286 radar, the first U-boat to fall victim to this technology. On the same day *Vanoc* and HMS *Walker* depth-charged its sister VIIB boat *U-99*, forcing it to the surface, where the crew scuttled it. On the previous day it had sunk six Allied merchant ships, making a total of 38 sunk, a GRT of 244,658.

'Stay hard' – the Laconia Incident

On 12 September 1942, *U-156* sank the British liner *Laconia* in the South Atlantic. It proved to be transporting 1800 Italian prisoners of war. Three U-boats and the Italian submarine *Cappelini* picked up survivors, but they and the lifeboats were attacked by a US Liberator aircraft. This resulted in Dönitz's

▼ **Wolfpack group *West***

North Atlantic, June 1941

Formed in June 1941 from Type VII boats, mostly from 7th Flotilla and 1st Flotilla, together with a number of larger Type IX boats from 2nd Flotilla, the West group gathered southeast of the Newfoundland Bank. However, even in summer it was hard to find targets in the North Atlantic. On 20 June, the group spread out northeastwards, forming a widely spaced line in the centre of the North Atlantic. No convoys were encountered, but a number of independently sailing merchantmen were sunk. Late in June, Group West, together with some independent boats, was ordered eastwards after a Focke-Wulf Fw 200 Condor aircraft sighted Convoy OG 66 about 500km (290nm) west of Ireland. The OG convoys were routed from Britain to Gibraltar and West Africa, and the 55 ships of OG 66 had left Liverpool on 24 June. Further aircraft sightings were made on 30 June and 1 July, but the wolfpack was unable to close because of poor visibility caused by fog and bad weather.

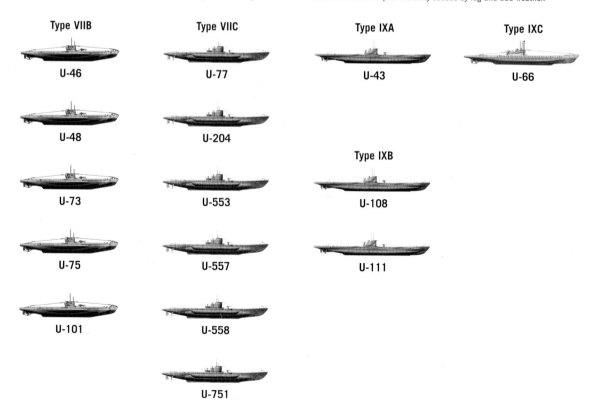

Type VIIB	Type VIIC	Type IXA	Type IXC
U-46	U-77	U-43	U-66
U-48	U-204		
U-73	U-553	Type IXB	
U-75	U-557	U-108	
U-101	U-558	U-111	
	U-751		

order to U-boats not to pick up survivors, unless for interrogation. 'Stay hard,' it said. 'Remember, the enemy does not care about women and children when he bombs Germany's towns and cities.' *U-156* was a member of the four-strong *Eisbär* wolfpack, based at Lorient but operating in the South Atlantic, where they sank 24 ships off the South African coast in October to November 1942.

At the end of 1942, two wolfpack groups, *Falke* and *Habicht*, were operating west of Ireland, with a total of 29 boats. But by this time, however, the work of the Ultra codebreakers, and the use of high-frequency direction-finding equipment, helped the Allies to identify U-boat locations and re-route convoys accordingly. The wolfpacks enjoyed less

success, though appalling weather conditions also played a part. Convoy TM 1, of nine oil tankers sailing from the Caribbean to North Africa, was intercepted in the Atlantic west of Gibraltar on 3–5 January 1943 by the 10 U-boats of the *Delfin* wolfpack, plus four others. Only two of the nine tankers reached Gibraltar.

U-106 was a typical Type IXB boat. Laid down on 26 November 1939 at AG Weser, Bremen, it was launched on 17 June 1940 and commissioned on 24 September. The speed of construction meant that the U-boats had few refinements. US submariners in particular would be struck by the austerity of their operating conditions. *U-106* sank 22 ships during its career, with a total GRT of 138,581, and survived

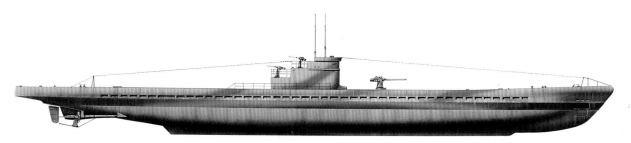

Specifications

Crew: 48–50

Powerplant: Diesel; electric motors

Max Speed: 33.7/13.5km/hr (18.2/7.3kt)
  surf/sub

Surface Range: 16,110km (8700nm)

Displacement: 1068/1197t (1051/1178 tons)
  surf/sub

Dimensions (length/beam/draught): 76.5 x 6.8
  x 4.7m (251 x 22.31 x 15.42ft)

Commissioned: 30 April 1940

Armament: 22 torpedoes (four bow/two stern
  tubes); one 10.5cm (4.1in), one 3.7cm (1.5in)
  and one 2cm (0.8in) gun

▲ U-106

German Navy, Type IXB attack submarine, Atlantic, January 1942

The 14 Type IXB boats each sank over 100,000GRT of Allied shipping. They carried a stock of 22 torpedoes, and a range extended by 1100km miles (700) over the *IXA*'s 15,000km (9321 miles). The dimensions were almost identical, though the *IXB*'s beam was 0.3m (1ft) wider. *U-106* torpedoed and severely damaged the battleship HMS *Malaya* in March 1941.

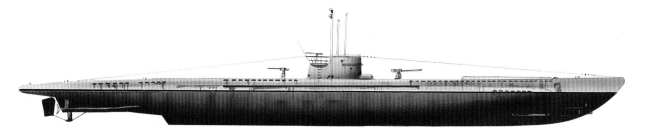

▲ U-118

German Navy, Type VIIC attack submarine, North Atlantic, 1943

U-118 was at first with the 4th Training Flotilla at Stettin (Szceczin) on the Baltic, then was attached to the 10th Flotilla at Lorient in October 1942, and finally the 12th at Bordeaux. Germany used 11 mine types, several of which could be launched from torpedo tubes, but the SM moored magnetic type required a minelaying tube.

Specifications

Crew: 52

Powerplant: Diesel; electric motors

Max Speed: 30.4/13km/hr (16.4/7kt) surf/sub

Surface Range: 26,760km (14,450nm)

Displacement: 1763/2143t (1735/2143 tons)
  surf/sub

Dimensions (length/beam/draught): 89.8 x 9.2
  x 4.7m (294.58 x 30.16 x 15.42ft)

Commissioned: 6 December 1941

Armament: 66 mines; 11 torpedoes (2 stern
  tubes); one 10.5cm (4.1in), one 3.7cm
  (1.5in) and one 2cm (0.8in) gun

three depth-charge attacks before being sunk off Spain by British and Australian Sunderlands on 2 August 1943.

Type XB, designed as minelayers, were the largest of the World War II U-boats. Eight were commissioned, capable of carrying 66 mines of SMA (Schachtmine A) moored type, with 18 placed in vertical shafts set forward and independent of the pressure hull. A further 48 were in side-shafts set into the saddle tanks. *U-118*, commissioned on 6 December 1941, made four operational patrols, but only one sortie as a minelayer, in January to February 1943, sinking four merchant vessels.

Before and and after that, it was used as a supply boat for attack submarines operating in the West Atlantic. On 12 June 1943, it was sunk to the southwest of the Canary Islands by air-dropped depth depth charges from Avengers flying from the US escort carrier *Bogue*. The XB boats had a slow diving time compared to the smaller German submarines and this made them particularly vulnerable to air attack. Only two survived the war.

At the start of 1943, over two hundred U-boats were available for operations. In the war's largest convoy action, in March, 40 U-boats attacked convoys HX229 and SC122, sinking 22 ships for the loss of one U-boat. It seemed that the concerted onslaught of submarines in large numbers might defeat the convoy system. But this was the last great success of the wolfpacks. The turn of fortune was due to several factors, including the Allied deployment of long-range reconnaissance aircraft, the improvement of radar systems, the use of escort carriers to despatch attack planes, the use of larger convoys, and more effective deployment of surface ASW forces in fast-moving support groups. Improved efficiency of British and US radar meant that the favoured night surface attacks by U-boats were no longer safe. Above and below the surface, they were detectable at all times. In May 1943, 26 convoy ships were sunk, but 27 U-boats were lost in the process. Overall, U-boat casualties outnumbered the new commissions, and Allied air patrols turned the Bay of Biscay into the 'valley of death'. Six U-boats were destroyed there by aircraft in May 1943. The U-boats were withdrawn from the North Atlantic. In late 1943, the combination of intercepted intelligence and increasing ASW skills by both aircraft and surface ships made any part of the Atlantic area an increasingly risky place for U-boats. In one attack on

▶ **April to December 1941**

In 1941, the *Kriegsmarine* still had too few U-boats to control the convoy routes. Improvements in British convoy tactics and the advent of a new type of escort, the corvette, made the U-boat mission harder. Increasing Canadian strength and the decision by the United States to escort convoys out of their ports further strengthened the British position. The American decision involved the US Navy in a 'secret' shooting war, in which US escorts attacked if first attacked by U-boats. However, the introduction of Wolfpack tactics – the use of multiple boats making co-ordinated attacks on a single convoy – negated the effects of improved British convoy tactics.

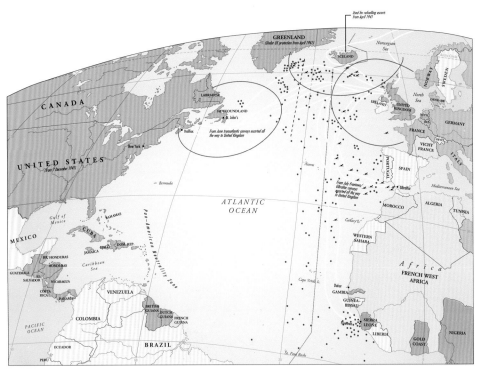

the combined convoys ON 202 and ONS 18, on 20 September 1943, the 14 boats of the *Leuthen* wolfpack concentrated their initial attack on the escort vessels, sinking three but losing two of their number in the process.

Throughout the war, the Type VII, in its various sub-classes, remained the *Reichsmarine*'s main attack submarine. A total of 709 were built. For the purposes of the German Navy as understood in 1935, its size, range, seaworthiness, speed, armament, manoueuvrability, construction cost and crewing requirement were all adequate and added up to an effective war machine that was further improved in its later variants, of which the most numerous was the VIIC, with 507 commissioned. *U-210*, which was commissioned in February 1942, a typical Type VIIC in design, exemplified the increasing hazards faced by the German submarine fleet. It would have joined the 9th Flotilla at Brest, but its first and only patrol lasted from 18 July to 6 August 1942. Having set off from Kiel, it was ordered to join the Atlantic *Pirat* wolfpack, which had a patrol line across the standard convoy route; then the *Steinbrinck* pack in the North Atlantic, about 645km (400 miles) northeast of

▲ **Concrete protection**

The massive concrete U-boat pens built by the *Organization Todt* on the French Atlantic coast proved impervious to Allied air attack.

▶ **January 1942 to February 1943**

In July 1942, the United States finally instituted a convoy system, so the U-boats moved south to the Caribbean, where they were able to strike at the vital oil supplies coming out of Maracaibo. As the US convoy system expanded to include these areas, the U-boats prepared to move back to the shipping lanes of the North Atlantic. By now, the *Kriegsmarine* had more than 300 U-boats in service, and by November 1942 Allied shipping was being sunk at a rate of more than 700,000 tonnes (689,000 tons) every month.

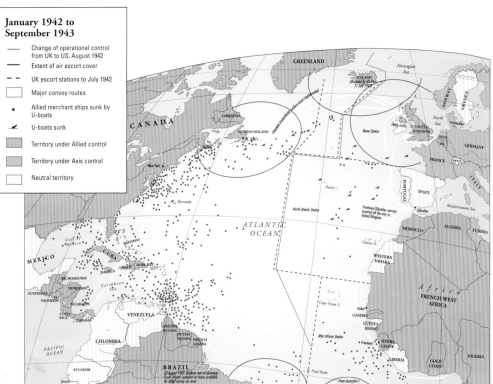

January 1942 to September 1943

- — — Change of operational control from UK to US, August 1942
- ——— Extent of air escort cover
- – – UK escort stations to July 1942
- ☐ Major convoy routes
- • Allied merchant ships sunk by U-boats
- ⚓ U-boats sunk
- ▨ Territory under Allied control
- ▨ Territory under Axis control
- ☐ Neutral territory

Newfoundland. Eastbound Convoy SC 94 was spotted on 5 August, but on the 6th, as *U-210* closed in, it was detected by the Canadian destroyer *Assiniboine*. Forced by depth charges to surface, the submarine engaged the destroyer in a gun battle that ended when *Assiniboine*, its bridge on fire, rammed and sank the U-boat. Nevertheless, the *Steinbrinck* pack sank 11 out of 36 ships in the convoy.

U-511 (Type IXC) was commissioned at DeutscheWerft, Hamburg, on 8 December 1941. Initially, it was used as a test platform for experimental rockets at the Peenemünde base. A rack for six 30cm (11.8in) Wurfkörper 42 Spreng artillery rockets was fitted to the deck. These were successfully

fired from a depth of 12m (39ft), and might with further development have become a major weapon. However, the problem of accurate aiming was not resolved and *U-511* was assigned from August 1942 to the 10th Flotilla at Lorient, making four patrols as far as the Caribbean Sea, and sinking three merchant ships. Its final mission for the *Reichsmarine* was to carry passengers and cargo to Penang, Malaya, between May and August 1943, sinking two ships en route. Passed on to a Japanese crew, it was sold to Japan on 16 September, becoming *RO-500*. It was scuttled by the Americans on 30 April 1946.

U-459 (Type XIV) was the first purpose-built refuelling and supply boat, of which 10 were

Specifications

Crew: 44	Dimensions (length/beam/draught): 67.1 x 6.2
Powerplant: Diesel; electric motors	x 4.8m (220.1 x 20.34 x 15.75ft)
Max Speed: 31.5/14.1km/hr (17/7.6kt) surf/sub	Commissioned: 21 February 1942
Surface Range: 12,040km (6500 nm)	Armament: 14 torpedoes (4 bow/1 stern tubes);
Displacement: 773/879t (761/865 tons)	one 8.8cm (3.5in) and two 2cm (0.8in) guns
surf/sub	

▲ U-210

German Navy, Type VIIC attack submarine, North Atlantic, August 1942

The Type VIIC had GHG underwater listening devices set in arrays of 24 7.5cm (3-in) crystal microphones on each side of the bows, providing a form of passive sonar detection. *U-210* did not survive long enough to have a snorkel tube fitted, as was done to most surviving U-boats in 1944–45.

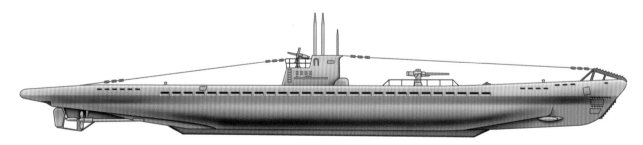

▲ U-511

German Navy, Type IXC attack submarine, Atlantic, 1943

Wolfpack groups to which *U-511* was assigned were *Pirat*, from 29 July to 3 August 1942, *Schlagetot* from 9 to 21 November 1942, *Delphin* from 3 January 1943 to 14 February; and *Robbe* from 16 February to 5 March 1943. On these patrols it sank only one ship, the British merchantman *William Wilberforce* (January 1943).

Specifications

Crew: 48–50	Dimensions (length/beam/draught): 76.8 x 6.8
Powerplant: Diesel; electric motors	x 4.7m (252 x 22.31 x 15.42ft)
Max Speed: 33.9/13.5km/hr (18.3/7.3kt)	Commissioned: 8 December 1941
surf/sub	Armament: 22 torpedoes (4 bow/2 stern tubes);
Surface Range: 20,370km (11,000nm)	one 10.5cm (4.1in), one 3.7cm (1.5in) and
Displacement: 1138/1252t (1120/1232 tons)	one 2cm (0.8in) gun
surf/sub	

commissioned between November 1941 and March 1943. It had no torpedo tubes but carried two 3.7cm (1.5in) and one 200mm (0.8in) AA guns. Its supply tanks held 439 tonnes (432 tons) of fuel oil. From the bases at St Nazaire, and then Bordeaux, *U-459* made six Atlantic patrols, with 63 refuelling meetings, between 29 March 1942 and 24 July 1943; on one occasion running so short itself that another 'milch cow', *U-462*, had to refuel it.

Attacked off Cape Ortegal, Spain by RAF Wellingtons on 24 July 1943, *U-459* was severely damaged and scuttled. By the end of 1943, the Type XIV boats had been virtually eliminated and, in May 1944, work on a planned further 14 was cancelled,

together with plans for a larger version to be known as Type XX.

U-530 (Type IXC/40) was commissioned in October 1942 and spent its career in the Atlantic with the 10th and 33rd Flotillas. The 10th was based at Lorient, the 33rd notionally at Flensburg, though many of its boats were still on service in the Atlantic.

U-530 did not have a particularly distinguished record as an attack boat, and was used on at least one patrol as a fuel tanker, but on 23 June 1944 it made an important mid-ocean rendezvous with the Japanese *I-52,* to transfer a Naxos radar detector, two operators, and a navigator to guide the huge Japanese submarine, with a cargo of gold and strategic

Specifications

Crew: 53	Dimensions (length/beam/draught): 67.1 x 9.4
Powerplant: Diesel; electric motors	x 6.5m (220.16 x 30.83 x 21.33ft)
Max Speed: 26.7/11.7km/hr (14.4/6.3kt)	Commissioned: 15 Nov 1941
surf/sub	Armament: Two 3.7cm (1.5in) and one 2cm
Surface Range: 17,220km (9300nm)	(0.8in) gun
Displacement: 1688/1932t (1661/1901 tons)	Fuel load: 439t (432 tons)
surf/sub	

▲ **U-459**

German Navy, Type XIV supply submarine, Atlantic, 1942

Commissioned on 15 November 1941, *U-459* went to the 4th Training Flotilla until 31 March 1942, then to the 10th Flotilla at Lorient from April to October 1942, and finally to the 12th Flotilla at Bordeaux from 1 November 1942. It made six war patrols in all, including one with wolfpack *Eisbär*, 25 August – 1 September 1942.

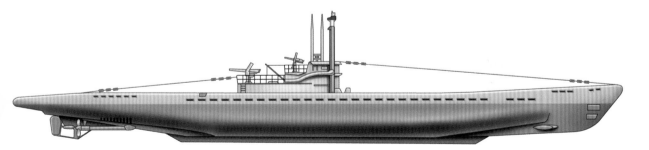

▲ **U-530**

German Navy, Type IXC/40 attack submarine, Atlantic, 1945

U-530 made seven patrols in total. It was one of the few Type XC boats fitted with the Lorenz Co.'s FuMO61 Hohentwiel U radar transmitter, and a retractable FuMB-26 Tunis antenna, as a marine version of the German radar developed for aircraft use. The range was 8–10km (5–6 miles) on the surface.

Specifications

Crew: 48–50	surf/sub
Powerplant: Diesel; electric motors	Dimensions (length/beam/draught): 76.8 x 6.9
Max Speed: 33.9/13.5km/hr (18.3/7.3kt)	x 4.7m (252 x 22.6 x 15.42ft)
surf/sub	Commissioned: 14 October 1942
Surface Range: 20,370km (11,000nm)	Armament: 22 torpedoes; one 10.5cm (4.1in)
Displacement: 1138/1252t (1120/1232 tons)	one 3.7cm (1.5in) and one 2cm (0.8in) gun

CONVOY PQ 17 BATTLE TIMETABLE, 27 JUNE – 13 JULY 1942	
Date	Event
27 June 1942	At 16:00 the ships of convoy PQ 17 leave their anchorage in Hvalfjordur, Iceland, and head northwards. The convoy consists of 35 ships and is heavily loaded with 297 aircraft, 594 tanks, 4246 lorries and gun carriers and 158,503 tonnes (156,000 tons) of cargo. (This was enough to equip an army of 50,000 men and was valued at $700 million at the time.) Shortly after leaving, one ship runs aground and returns to port
29 June	The convoy encounters heavy drift ice. Four merchantmen are damaged, with one having to return to port. This leaves 33 ships en route to Russia
1 July	The convoy is spotted by *U-255* and *U-408*. *U-456* joins the other boats and begins tracking the convoy. Further reconnaissance information is provided by BV 138 flying boats of the *Luftwaffe*
2 July	A number of U-boats attempt attacks on the convoy, but to little effect. They are joined in the evening by the first in a series of *Luftwaffe* torpedo attacks
3 July	U-boats and *Luftwaffe* torpedo planes continue to attack without success. However, British intelligence receives reports that a powerful German surface force is leaving Norwegian waters and heading northwards. The Admiralty calculates that *Tirpitz*, *Hipper*, *Scheer* and *Lützow* would intercept the convoy on the evening of 4 July
4 July	Two ships are sunk by *U-457* and *U-334*. At around 22:00, the British Admiralty, fearing that *Tirpitz* and her consorts are about to strike, and knowing that the battleships of the Home Fleet are too far away to intervene, orders the escorts to run westwards and for the convoy to scatter and proceed independently towards Russia
5 July	Even though the German surface forces have not left port, the scattered merchantmen are vulnerable to U-boats and air attack. The slaughter begins almost immediately. *Luftwaffe* aircraft sink six ships, while the U-boats account for a similar number (*U-88* and *U-703* sinking two each, while *U-334* and *U-456* sink the others)
6 July	Two more vessels are lost, one to the *Luftwaffe* and one to *U-255*
7 July	The *Luftwaffe* sinks another ship, while *U-255*, *U-457* and *U-355* account for three more
8 July	*U-255* sinks her third ship
10 July	*U-251* and *U-376* each sink one merchantman
13 July	*U-255* sinks a derelict merchant ship that has been adrift since being struck by *Luftwaffe* bombs on 5 July

materials, to Germany. *I-52* was soon afterwards sunk by depth charges and homing torpedoes from USS *Bogue*'s Avengers. *U-530* proceeded to make the last U-boat patrol into the Caribbean. At the end of the war the boat surrendered in Mar del Plata, Argentina. Transferred to the United States, it was sunk, after tests, as a target on 28 November 1947.

By early 1943, air attacks were taking such a toll of U-boats in the Atlantic that some submarines were converted as 'flak-boats' to provide anti-aircraft protection, especially for the 'milch-cow' supply boats. A Type VIIC, *U-441*, commissioned in February 1942, attached to the 1st Flotilla at Brest, and part of the big *Haudegen* wolfpack of January 1943, was the first of four boats to complete conversion. The bridge was extended fore and aft in an enlarged 'wintergarden' to allow for two fast-firing quadruple 2cm (0.8in) Flakvierling guns and a 3.7cm (1.5in) Flak gun, as well as additional MG42

machine guns. Around 20 additional crew were needed, bringing the total to 67. On its first flak patrol as *Uflak-1*, it shot down an RAF Sunderland, but was badly damaged by three Beaufighters on its second patrol. A flak boat could not cope with concerted attack by several aircraft, and *U-441*, like the others involved, was re-converted from October 1943 and resumed basic combat duties. Ironically, an aircraft was its downfall: sunk on 8 June 1944 in the English Channel by depth charges from a Liberator of No. 224 Squadron RAF.

British Production

Germany's drive to build more and more U-boats gave it the world's largest submarine fleet, despite the ever-increasing rate of destruction. The British rate of increase was far more modest, but there were very few German merchantmen for the Royal Navy to attack, and the task of the British submarines was to attack

German and Italian naval craft, including, of course, submarines. British submarines played virtually no part in the wider Battle of the Atlantic, though actively engaged on patrols in the approaches to the British Isles. The S-class was chosen for an accelerated construction programme in 1941, with 50 being built between 1941 and 1945, in three groups with slightly varying specifications. Though bigger than the original S-boats, they were still only medium-large compared to many of their adversaries. Powered on the surface by two Admiralty-pattern diesel engines, many made by Paxman (who provided engines for over half the British wartime submarine fleet), the two electric motors were rated at 1300hp (969kW). These could be used as generators when the diesels were engaged in direct drive, either to recharge the batteries or to provide auxiliary power.

The third group, including HMS *Seraph*, had an additional torpedo tube, stern-facing and externally mounted, and some later boats mounted a 100mm (4in) gun. The S-class was an effective design, serving mainly around the British coasts and in the Mediterranean, though some were fitted with external fuel tanks and operated in the Far East. Fast to dive, they had an operational depth of 76m (249ft). Seventeen were lost to enemy action and one, HMS *Seal*, was captured by the Germans. From 1943 to 1945, one of the class, HMS *Sturgeon*, was manned by a Dutch crew as Zeehond.

The British V-class, of which 42 were ordered but only 22 completed, was a development of the slightly smaller U-class. Official designation was 'U-class long-hull'; they were 62.33m (204ft 6in) long

compared with the the U-class length of 58m (191ft). To create further confusion, seven V-class had U-names and four U-class had V-names. The V-class had thicker steel plates, 19.05mm (.75in) rather than 12.7mm (.5in), and a greater degree of welding in construction, enabling them to dive faster and deeper. The U- and V-classes were the first British submarines to have diesel-electric drive, with the diesels feeding two Paxman diesel generators. British submarines had been most active in the Mediterranean Sea, and the reduction of combat operations following the collapse of Italy deprived the V-class of much possible action. Two V-class went to the Free French Navy, and one each to the Norwegian and Greek free forces.

Between August 1941 and May 1945, 78 convoys sailed to North Russian ports, tagged as 'PQ outward bound' and 'QP or RA homewards'. Convoy PQ 17, of 35 ships, lost 24 of them between 1 and 13 July 1942 to a sustained attack by 10 U-boats and a large force of *Luftwaffe* dive-bombers and torpedo planes. Believing mistakenly that German capital ships were on the way, the British Admiralty ordered the convoy to scatter, leaving the merchant ships open to U-boat attack. It was the biggest convoy disaster of the war.

Norwegian harbours at Narvik and Hammerfest were added to Trondheim as forward bases, both for convoy attack and for weather reporting and

Specifications

Crew: 67

Powerplant: Diesel; electric motors

Max Speed: 31.5/14.1km/hr (17/7.6kt) surf/sub

Surface Range: 12,040km (6500nm)

Displacement: 773/879 tonnes
(761/865 tons) surf/sub

Dimensions (length/beam/draught): 67.1 x
6.2 x 4.8m (220.1 x 20.34 x 15.75ft)

Commissioned: 21 February 1942

Armament: 14 torpedoes; one 3.7cm (1.5in)
and two quad 2cm (0.8in) guns

▼ **U-441**

German Navy, flakboat conversion of Type VIIC, North Atlantic, 1943

In April–May 1943, *U-441* was rebuilt as *U-Flak 1*, the first of three U-Flak boats. Designed to lure aircraft into battle, she was equipped with an enlarged bridge on which were mounted two Flakvierling 0.8in (2cm) quad mounts and a 3.7cm (1.5in) Flak gun, along with extra MG 42 machine guns. On her first patrol, *U-441* shot down a Sunderland but was still vulnerable. With the boats unable to fight off Allied air attacks, Admiral Dönitz decided that the U-Flak experiment had failed. In late 1943, *U-Flak 1* was converted back to a more conventional configuration.

U-441 was sunk with all hands on 8 June 1944 in the English Channel by depth charges from a Liberator of No. 224 Sqn RAF.

intelligence-gathering. The 13th Flotilla, based at Trondheim, formed of 55 Type VIIC and VIIC/41 boats, was operational right up to the final surrender in May 1945. Formed into two wolfpacks, *Keil* and *Donner*, in April 1944 they made repeated attacks on the returning convoy RA 59, sinking one freighter but losing *U-277*, *U-959* and *U-674*, all Type VIIC boats. The scale of the German effort was prodigious. From September 1939 until May 1943, almost 600 U-boats were built and put into action (not all in the Atlantic campaigns) and 250 had been lost. They still had over 400 in service, far more than any other navy. But in their prime purpose, in this war, they had been defeated.

The U-Boats wrought massive destruction on Allied shipping, sinking 14,732,680 tonnes (14,500,000) tons over all the oceans of the world. Out of this total, some 12,095,992 tonnes (11,904,954 tons) was sunk in the North Atlantic alone. Although the U-Boats were eventually fitted with Dutch-invented 'Schnorchel' tubes, allowing them to charge their batteries while operating below the surface, thus making them harder to find, between June and December 1944, 140 did not return to their bases. The U-Boat Command paid a huge price in the loss of their personnel: of 40,900 officers and men involved, 25,870 were killed (63 per cent) and another 5338 taken prisoner of war.

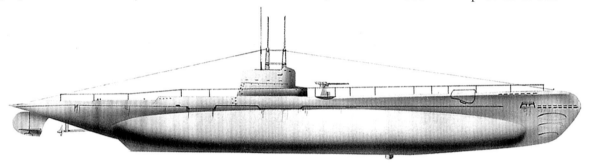

▲ Seraph

Royal Navy, S-class patrol submarine, Mediterranean, 1943

Seraph played a key role in the secret preparations for the Allied landings in North Africa, including the depositing of the body of 'the man who never was' on the Spanish coast in Operation Mincemeat in early 1943. In 1944, it was converted as a fast target boat for ASW exercises and was stricken in 1963.

Specifications

Crew: 44	Submerged: 1005 tonnes (990 tons)
Powerplant: Twin screw diesel; electric motors	Dimensions (length/beam/draught): 66.1m x
Max Speed: Surfaced: 14.7 knots; Submerged:	7.2m x 3.4m (216ft 10in x 23ft 8in x 11ft 2in)
9 knots	Commissioned: October 1941
Surface Range: 11,400km (6144nm) at 10 knots	Armament: Six 533mm (21in) torpedo tubes; one
Displacement: Surfaced: 886 tonnes (872 tons);	76mm (3in) gun

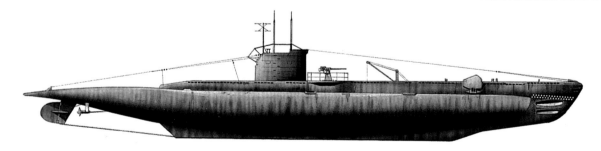

Specifications

Crew: 37	Submerged: 752 tonnes (740 tons)
Powerplant: Twin screw diesel; electric motors	Dimensions (length/beam/draught): 61m x 4.8m
Max Speed: Surfaced: 11.25 knots; Submerged:	x 3.8m (200ft x 16ft x 12ft 9in)
9 knots	Commissioned: September 1944
Surface Range: 7041km (3800nm) at 8 knots	Armament: Four 533mm (21in) torpedo tubes;
Displacement: Surfaced: 554 tonnes (545 tons);	one 76mm (3in) gun

▲ HMS Vagabond

Royal Navy, V-class patrol submarine

Commissioned on 19 September 1944, *Vagabond* was powered by two 6-cylinder Davey-Paxman engines generating 400hp (298kW) compared to the original U-class's 307hp (229kW) Admiralty diesels. Diving depth was 91m (300ft). V-boats carried the DF loop at the rear of the tower casing, not on top as in the U-class.

The Mediterranean and Black Seas
1940–45

The Mediterranean, lined on its south coast by French and Italian colonies and with the British protectorate of Egypt at the east end, was a strategic sea, made even more so as it was the passage to the Suez Canal and the short route to India and Africa.

AXIS POSSESSION OF SUEZ would be a major blow to the Allied war effort. When hostilities with Italy began in June 1940, the British Navy was in effective control of the eastern and western Mediterranean, with the Italians in control of the central area. With aircraft able to overfly any part, the role of submarines was all the more important, although they were dangerously visible at low depths.

Early Deployment

Italy had 49 submarines in three main groups, a western one operating between Gibraltar and Siciliy, a second centred in the Gulf of Genoa, and the third between Greece and Alexandria. The Royal Navy moved 10 submarines to Alexandria in 1940 and further deployments followed, though between surface ships and mines, nine were sunk by the end of 1940. Five Greek boats joined the British squadron, and a flotilla of 10 U-class boats were based at Malta from early 1941, and these smaller craft turned out to be very effective performers in the Mediterranean. In June 1941, 25 British and Allied boats were on service, but

ITALIAN SUBMARINE CLASSES, 1939–45			
Class	Number	Launched	Note
CA1-2	2	1938–39	Midget sub
Liuzzi	4	1939–40	Larger version of pre-war Brin class
Marconi	6	1939–40	Ocean-going
Cagni	4	1940	Ocean-going; largest Italian WWII sub
Acciaio	13	1941–42	Last survivor discarded 1966
CB	21	1941–43	Midget sub; 9 completed after Sep 1943
CA3-4	2	1942	Modified CA1; scuttled 1943
Flutto Type 1	9	1942–43	12 originally ordered
Flutto Type 2	3	1944	15 originally ordered
Romolo	2	1943	Transport sub; 12 originally ordered
S1	11	1943	Ex-U-boats repossessed by Germany 1943

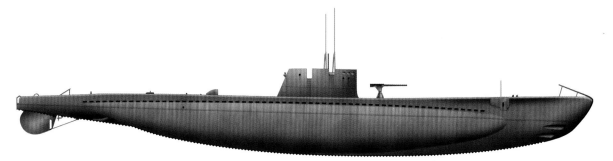

Specifications

Crew: 45

Powerplant: Twin screw diesel engines; electric motors

Max Speed: Surfaced: 14 knots; Submerged: 8 knots

Surface Range: 4076km (2200nm) at 10 knots

Displacement: Surfaced: 690 tonnes (680 tons);

Submerged: 861 tonnes (848 tons)

Dimensions (length/beam/draught): 60m x 6.5m x 4m (197ft 6in x 21ft x 13ft)

Commissioned: November 1936

Armament: Six 533mm (21in) torpedo tubes; one 100mm (3.9in) gun

▲ **Dagabur**

Italian Navy, patrol submarine, Mediterranean/Red Sea, 1941

Built at the Tosi yard, Taranto, *Dagabur* was completed in April 1937. Several of the Adua class had their conning towers reduced in size during the war, and two, *Gondar* and *Scirè*, were fitted with cylindrical containers for three SLC manned torpedoes. Only one of the class, *Alagi*, survived the war, though three were sold to Brazil in 1937.

failed to do more than slightly hinder the transfer of the *Afrika Korps* to North Africa. Sixty-nine Axis ships were sunk by submarines, with a GRT of 305,000 during 1941. By the end of 1941, despite losses, there were 28 Allied submarines in the Mediterranean.

For most of the year only 10 Italian submarines had been operational, but from September 10 U-boats entered this theatre, and by the end of the year they had put Britain's eastern Mediterranean battle squadron out of action, with the loss of the carrier *Ark Royal* and the sinking or disabling (with Italian help) of three battleships and a cruiser. In April 1943, the British flotilla moved from Malta to Alexandria, but continuing losses held the Allied number down to 12 in April 1942, compared to 16 U-boats plus the Italians. By summer, reinforcements had brought the numbers up to 23 British boats. Further temporary reinforcements arrived to support the Allied landings in North Africa in October 1942.

The constant crossings of the Mediterranean by Axis supply convoys offered many attack opportunities but they were normally heavily escorted, and Allied forces never succeeded in more than partial disruption, though in some cases three quarters of a convoy's strength was sunk. In September 1943, the Italian war effort collapsed and an armistice was sought, but U-boats remained highly active.

Submarine Actions

Dagabur, completed in 1937, was one of 17 Adua-classboats, very similar to the Perla class, but of more restricted range, and able to go slightly deeper, to 80m (262ft). *Dagabur* attacked the cruiser HMS *Bonaventure* on 30 March 1941, but the Perla class *Ambra* successfully sank it. As the Malta-bound convoy of Operation Pedestal ploughed its way eastwards in August 1942, *Dagabur* was among the forces sent to prevent it. On 12 August, the destroyer HMS *Wolverine*, having located it on the surface through Type 271 radar, charged at a full 27 knots and rammed *Dagabur*, sinking it instantly.

A much larger boat was *Remo*, one of only two completed submarines of its class, intended to form 12 cargo-carrying long-range boats between Europe and Japan. Cargo capacity was 610 tonnes (600 tons). Its limited armament was intended for self-defence. *Remo* never got very far, being sunk in the Gulf of Taranto by the U-class HMS *United* on 15 July 1943.

Flutto was the lead boat of eight medium-range submarines (four others were cancelled or uncompleted) intended to form part of a large wartime building programme, though two others, *Tritone* and *Gorgo*, were completed before it. By now, Italian conning towers had a lower profile. During the Allied landings on Sicily, *Flutto* was operating in the Straits of Messina, when it was sunk on 11 July 1943 by three British motor torpedo boats, one of six Italian submarines sunk in the same week. One of the Flutto class, *Marea*, was involved in secret intelligence missions on the Italian coast in November to December 1943, on behalf of the Allies.

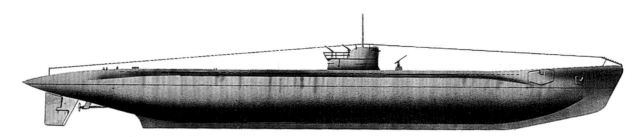

▲ Remo

Italian Navy, transport submarine, 1943

The large hull extended over four watertight holds. Two 450mm (17.7in) torpedo tubes were mounted in the bow. *Remo* was torpedoed while on the surface; *Romolo* was also sunk three days later. None of the other boats in the class were completed, though two, R-11 and R-12, were scuttled, refloated and used as oil storage hulks after the war.

Specifications

Crew: 63

Powerplant: Twin screws, diesel/electric motors

Max Speed: Surfaced: 13 knots; Submerged:

6 knots

Surface Range: 22,236km (12,000nm) at 9 knots

Displacement: Surfaced: 2245 tonnes (2210

tons); Submerged: 2648 tonnes (2606 tons)

Dimensions (length/beam/draught): 70.7m x

7.8m x 5.3m (232ft x 25ft 9in x 17ft 6in)

Commissioned: March 1943

Armament: Two 450mm (17.7in) torpedo tubes;

three 20mm (0.8in) guns

Midget Submarines

Midget submarines had always been a specialism of the Italian Navy, and semi-submersible 'human torpedoes' manned by frogmen, deployed from the specially modified Adua class submarine *Scirè*, made several attempts on shipping at Gibraltar, and seriously damaged the British battleships *Valiant* and *Queen Elizabeth* in Alexandria harbour in December 1941. Between June 1940 and September 1943, Italian underwater craft and explosive motor torpedo boats sank seven merchant vessels and five British warships.

Black Sea

During the war, the CB midget class, intended as an anti-submarine weapon, was designed. Of 72 planned, only 22 were laid down, with six built in January to May 1941 and transferred to the Black Sea in early 1942, based at Yalta. *CB2* has been credited with the torpedoing of a Soviet submarine, *Shch-208*, on 18 June 1942, though Soviet records ascribe the loss to a mine in August. With the Italian surrender the CBs passed into Romanian hands and were scuttled in 1944. A further 16 were wholly or partially completed in 1943; five were surrendered to

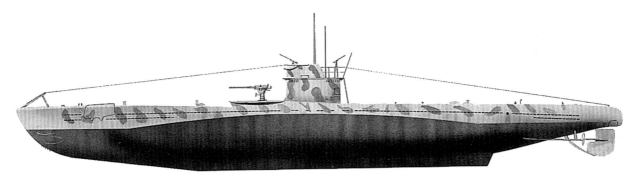

▲ Flutto

Italian Navy, patrol submarine, 1942

Completed in March 1943, *Flutto* was one of only three of its class to be engaged in action; all were lost. Two were fitted with cylinders for manned torpedoes, set alongside the tower and not replacing the gun as happened with the Adua class. After the war, *Nautilo* was passed to the Yugoslav Navy, and *Marea* to the Soviets.

Specifications

Crew: 50	Displacement: Surfaced: 973 tonnes (958 tons);
Powerplant: Twin screw diesel engines; electric	Submerged: 1189 tonnes (1170 tons)
motors	Dimensions (length/beam/draught): 63.2m x 7m
Max Speed: Surfaced: 16 knots; Submerged:	x 4.9m (207ft x 23ft x 16ft)
7 knots	Commissioned: November 1942
Surface Range: 10,000km (5400nm) at 8 knots	Armament: Six 533mm (21in) torpedo tubes; one
	100mm (3.9in) gun

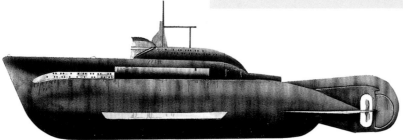

Specifications

Crew: 4	Displacement: Surfaced: 25 tonnes (24.9 tons);
Powerplant: Single screw diesel; one electric	Submerged: 36 tonnes (35.9 tons)
motor	Dimensions (length/beam/draught): 15m x 3m x
Max Speed: Surfaced: 7.5 knots; Submerged:	2m (49ft 3in x 9ft 10in x 6ft 9in)
6.6 knots	Commissioned: August 1943
Surface Range: 2660km (1434nm) at 5 knots	Armament: Two 450mm (17.7in) torpedoes in
	external canisters

▲ CB12

Italian Navy, midget submarines, Black Sea, 1942

These were built far inland, in Milan by Caproni Toliedo, but could be moved on special rail trucks. The torpedoes were mounted in external collars. Maximum diving depth was 55m (180ft), and they were equipped to carry 10 man-days of provisions. They were of very similar dimensions to the British X-boats, and, though still slow-speed, were slightly faster.

Great Britain, the others were taken over by the German Navy. None of these saw active service, as far as is known, though *CB20* passed to the post-war Yugoslav Navy and remained in service until 1959.

U-boats in the Med

Germany's 23rd U-boat Flotilla was formed at Salamis, Greece, on 11 September 1941, with nine boats, three Type VIIB and six VIIC, moved from Lorient. *U-331* sank the British battleship *Barham* on 25 November, but the U-boat deployment was not a general success. The 23rd Flotilla was merged into the larger 29th, based first at La Spezia, Italy, then Toulon, France.

In all, 68 U-boats were sent to the Mediterranean, against the wishes of Dönitz; none survived the war. A small contingent of Type II coastal U-boats, six in all, were transported to the Black Sea as the 30th Flotilla, based at Constanta, Romania, and disturbing the Soviet hegemony of that water; one was sunk by aircraft and the rest were scuttled, in August to September 1944.

U-73 (Type VIIB), commissioned on 30 September 1940, was stationed with the 7th Flotilla at St Nazaire before transferring to the Mediterranean in January 1942 to join the 29th Flotilla at Salamis. Five other Type VIIBs, known as the Goeben group, were deployed there around this time. The aim was to assist the Afrika Korps by cutting off the British supply line between Alexandria and Tobruk. On 11 August 1942,

U-73 made a major contribution by sinking the carrier HMS *Eagle*, with four torpedoes. It was sunk by American destroyers on 16 December 1943.

Black Sea Patrols

U-19 (Type IIB), commissioned on 16 January 1936, had had a distinguished record with the 1st Flotilla at Brest, sinking 14 merchant ships and one warship in the course of 20 patrols. In October 1942, it was assigned to the newly formed 30th Flotilla based at Constanza, Romania. The six boats, all Type IIB, had to be dismantled in order to be transferred to the Black Sea. The sections were transported by barge up the Elbe to Dresden, then overland to Linz on the Danube, where they were reassembled and made their own way down the Danube to Constanza.

Between 21 January 1943 and 10 September 1944, *U-19* carried out 11 patrols. The U-boats had only limited success, though Soviet supremacy in the Black Sea was challenged. In August 1944, Romania surrendered and the Constanza base was no longer tenable. *U-19* was scuttled off the Turkish

29TH FLOTILLA INSIGNIA

The 29th Flotilla's insignia was originally worn by *U-338*. The boat rammed a dock crane on being launched, and became known as the 'Wild Donkey'. Three or four of the flotilla's boats used this emblem.

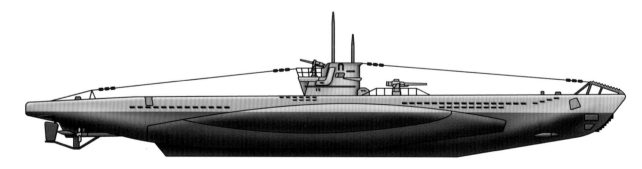

▲ **U-73**

German Navy, Type VIIB attack submarine, Mediterranean, 1943

The sinking of HMS *Eagle*, escorted by numerous destroyers and other craft, from 500m (547yds), was a remarkable feat. *U-73* accounted for eight merchant ships and four warships in five Atlantic and 10 Mediterranean patrols; on the last of these, with the *Wal* wolfpack, it sank a 7572.5-tonne (7453-ton) ship two days before its own destruction.

Specifications

Crew: 44

Powerplant: Diesel; electric

Max Speed: 31.9/14.8km/hr (17.2/8kt) surf/sub

Surface Range: 12,040km (6500nm)

Displacement: 765/871t (753/857 tons) surf/sub

Dimensions (length/beam/draught): 66.5 x 6.2 x 4.7m (218.1 x 20.34 x 15.4ft)

Commissioned: 31 October 1940

Armament: 14 torpedoes (4 bow/1 stern tubes); one 8.8cm (3.5in) and one 2cm (0.8in) guns

BOATS THAT SERVED WITH 30TH FLOTILLA (6 BOATS)					
U-Boat	Type	Commissioned	Flotilla(s)	Patrols	Fate
U-9	IIB	21 Aug 35	1 Oct 1942 – 20 Aug 1944 from 24. Flottille	19 patrols. 7 ships sunk: total 16,669GRT; 1 warship sunk: total 561t/552 tons; 1 warship damaged: total 419t/412 tons	Sunk by Soviet aircraft 20 Aug 1944 at Konstanza, Black Sea
U-18	IIB	4 Jan 36	6 May 1943 – 25 Aug 1944 from 24. Flottille	14 patrols. 3 ships sunk: total 1985GRT; 1 ship damaged: total 7745GRT; 1 warship damaged: total 57t/56 tons	Scuttled 25 Aug 1944 at Konstanza, Black Sea
U-19	IIB	16 Jan 36	1 Oct 1942 – 10 Sep 1944 from 22. Flottille	20 patrols. 14 ships sunk: total 35,430GRT; 1 warship sunk: total 448t/441 tons	Scuttled in the Black Sea 10 Sep 1944 off the coast of Turkey
U-20	IIB	1 Feb 36	1 Oct 1942 – 10 Sep 1944 from 21. Flottille	17 patrols. 14 ships sunk: total 37,669GRT; 1 ship damaged beyond repair: total 844GRT; 1 ship damaged: total 1846GRT	Scuttled in the Black Sea 10 Sep 1944 off the coast of Turkey
U-23	IIB	24 Sep 36	1 Oct 1942 – 10 Sep 1944 from 21. Flottille	16 patrols. 7 ships sunk: total 11,094GRT; 2 warships sunk: total 1433t/1410 tons; 3 ships damaged beyond repair: total 18,199GRT; 1 ship damaged: total 1005GRT; 1 warship damaged: total 57t/56 tons	Scuttled in the Black Sea 10 Sep 1944 off the coast of Turkey
U-24	IIB	10 Oct 36	1 Oct 1942 – 25 Aug 1944 from 21. Flottille	20 patrols. 4 ships sunk: total 961GRT; 5 warships sunk: total 580t/571 tons; 1 ship a total loss: total 7886GRT; 1 ship damaged: total 7661GRT	Scuttled 25 Aug 1944 at Konstanza, Black Sea

coast on 10 September. Apart from *U-9*, which was sunk by Soviet aircraft on 20 August, the other boats of the flotilla were also scuttled in August to September.

Numbers and Losses

Over a hundred British submarines, with 10 French, eight Greek, four Dutch and two Polish boats, were involved in Mediterranean operations, and usually between 20 and 30 at a time. Their contribution in hindering supplies to Axis armies in North Africa was a vital one, with more than a million tons of shipping sunk.

Forty-five British submarines were lost in the Mediterranean, of which 22 probably succumbed to mines. Nineteen were sunk by surface ships, three by aircraft and only one by a submarine. Sixteen Italian and five German submarines were sunk by Allied submarines. Altogether, 136 Italian submarines were involved, but many had been converted to a transport role to help in getting supplies across. Sixty-six were lost in total, against 41 new boats completed during the time Italy was at war.

Sixty-two U-boats were deployed in the Mediterranean, though there were never more than 25 in action at any one time. Between them, they sank 95 ships, totalling some 500,000GRT, and forced Allied ships to move in convoy. By sinking the British depot ship *Medway*, they seriously affected the Royal Navy's submarine operations. By the end of the war, all U-boats operating in the Mediterranean had been destroyed.

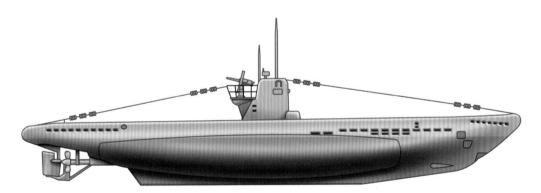

▲ U-19

German Navy, Type II coastal submarine, Black Sea, 1943

The Black Sea was the only theatre where Type II boats were deployed as a combat flotilla. Although they sank or damaged a number of Soviet tankers and claimed to have shot down at least two aircraft, and *U-19* sank a minesweeper on 29 August 1944, they did not paralyze Soviet shipping and their success was limited.

Specifications

Crew: 25

Powerplant: Diesel; electric motors

Max Speed: 33/15.4km/hr (17.8/8.3kt) surf/sub

Surface Range: 3334km (1800nm)

Displacement: 283/334t (279/329 tons) surf/sub

Dimensions (length/beam/draught): 42.7 x 4.1 x 3.8m (140.1 x 13.5 x 12.5ft)

Commissioned: 16 January 1936

Armament: Six torpedoes (3 bow tubes); one 2cm (0.8in) gun

Far East and Pacific

DECEMBER 1941 – AUGUST 1945

In this vast war theatre, the prime conflict was between the rapidly expanding American submarine fleet, mostly attack boats, and the Japanese submarine fleet, built primarily with fleet operations in view.

WHEN THE JAPANESE ATTACKED Pearl Harbor on 7 December 1941, Japan had 63 operational submarines, the Dutch had 15 based at Surabaya, Java, and the Americans had 55. Great Britain had no submarines in the Pacific, and only two between February 1942 and July 1943.

British Submarines

HMS *Storm* was one of 15 S-class boats ordered in Britain's 1941 building programme. Commissioned on 23 July 1943, it made one patrol into the Arctic Ocean before being despatched to the Royal Navy base at Trincomalee, Ceylon, arriving on 20 February 1944. It operated in the Bay of Bengal and the Malacca Straits, on ocean patrol and covert missions. Two Japanese destroyers and a merchant vessel were sunk.

In September 1944, *Storm* was deployed to Fremantle, Western Australia, with one ballast tank modified to hold the extra fuel required to maintain patrols as far out as Java. The boat returned to Britain in April 1945, having travelled 114km (71,000 miles)

and spent over 1400 hours submerged. It was scrapped in September 1949.

German Submarines

German U-boats also found their way into eastern waters. Eleven were to be transferred to a base in Japanese-held Penang, Malaya (12th, later 33rd, Flotilla) in mid-1943. But only five made it all the way, and their raiding activities in the Indian Ocean were of minor concern, largely through Allied decoding of their radio transmissions.

Japan

At the start of hostilities, Japan had 48 ocean-going I-class submarines and 15 were smaller RO-class; 29 were under construction; and 41 carried from one to three aircraft, a facility dropped by all other navies in the 1920s. Japanese submarines, though quite fast, were slow to dive and vulnerable to ASW techniques, while the Japanese Navy was surprisingly slow to develop its own radar and ASW capacity.

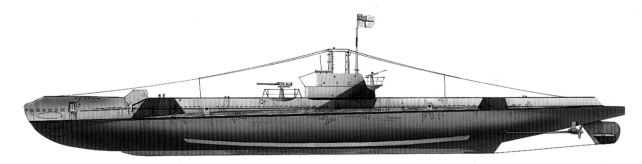

▲ HMS Storm

Royal Navy, S-class patrol submarine, Pacific, 1944

One of the third group of S-class boats, from the 1941 programme, *Storm* had a seventh external torpedo tube at the stern. Thirteen torpedoes were carried. D/F and radar aerials were added in 1944. It sank two Japanese warships, an army transport and 22 small craft. As with almost all submarines, its gunners had zero protection.

Specifications

Crew: 44	Submerged: 1006 tonnes (990 tons)
Powerplant: Twin screw diesel; electric motors	Dimensions (length/beam/draught): 61.8m x
Max Speed: Surfaced: 14.75 knots; Submerged:	7.25m x 3.2m (202ft 6in x 23ft 9in x 10ft 6in)
9 knots	Commissioned: May 1943
Surface Range: 15,750km (8500nm) at 10 knots	Armament: Six 533mm (21in) torpedo tubes; one
Displacement: Surfaced: 726 tonnes (715 tons);	76mm (3in) gun

The Japanese fleet had the most effective torpedoes available during World War II. The Type 95, a smaller submarine version of the Type 93 'long lance' (an American name, not used by the Japanese) developed from 1928, used pure oxygen to burn kerosene, instead of the compressed air and alcohol used in other nation's torpedoes. This gave them a range of up to 12km (7.5 miles) – about double that of their Allied counterparts – which also reduced their wake, making them harder to notice and avoid. The Type 95 also had by far the largest warhead of any submarine torpedo, initially 405kg (893lb), increased to 550kg (1210lb) late in the war.

Most importantly, the Type 95 used a simple contact exploder, and was far more reliable than its American counterpart, the Mark 14, until the latter was improved in late 1943. Japanese submarines also made extensive use of an electric torpedo, the Type 92. This weapon, with a 299kg (661lb) warhead, had modest performance compared to the Type 95, but emitted no exhaust and left no wake.

In one celebrated instance, *I-19* of the 1st Submarine Flotilla fired six torpedoes at the carrier USS *Wasp* on 15 September 1942. Three hit the carrier, effectively destroying it. Of the three that missed, two travelled on into the path of another US task force, hitting and causing serious damage to the destroyer *O'Brien* and the battleship *North Carolina*.

RO-100 Series

The RO-100 series, also known as 'Kaisho' (small) or Type KS was an 18-strong class developed from 1940 and completed by 1944. Intended for coastal defence, with an operating depth of 75m (245ft), its size meant it carried a limited payload of eight 533mm (21in) torpedoes. During the war, the need to operate further out made life difficult for the class. *RO-108* sank the US destroyer *Henley* off New Guinea in 1943 and RO-100s sank 33,021 tonnes (32,500 tons) of Allied merchant shipping, but the class was severely overextended. None survived the war, most of them sunk by American destroyers. The original *RO-100* made eight patrols before being sunk by a mine off the Solomon Islands in November 1943.

The C1 Hei gata class of attack submarine was laid down in 1937–38 but not commissioned until March 1940 to October 1941. In all there were five: *I-16*, *I-18*, *I-20*, *I-22* and *I-24*, intended specifically for attack on surface warships. Operational depth was

100m (330ft), and the class had a range of almost 26,000km (16,155 miles) and could remain at sea for up to 90 days. Twenty torpedoes were carried.

All participated in the surprise attack on Pearl Harbor by launching midget submarines, and *I-24* also took part in the Battle of the Coral Sea and the attack on Sydney Harbour (May and June 1942). *I-16* was converted to a transport in early 1943, carrying a landing craft. It was sunk off the Solomon

JAPANESE SUBMARINE CLASSES, 1939–45			
Class	Number	Launched	Note
C1	5	1940–41	Midget sub carrier
B1	20	1940–43	Patrol boat with seaplane or Kaiten
A/B	50	1940–43	Midget sub; 2-man crew
A1	3	1941–42	Seaplane carrier developed from J3
KD7	10	1942–43	Attack submarine
Kaisho type	18	1942–44	Coastal defence
Kaichu type	20	1943–44	Patrol submarine
B2	6	1943–44	Patrol submarine with seaplane or Kaiten
C3	3	1943–44	Long-range cruiser; cargo capacity
D1	12	1943–44	Landing craft; 110 troops
A2	1	1944	Long-range seaplane carrier
B3	3	1944	Patrol submarine with seaplane or Kaiten
C-type	15	1944	3-man crew; 47 completed by end of war
D-type	115	1944–45	5-man crew; 496 under construction mid-1945
AM	2	1944–45	Carried 2 seaplane bombers
Sen Toku I-400	3	1944–45	Long range; carried 3 float-planes
D2	1	1945	Cargo plus landing craft
Sen Taka	3	1945	Snorkel-fitted. Too late for combat duty
Sen Taka Sho	10	1945	Coastal patrol. 22 laid down
Sen Yu Sho	10	1945	Small supply boat
Sen Ho	1	1945	Submarine tanker and armament carrier

Islands by charges from a 'Hedgehog' ASW mortar from the US destroyer *England*, and none of the others survived the war.

In 1938, the Imperial Japanese Navy had built a small high-speed experimental submarine, designated 'Vesssel No. 71', capable of making over 21 knots (39km/h) submerged. From this, the much larger attack boat of class *I-201* was developed, with 23 ordered from the Kure Navy Yard in 1943. But only eight were laid down, and three were completed before the Japanese surrender, but not put into operational service. These were among the first

submarines to travel faster when submerged than on the surface.

Faced with ever-more effective and aggressive ASW techniques, the Japanese desperately needed a boat that combined speed, fast diving, good underwater handling and quietness of operation along with its offensive capacity. Four electric motors developing 5000hp (3700kW) provided the underwater power.

The I-201 class, single-hulled, of streamlined design, with retractable deck guns, and snorkels, planned for large-scale production using prefabricated

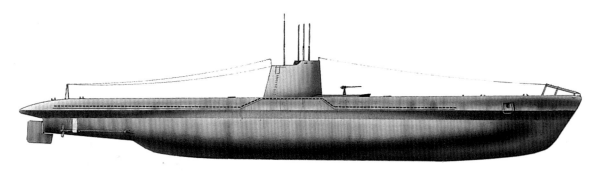

▲ RO-100

Imperial Japanese Navy, Type KS patrol submarine, Western Pacific, 1943
Completed in August 1942, this was the class leader. Assigned to SubRon 7, Submarine Division 13, of Japan's 8th Fleet, it was based at Rabaul, New Guinea, making combat patrols and supply runs in the region until sunk by a mine near Buin, Bougainville, on 25 November 1943.

Specifications

Crew: 75

Powerplant: Twin shaft diesel; electric motors

Max Speed: Surfaced: 14 knots; Submerged: 8 knots

Surface Range: 6485km (3500nm) at 12 knots

Displacement: Surfaced: 611 tonnes (601 tons); Submerged: 795 tonnes (782 tons)

Dimensions (length/beam/draught): 57.4m x 6.1m x 3.5m (188ft 3in x 20ft x 11ft 6in)

Commissioned: August 1942

Armament: Four 533mm (21in) torpedo tubes; one 76mm (3in) gun

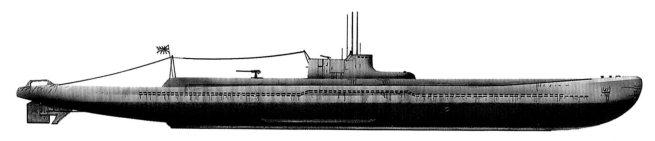

▲ C-1

Imperial Japanese Navy, midget submarine carrier
Based on the KD 6A type, though considerably larger, this was a fast boat on the surface. Unlike most big Japanese submarines, none of the class carried a float-plane. The midget submarine fittings were later replaced by attachments to hold small supply barges for landing supplies.

Specifications

Crew: 100

Powerplant: Twin shaft diesel; electric motors

Max Speed: Surfaced: 23.5 knots; Submerged: 8 knots

Surface Range: 25,928km (14,000nm)

Displacement: Surfaced: 2605 tonnes (2564 tons); Submerged: 3761 tonnes (3701 tons)

Dimensions (length/beam/draught): 108.6m x 9m x 5m (256ft 3in x 29ft 5in x 16ft 4in)

Commissioned: July 1938

Armament: Eight 533mm (21in) torpedo tubes; one 140mm (5.5in) gun

▲ **I-400 class**
The I-400 class was a serious attempt by the Imperial Japanese Navy to create a submarine aircraft carrier. The experiment proved to be an expensive flop and the class made no contribution to the war effort.

parts, was a potentially formidable submarine. But they had no influence on the war and were sunk or scuttled by the US Navy in the course of 1946.

I-351 (Sen-Ho or Sensuikan-Hokyu, 'submarine tanker') was planned in 1941 as a refuelling and supply craft for the Kawanishi H6K flying boats in remote places where onshore facilities could not be set up. Three were planned but only *I-351* was operational during the war, launched early in 1945 at Kure Navy Yard. With a capacity of 371 tonnes (365

tons) of gasoline fuel, twenty 250kg (550lb) bombs and 15 Type 91 aerial torpedoes, in addition to 11 tonnes (10.8 tons) of fresh water, it could substantially extend the striking range of the aircraft. It was well protected with four 533mm (21in) torpedo tubes, four 81mm (3in) mortars, and a battery of seven Type 96 25mm AA guns. It also carried 13-go radar equipment. *I-351* survived in action for only six months before being sunk by the US Gato class submarine *Bluefish* on 14 July 1945.

I-400 Class

The Sen-Toku I-400 class were the largest submarines built by any country before the appearance of nuclear-powered ballistic missile submarines. It was originally meant to number 18, and work started in January 1943. Within the partial double hull were two parallel cylindrical hulls. After the death of Admiral Yamamoto, sponsor of the class, the number was scaled back to five, of which only three were completed.

Unlike other Japanese aircraft-carrying submarines, they were attack rather than scouting vessels, with an operating range sufficient to make three round trips across the Pacific, or to circumnavigate the globe. To accommodate a hangar for three Aichi M6A Seiran bombers, the conning tower was offset to port.

A compressed-air 26m (85ft) catapult on the forward deck launched the aircraft, loaded with a 1800lb (800kg) bomb. An attack on the Panama Canal locks by Submarine Squadron 1, formed of the operational I-400 boats plus the aircraft-carrying *I-13* and *I-14*, was devised in 1944–45, but abandoned in

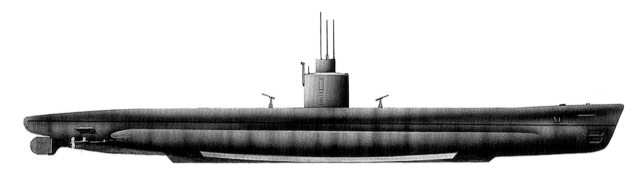

Specifications

Crew: 100	Displacement: Surfaced: 1311 tonnes (1291
Powerplant: Twin screws diesel; electric motors	tons); Submerged: 1473 tonnes (1450 tons)
Max Speed: Surfaced: 15.7 knots; Submerged:	Dimensions (length/beam/draught): 79m x 5.8m
19 knots	x 5.4m (259ft 2in x 19ft x 17ft 9in)
Surface Range: 10,747km (5800nm) at 14 knots	Commissioned: July 1944
	Armament: Four 533mm (21in) torpedo tubes

▲ I-201

Imperial Japanese Navy, fast attack submarine, 1945

I-201 was completed on 2 February 1945 and assigned to various subdivisions of the 6th Fleet. An anechoic rubberized coating was applied to reduce noise. The bow planes were retractable. Ten Type 95 torpedoes were carried. The conning tower is notably small. It was sunk as a target on 23 May 1946.

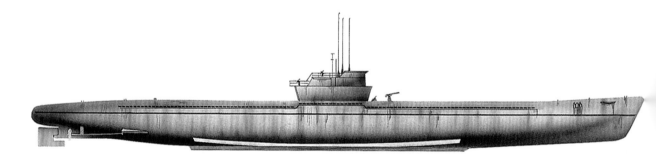

▲ I-351

Imperial Japanese Navy, flying-boat tender/transport submarine

Attached to Submarine Division 15 of the 6th Fleet, this boat made two return trips between its Sasebo base and Singapore in May to July 1945, picking up loads of rubber and other goods for the war effort. It never fulfilled its intended role as a flying-boat tender.

Specifications

Crew: 90	Displacement: Surfaced: 3568 tonnes (3512
Powerplant: Twin screws, diesel/electric motors	tons); Submerged: 4358 tonnes (4290 tons)
Max Speed: Surfaced: 15.8 knots; Submerged:	Dimensions (length/beam/draught): 110m x
6.3 knots	10.2m x 6m (361ft x 33ft 6in x 19ft 8in)
Surface Range: 24,076km (13,000nm) at	Commissioned: February 1944
14 knots	Armament: Four 533mm (12in) torpedo tubes

July 1945 in favour of attacking US carriers at the Ulithi Atoll base. Japan's surrender in August pre-empted this operation.

US Navy Submarines

Though originally planned as fleet boats, the US Navy's Gato class turned out to be well suited to the different kind of naval war that developed in the Pacific. Construction began on 11 September 1940 with USS *Drum*, at Portsmouth, New Hampshire, which was also the first to be commissioned, on 1 November 1941. Diving depth was 90m (300ft). Emulating the Germans' wolfpack system, Gato class

submarines operated as co-ordinated groups in the Yellow Sea and other areas.

The Gato class was the first to be fitted with air conditioning from the start. Many detail modifications were made in the course of the war, usually in order to accommodate radar, direction-finding and sonar equipment. While the array on masts and periscopes above the conning tower became ever more complex, the tower itself was progressively reduced in the interest both of lowering the profile and of reducing drag. USS *Barb*, refitted in 1945, was the first submarine to launch rocket shells against mainland targets; in 1954, it was passed to the Italian Navy as

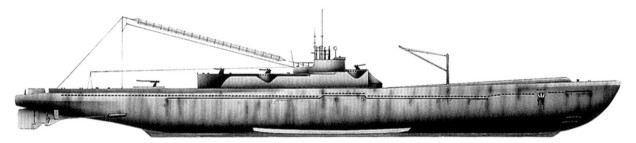

Specifications

Crew: 100	Displacement: Surfaced: 5316 tonnes (5233
Powerplant: Twin screw diesel; electric motors	tons); Submerged: 6665 tonnes (6560 tons)
Max Speed: Surfaced: 18.7 knots; Submerged:	Dimensions (length/beam/draught): 122m x 12m
6.5 knots	x 7m (400ft 1in x 39ft 4in x 24ft)
Surface Range: 68,561km (37,000nm) at	Commissioned: 1944
14 knots	Armament: Eight 533mm (21in) torpedo tubes;
	one140mm (5.5in) gun

▲ **I-400**

Imperial Japanese Navy, aircraft-carrying strategic raider, 1945

Great ingenuity went into the folding and collapsible equipment, including a retrieval crane. The three I-400s were fitted with Mk3 Model 1 air search radar, Mk2 Model 2 surface search radar, and an E 27 radar detector. *I-400* had a German snorkel system from May 1945. All were sunk as targets in 1946.

Specifications

Crew: 80	Displacement: Surfaced: 1845 tonnes (1816
Powerplant: Twin screw diesel; electric motors	tons); Submerged: 2463 tonnes (2425 tons)
Max Speed: Surfaced: 20 knots; Submerged:	Dimensions (length/beam/draught): 94m x 8.2m
10 knots	x 5m (311ft 3in x 27ft x 17ft)
Surface Range: 19,311km (10,409nm) at	Commissioned: April 1942
10 knots	Armament: 10 533mm (21in) torpedo tubes

▲ **USS Barb**

US Navy, Gato class patrol/attack submarine, Pacific 1944

Barb made five patrols off Europe before deploying to Pearl Harbor in September 1943. On seven Pacific patrols it sank 17 ships of 96,628GRT, including the escort carrier *Unyo* on 17 September 1944, making it the US Navy's most successful combat submarine. Members of its crew mounted the only land incursion into Japan, in July 1945.

Enrico Tazzoli; the profile shows its post-Guppy programme appearance.

Another Gato boat, USS *Grouper*, was refitted as a model of the post-war hunter-killer *SSK*. From 4 February 1943, when USS *Balao* was commissioned, the Gato class was supplemented by 122 boats of a similar – but in various ways – improved version, which was capable of operating down to 122m (400ft) with a range of 20,000km (12,400 miles), and able to remain submerged for 48 hours at a stretch. By August 1945, 56 Japanese submarines remained in service, many of them by now in bad or damaged condition; and, of these, only nine were large attack submarines. In the course of the war 126

were built (excluding midget submarines) and 127 were lost: 70 to surface ships, 19 to other submarines, 18 to aircraft, and the remainder to other causes.

US SUBMARINE CLASSES, 1940–45			
Class	Number	Launched	Note
Tambor	6	1940–41	2 lost
Mackerel	2	1941	
Gar	6	1941	5 lost
Gato	73	1941–44	19 lost
Balao	113	1943–45	9 lost
Tench	28	1944–45	

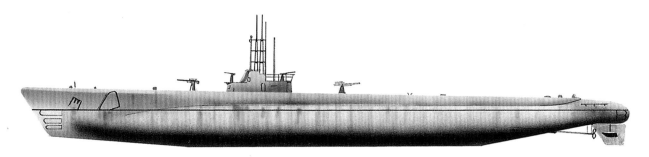

▲ USS Drum (Gato class)

US Navy, Gato class patrol/attack submarine

The first Gato-boat to be commissioned and enter combat, it is seen in WWII mode. After heavy depth-charging it was given a Balao-type conning tower at the end of 1943. The complex rig above the shears reflects the variety of sensory and communications equipment now carried.

Specifications

Crew: 80

Powerplant: Twin screw diesels; electric motors

Max Speed: Surfaced: 20 knots; Submerged: 10 knots

Surface Range: 22,236km (12,000nm) at 10 knots

Displacement: Surfaced: 1845 tonnes (1816 tons); Submerged: 2463 tonnes (2425 tons)

Dimensions (length/beam/draught): 95m x 8.3m x 4.6m (311ft 9in x 27ft 3in x 15ft 3in)

Commissioned: May 1941

Armament: 10 533mm (21in) torpedo tubes

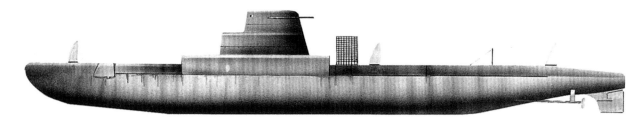

Specifications

Crew: 80

Powerplant: Twin screw diesels; electric motors

Max Speed: Surfaced: 20 knots; Submerged: 10 knots

Surface Range: 19,300km (10,416nm) at 10 knots

Displacement: Surfaced: 1845 tonnes (1816 tons); Submerged: 2463 tonnes (2425 tons)

Dimensions (length/beam/draught): 94.8m x 8.2m x 4.5m (311ft 3in x 27ft x 15ft)

Commissioned: February 1942

Armament: 10 533mm (21in) torpedo tubes

▲ USS Grouper (Gato class)

US Navy, Gato class patrol/attack submarine, later test-boat

Commissioned on 12 February 1942, *Grouper* made nine war patrols, and in 1946 was the first submarine fitted with a combat information centre. From then on it was a test boat, becoming the first designated SSK on 2 January 1951. Later a floating laboratory, *AGSS-214*, it was finally scrapped in 1970.

Late war submarine development
1944–45

While Britain and the United States concentrated on enlarging their fleets of proven designs, Germany worked to develop new and more efficient submarine types, while also building huge numbers to established designs.

GERMANY PROVED TO BE ahead of the Allies in submarine design, although by this point in the war the Allies had developed effective air and sea submarine counter-measures.

Germany

Between 1943 and 1945, 118 U-boats of Type XXI were commissioned. Effectively this introduced a new generation of combat submarine. The streamlined outer hull covered a pressure-hull in figure-of-eight cross-section, the upper section of greater diameter than the lower.

The Type XXI had much improved crew facilities with a deep-freeze for food, a shower compartment and better accommodation. A hydraulic reload system enabled all six tubes to be reloaded in 10 minutes, less than the manual loading time of one tube on the Type VIIC. Greater electrical power, with three times the battery capacity of the Type VIIC, gave the Type XXI a much wider underwater range, enabling it to traverse the Bay of Biscay at a depth that minimized the risk of detection. It could reach

280m (919ft), a greater depth than any other submarine of the time. The four electric motors, two of them designed for silent running, gained it the name of 'Elektroboot'. Prefabrication and welding of eight separate sections were used to speed up building time to a hoped-for six months.

Seventeen completed or almost-completed Type XXIs were destroyed in yards between December 1944 and May 1945. As a result, only four were combat ready at the time of Germany's surrender, and only *U-2511* and *U-3008* undertook any offensive patrols. Neither sank anything, though on the day of surrender, 4 May, *U-2511* made a demonstration run at the British cruiser *Suffolk*, which did not even notice the U-boat's presence.

U-3001 was one of the first Type XXI submarines to be commissioned, on 20 July 1944, and was assigned to the 32nd Training Flotilla at Konigsberg (now Kaliningrad), but quickly passed on to the 4th, at Stettin (Szczecin). From November 1944 to May 1945, it was based at KLA (Warship Training Section), Bremen. Always a training boat, it made no

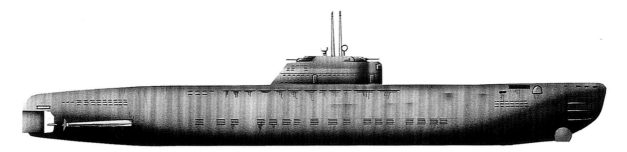

▲ 'Elektroboot' U-3001

German Navy, Type XXI, 'Elektroboot,' coastal submarine, Stettin, 1944

Twenty-three torpedoes could be carried, or a split load of 14 torpedoes and 12 TMC mines. Passive/active sonar enabled blind firing from 49m (160ft), using LUT guidable torpedoes. It could travel submerged for three days before recharging. With no open deck top, its tower heralded the later fin or sail type.

Specifications

Crew: 57	surf/sub
Powerplant: Diesel; electric motors	Dimensions (length/beam/draught): 76.7 x
Max Speed: 28.9/31.9km/hr (15.6/17.2kt)	6.6 x 6.3m (251.7 x 21.7 x 20.7ft)
surf/sub	Commissioned: 20 July 1944
Surface Range: 20,650km (11,150nm)	Armament: 23 torpedoes (6 bow tubes);
Displacement: 1647/1848t (1621/1819 tons)	two twin 2cm (0.8in) gun turrets

wartime patrols, and was scuttled on 3 May 1945 northwest of Wesermünde.

By the end of 1941, the Type II submarine was in active service only in the Black Sea. A new smaller boat was needed to work in the North and Baltic Seas, to which Dönitz added the Mediterranean and Black Seas. This required the hull to be sectionable to sizes that could be carried by railway. The initial design was complete by 30 June 1943 and construction began not only in Germany but also at shipyards in occupied territories. The first was *U-2321*, launched on 17 April 1944 and commissioned 12 June. The Type XXIII was a single-hull boat, of all-welded construction. Like the Type XXI, being built in parallel, it was of streamlined

construction and had a 'creep' electric motor. From April 1944 to May 1945, 61 entered service, out of 280 ordered, though only six are known to have carried out operational patrols, resulting in the sinking of five Allied ships.

Most Type XXIII boats were assigned to the 32nd Training Flotilla, though 13 joined the 5th Flotilla at Kiel, and 10 were active with the 11th Flotilla at Bergen, Norway. Despite having only two torpedo tubes, no gun and no spare torpedoes, the Type XXIIs, because of their speed and stealth, could have been a powerful aid to Germany's war effort.

U-2326 was one of only three Type XXIII boats to survive the war. Surrendered at Dundee, Scotland, it became the British *N25*, then was passed to France

Specifications

Crew: 14	Displacement: 236/260t (232/256 tons)
Powerplant: Diesel; electric motors	surf/sub
Max Speed: 18.5/23.2km/hr (10/12.5kt)	Dimensions (length/beam/draught): 34.1 x 3 x
surf/sub	3.75m (112 x 10 x 12ft)
Surface Range: 2500km (1350nm)	Commissioned: 10 August 1944
	Armament: Two torpedoes (2 bow tubes)

▲ Elektroboot U-2326

German Navy, Type XXIII, Elektroboot, attack submarine, Bergen, December 1944

Front hydroplanes were a later addition to the Walter design. A 62-cell battery was in the lower hull. The hump behind the tower covered the silencing system of the MWM RS-348 4-stroke diesel engine. These boats could crash-dive in 9 seconds and vanish in virtual silence using the 'creep' electric motor.

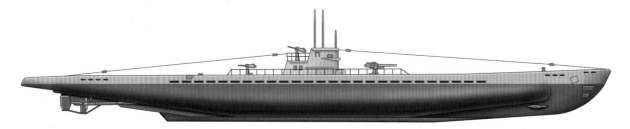

▲ U-195

German Navy, Type IXD/1 attack submarine, Atlantic/Indian Ocean 1944–45

U-195 made three combat patrols with the 10th Flotilla, lasting up to 126 days, and sank three ships, before removal of its weapons. In 1944, it carried V2 rocket parts and uranium oxide to Batavia (Java) for onward transport to Japan. Its engines were considered too unreliable for a return to Europe.

Specifications

Crew: 55	surf/sub
Powerplant: Diesel; electric motors	Dimensions (length/beam/draught): 87.6 x 7.5
Max Speed: 38.5/12.8km/hr (20.8/6.9kt)	x 5.4m (287.42 x 24.58 x 17.75ft)
surf/sub	Commissioned: 11 September 1942
Surface Range: 18,335km (9900nm)	Armament: 24 torpedoes; one 10.5cm (4.1in),
Displacement: 1636/1828t (1610/1799 tons)	one 3.7cm (1.5in) and one 2cm (0.8in) gun

in 1946, but sank in an accident off Toulon in the same year.

Two Type IXD boats were commissioned in September 1942, *U-195* as *IXD1* and *U-196* as *IXD2*, as large fast attack boats. *U-196* made the longest patrol of any World War II submarine, from 13 March to 23 October 1943, to the Indian Ocean. *U-195* sank three ships off South Africa in March to July 1943, but in the following year it was disarmed and converted at Bordeaux as a transport, carrying 256 tonnes (252 tons) of strategic war materials. Originally fitted with experimental high-speed diesel engines, these proved unreliable and smoky, and were replaced by standard Type IX diesels. In May 1945, *U-195* was taken over by the Japanese Navy at Batavia as *I-506*, for a brief period before being surrendered to the Americans in August.

Other Navies

HMS *Sanguine* was one of the last of the S-class to be completed before the end of the war brought the building programme to a halt. It was commissioned on 13 May 1945, too late for active service in European waters. In 1958, it was sold to the Israeli Navy, as was a sister boat, *Springer*, in 1959; they were renamed *Rahav* and *Tanin*. Numerous S-class boats were disposed of to other navies in the post-war years. Three, *Saga*, *Spearhead* and *Spur*, went to Portugal in 1948–49; and *Spiteful*, *Sportsman*, *Statesman* and *Styr* were passed to France in 1951–52. The last British S-class was scrapped in 1962.

In the course of the war the Italian Navy developed the Flutto class of medium submarines. Twelve of Type 1 were ordered and 10 completed by August 1943. Orders were placed for 24 of Type 2, but only three were launched and none commissioned during the war; all were captured at Monfalcone by German forces after Italy's surrender. Type 3 was to consist of 12 boats but none was completed. The design was very much in line with Italian practice, but with a conning tower of reduced size.

Eight of the Flutto 2 boats were given UIT numbers to indicate U-boats of Italian provenance. One of the Flutto 1 class, *Nautilo*, scuttled in 1945, was raised and served in the Yugoslav post-war fleet as *Sava*. *Marea* was passed to Soviet Russia in 1949. The only surviving Flutto 1 boat in Italian hands was *Vortice*. After a major refit in 1951–53, it was recommissioned into the Italian Navy and served until August 1967.

Japan's Ha 201 Sensuikan Taka-Ko gata (small fast submarine) was comparable in type and purpose to Germany's Type XXIII, and constructed in a similar manner, in prefabricated sections using five different yards. Experience gained in the testing of 'Vessel No. 71' in 1938 was incorporated into the streamlined design. Home defence was the aim and 79 boats were planned for production in a crash programme beginning in January 1945.

Only 10 were completed and none undertook active patrols. Armed with only four torpedoes, they

GERMAN SUBMARINE CLASSES, 1935–45			
Class	**Number**	**Launched**	**Note**
Type IIA	6	1934–35	Double-hull design; coastal boats
Type IIB	24	1935–36	
Type IA	2	1936	
Type VIIA	10	1935–37	Two served in Spanish Civil War
Type IX	8	1936–39	Ocean-going; double hull
Type VIIB	24	1936–40	
Type IIC	8	1937–40	
Type IXB	14	1937–40	
Type VIIC	568	1938–44	Attack boat; single hull
Type IID	16	1939–40	
Type IXC	54	1939–42	
Type XB	8	1939–44	Minelayer
Type VIID	6	1940–42	Minelayer
Type XIV	10	1940–43	'Milch Cow' supply boats
Type IXC/40	87	1940–44	
Type IXD1	2	1940–42	
Type IXD2	28	1940–44	
Type VIIC/41	91	1941–45	
Type VIIF	4	1941–43	Supply boats
Type IXD42	2	1942–44	
Type XVIIA	6	1942–44	Experimental
Type XVIIB	3	1943–44	Experimental
Type XVIII	1	1943–44	Experimental; not completed
Type XXI	118	1943–45	'Elektroboot' developed from Type XVIII
Type XXIII	61	1943–45	Coastal; only 6 operational

were highly manoeuvrable and capable of short bursts of high speed while submerged, which would have made them dangerous to surface craft. They could dive to 100ms (330ft). With only a 7.7mm (0.3in) AA machine gun, they were vulnerable to air attack, but a form of snorkel allowed them to stay submerged for lengthy periods. Limited storage space restricted their sea-time to 15 days.

Midget Submarines

Numerous countries, notably Italy and Japan on the Axis powers, and Great Britain among the Allies, invested in midget submarines: boats of under 150 tonnes (148 tons) with a crew in single numbers,

normally operated from a mother ship. The Japanese 'Kaiten' craft were really manned torpedoes and their construction in the later phase of the war was an act of desperation.

The British and Italian designs, though certainly high risk, were not suicide craft. Their aim was to engage in covert operations where a large vessel would not be able to penetrate. After 1939, the Royal Navy took an interest in the midget submarine, and two prototypes, *X-3* and *X-4*, were built, leading to the *X-5*, with a four-man crew, and 20 were constructed. The most celebrated exploit of these X-boats was the attempt on the German battleship *Tirpitz* and other capital ships anchored in the

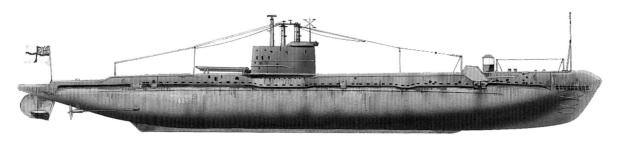

▲ HMS Sanguine

Royal Navy, S-class patrol submarine

S-boats had served in the Mediterranean during World War II, and *Sanguine*, without air conditioning, was often uncomfortable for its crew. Internal temperatures sometimes reached 40°C (104°F). But it remained active until 1966. *Tanin* participated in the Six-Day War of June 1967. Both were scrapped in 1968.

Specifications

Crew: 44	Submerged: 1006 tonnes (990 tons)
Powerplant: Twin screw diesel; electric motors	Dimensions (length/beam/draught): 61.8m x
Max Speed: Surfaced: 14.7 knots; Submerged:	7.25m x 3.2m (202ft 6in x 23ft 9in x 10ft 6in)
9 knots	Commissioned: February 1945
Surface Range: 15,750km (8500nm) at 10 knots	Armament: Six 533mm (21in) torpedo tubes; one
Displacement: Surfaced: 726 tonnes (715 tons);	76mm (3in) gun

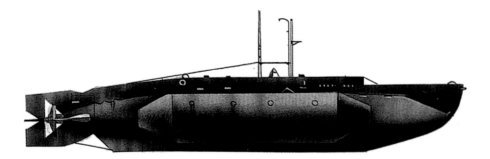

Specifications

Crew: 4	Submerged: 30 tons (29.5 tons)
Powerplant: Single screw diesel; electric motors	Dimensions (length/beam/draught): 15.7m x
Max Speed: Surfaced: 6.5 knots; Submerged:	1.8m x 2.6m (51ft 6in x 6ft x 8ft 6in)
5 knots	Commissioned: March 1942
Surface Range: 926km (500nm)	Armament: Two 1994kg (4400lb) detachable
Displacement: Surfaced: 27 tonnes/tons;	amatol charges

▲ HMS X-5

Royal Navy, midget submarine type, Norway, 1943

The X-boats had a passage-crew in transit and an operations crew for combat. An airlock allowed a diver to leave and re-enter. They could dive to 91m (300ft). Twenty were built, seven lost in action or accident, and one is preserved. Six XE-boats, as used at Singapore, were also constructed.

▲ **HMS** *Sanguine*

Commissioned on 13 May 1945, this was the last S-class to be completed. Note the sonar dome, the absence of a deck gun and the redesigned conning tower.

Altafjord, on the Norwegian coast. X-craft were used in other theatres too, including successful missions to sink Japanese ships at Singapore in July 1945.

The Germans developed a range of midget submarines, including the Seehund type of 1944, of which 285 were built (1000 were intended), but their introduction had a negligible effect on the closing stage of the war. Japan used Ko-hyoteki type midget submarines in the attacks at Pearl Harbor (1941) and Sydney Harbour (29 May 1942); 101 were built in all. In 1945, Japan produced around 210 Kairyu 'sea dragon' two-man midget submarines and about 420 Kaiten 'human torpedoes'. Although Kaitens were sent on around 100 missions, only one significant strike was made, sinking the convoy escort USS *Underhill* on 24 July 1945.

Last US Wartime Classes

At the end of the war, the US Navy possessed a large and up-to-date submarine fleet, though many were

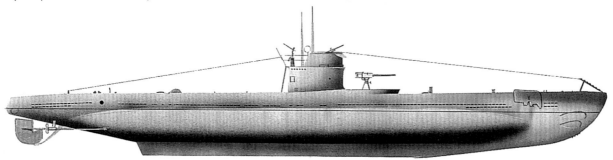

▲ **Ferro**

Italian Navy, Flutto II class patrol submarine

Ferro was given the German number *UIT-12*, but no further work was carried out and it was blown up on the slipway on 1 May 1945. One of the Flutto II boats, *Bario* (numbered *UIT 7* in 1943–45), was salvaged from the Monfalcone yards, rebuilt at Taranto in 1957–61, renamed *Pietro Calvi*, and served until 1972.

Specifications

Crew: 50

Powerplant: Twin screw diesel engines; electric motors

Max Speed: Surfaced: 16 knots; Submerged: 8 knots

Surface Range: 6670km (3600nm) at 12 knots

Displacement: Surfaced: 1130 tonnes (1113 tons); Submerged: 1188 tonnes (1170 tons)

Dimensions (length/beam/draught): 64m x 6.9m x 4.9m (210ft 7in x 22ft 11in x 16ft 2in)

Commissioned: Not launched

Armament: Six 533mm (21in) torpedo tubes; one 100mm (3.9in) gun

SOVIET SUBMARINE CLASSES, 1939–45			
Class	Number	Launched	Note
Series XIIIb L20	6	1940–41	Minelayer
Series Xb Shch 135	20	1940–47	Patrol
Series XIIb M30	45	1937–41	Coastal patrol
Series IXb S4	31	1939–41	Pre-war class; 4 to China, 1955
Series XIV K1	7	1939–41	Minelayer; continuation of pre-war type
Series XV M204	10	1941	Continuation of pre-war class
Ronis	2	1927	Seized from Latvia, 1940; coastal
Kalev	2	1936	Seized from Estonia 1940; minelayer
S3-4	2	1941	Seized from Romania 1944
TS4	1	1936	Seized from Romania 1944

battle-worn and in need of reconditioning. *Entemedor* of the Balao class (originally to be named 'Chickwick') was commissioned in April 1945 and made only one wartime patrol.

In 1945–48, it was based at West Coast ports and made several cruises in Far Eastern waters, based at Subic Bay. Placed on the reserve list in 1948, it was recommissioned in October 1950 during the Korean War. It saw service in the Atlantic in 1951–52, and was extensively modernized in 1952. In 1973, it was sold to Turkey and renamed *Preveze*, serving until 1987.

The Tench class was a refinement of the Balao type, which they resembled very closely. Originally 134 were to be constructed but, with the end of the war, 101 were cancelled or scrapped while under construction, and 33 remained as the United State's most up-to-date submarine prior to the post-war modernization programmes. While exceeding the Balao class in displacement by only some 40.6 tonnes (40 tons), they did have a better-organized interior layout as well as greater hull strength. Only a few of the class, including *Tench* itself, participated in wartime operations. USS *Pickerel* was one of those not completed until after the war, in 1949. Fourteen were sold to other navies between 1964 and 1973: four to Brazil, two each to Turkey and

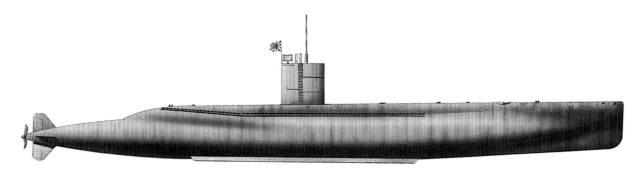

Specifications

Crew: 22

Powerplant: Single shaft diesel; electric motor

Max Speed: Surfaced: 10.5 knots; Submerged: 13 knots

Surface Range: 5559km (3000nm) at 10 knots

Displacement: Surfaced: 383 tonnes (377 tons);

Submerged: 447 tonnes (440 tons)

Dimensions (length/beam/draught): 50m x 3.9m x 3.4m (164ft x 13ft x 11ft 3in)

Commissioned: May 1945

Armament: Two 533mm (21in) torpedo tubes; one 7.7mm AA gun

▲ **Ha 201**

Imperial Japanese Navy, coastal defence submarine

The class was intended to work in co-ordinated groups, but this never happened. *Ha 201* was first of the class, completed on 31 May 1945, and assigned to Submarine Division 33, then Submarine Division 52. Surrendered at the Sasebo base on 2 September 1945, it was used for target practice, tied against the large *I-402*, in April 1946, and finally scuttled.

Italy, and one each to Canada, Greece, Pakistan, Peru, Taiwan, and Venezuela.

A combination of damage repair, major refits, different techniques at the various shipyards, and constant efforts to reduce the submarines' profile, both against visual and electronic reconnaissance, plus the requirement for ever-faster diving times, meant that although the Gato-Balao-Tench classes all had an overall resemblance, no two boats looked exactly the same and, in fact, were likely to show distinct differences, especially in the form of the conning tower and the arrangement of periscope shears, aerials and antennas.

SUBMARINE STRENGTHS, 1939 AND 1945 COMPARED				
Country	1939	1945	War Build	War Losses
Germany	57	448*	1171	780
Great Britain	60	162	178	76
Italy	107	57	38	88
Japan	63	46	111	128
Russia	218	163	54	109
United States	99	274	227	52

*Includes 222 U-boats scuttled in May 1945, 156 surrendered, and others never deployed in action

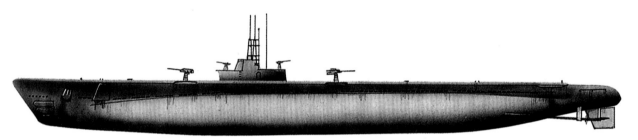

Specifications

Crew: 80

Powerplant: Twin screw diesel engines, electric motors

Max Speed: Surfaced: 20 knots; Submerged: 8.7 knots

Surface Range: 20,372km (11,000nm) at 10 knots

Displacement: Surfaced: 1854 tonnes (1825 tons); Submerged: 2458 tonnes (2420 tons)

Dimensions (length/beam/draught): 95m x 8.3m x 4.6m (311ft 9in x 27ft 3in x 15ft 3in)

Commissioned: December 1944

Armament: Ten 533mm (21in) torpedo tubes; one 127mm (5in) gun

▲ USS Entemedor

US Navy, Balao-class patrol submarine

Entemedor returned to base at Seattle on 22 September 1945, and served with the Pacific Fleet at Subic Bay in 1946-47. In reserve between 1948 and 1950, it was recommissioned in October 1950, joined the Atlantic Fleet, went through a GUPPY IIA refit in 1952, and did stints with the 6th Fleet in the Mediterranean up to 1962.

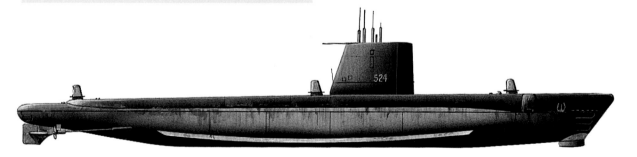

Specifications

Crew: 22

Powerplant: Four diesel engines; two electric motors

Max Speed: surfaced: 20.2 knots; Submerged: 8.7 knots

Surface Range: 20,372km (11,000nm) at 10 knots

Displacement: surfaced: 1595 tonnes (1570 tons); Submerged: 2453 tonnes (2415 tons)

Dimensions (length/beam/draught): 95.2m x 8.31m x 4.65m (311ft 8in x 27ft 3in x 15ft 3in)

Commissioned: December 1944

Armament: One or two 127mm (5in) guns; 10 533mm (21in) torpedo tubes for 28 torpedoes

▲ USS Pickerel

US Navy, Tench class patrol submarine, Pacific 1949

Pickerel was launched on 8 February 1944. In 1949, it deployed to Submarine Division II at Pearl Harbor, and thereafter remained in the Pacific. In 1962, it received a GUPPY III refit, then joined the 7th Fleet at Yokosuka, Japan. After Vietnam combat deployment on Yankee Station, it was transferred to Italy in 1972 as *Primo Longobardo*.

Chapter 4

The Cold War: 1946–89

Submarines had proved their worth so effectively
during the war years that it was beyond doubt they would be
key elements in future naval strategy. But there were big
challenges: how to arm them, how to extend undersea
cruising range and duration, and how to improve detection
and weapons-guidance systems. And not least, how to attack
and destroy a hostile and well-protected submarine.
Initially these challenges were met by seeking to develop
and improve on existing designs, but within 10 years this
gave way to a new approach, starting from first principles.
It became clear that application of new technologies,
from nuclear reactors to microchips, would expand the
role and power of the submarine in ways hardly
thought of in 1945.

◀ **USS *Dallas***

This boat of the Los Angeles class was the first to have the Mk 117 fire-control system installed. Service includes Indian Ocean, Mediterranean, Persian Gulf and North Atlantic deployments. It is currently fitted to deploy a Swimmer Delivery Vehicle, visible behind the sail.

Introduction

Modernization is the key-word as submarine requirements are re-assessed in the light of the increasingly tense relationship between the Western powers and the Soviet bloc.

THE END OF THE WAR brought rationalization of the submarine fleets of the victorious Allied powers, with the older and more decrepit boats going for scrapping or target practice. Following their surrender in May and August 1945, all submarine design and construction in Germany and Japan came to a sudden end.

But these countries had been the most inventive and original wartime submarine builders, so surviving boats, and future plans, were closely scanned by the Allies. This was particularly true of the German boats, since the merits of the Type XXI and XXIII were already well known. The US, British and Soviet navies all possessed intact vessels of Type XXI and were startled to find just how much more advanced the German boats were.

These formed the basis of experiment and design in the later 1940s and into the 1950s. Attention focused particularly on three aspects: the snorkel, which enabled the submarine to stay underwater; the improvement of submarine speed; and their ability to launch missiles against surface or land targets. A pattern was developed, of a smooth hull, uncluttered deck, no gun, streamlined fin or sail, and snorkel as a standard fitting.

The geopolitical background of the time was dominated by the hostile rivalry between the Soviet Union and the United States, each with its allies, forming the Warsaw Pact nations in the former case; and in the latter, the North Atlantic Treaty Organization (NATO), in 1949. The Soviet possession of nuclear technology and atomic weapons from 1949 raised the stakes enormously. A new arms race began, with the submarine an essential element. US production of a nuclear reactor compact enough to fit in a submarine's hull brought about the era of the 'true' submerged vessel that could travel underwater for weeks rather than days or hours. USS *Nautilus* and the hundreds of US and Soviet nuclear boats that followed, along with smaller British, French and, later, Chinese fleets revolutionized ideas about large-scale warfare. With such submarines,

▲ **HMS** *Explorer*

HMS *Explorer*, one of two experimental submarines, was nicknamed 'Exploder' as a consequence of her many accidents.

▲ **USS** *Philadelphia*
Launched in 1974, the USS *Philadelphia* is a Los Angeles class nuclear attack submarine. It was decommissioned in 2010.

armed with long-range nuclear missiles, came the concept of the 'deterrent'. Any first strike against a superpower would be answered by a retaliatory strike from submarines at unknown locations. Mutual devastation was assured.

Missile Platforms

From the 1950s, the development of the submarine was linked to that of rocket-type weapons that could be fired from under the surface. As the missiles became larger and heavier, so the boats had to be more capacious in order to maximize their firepower. This led to some strange-looking designs until massive submarines, which could hold vertically mounted intercontinental ballistic missiles (ICBMs) within the hull, were built. The difficulties and hazards of launching a jet-propelled missile from a submarine included the problems of powering the actual launch, of maintaining stability, and of guiding the missile towards a target. From the early firings of Loon rockets, derived from the German V-1 and launched from a deck-mounted rack on US test-vessels, remarkable progress was made. The United States pressed on with solid-fuel rocket engines, while the Soviets for a long time continued with liquid-fuel missiles.

Nuclear submarines required advanced technology, under strict (if sometimes broken) secrecy. Most navies continued to employ, and to improve, submarines with diesel-electric drive. These were smaller, far less expensive, and fitted a well-tried range of tactical roles and missions. Only the US Navy gave up on developing new conventional designs, though it continued to use existing classes through most of the Cold War period.

On several occasions the Cold War threatened to become a 'hot' one. The Korean War in 1951 led to the rapid recommissioning of many US submarines from reserve, though they played little part in the land-based conflict. Four British submarines were part of the Suez invasion force in 1956. Both sides deployed submarines in the Cuban Missile Crisis of October 1962.

War between India and Pakistan in 1971 included the first submarine battles since 1945. British and Argentinian submarines were in action in the Falklands/Malvinas War in 1982. But by the 1980s, the long stalemate was beginning to end. The Strategic Arms Limitation (SALT I) agreement reduced the number of land-based missiles but had little effect on submarine numbers.

America and the Soviet Union
1946–54

The US and Soviet navies push ahead with new submarine types and modifications, mostly taken from German designs.

IN THE SOVIET UNION, Project 613 was put in hand from 1946, for a new class of submarine, later codenamed 'Whiskey' by NATO, a further improved version of the Type XXI. Originally designated as coastal patrol submarines, they were in fact fully sea-going boats. At least 215 were built between 1951 and 1958, in five configurations. The peak years of construction were 1953–56. *Whiskey I* had twin 25mm (0.98in) guns mounted in the sail. *Whiskey II* had two additional 57mm (2.2in) guns. *Whiskey III* had no guns. *Whiskey IV* had the 25mm guns restored and was also fitted with a snorkel. *Whiskey V* had the guns removed and a streamlined sail fitted, and most of the class were modified to this design.

Whiskey class submarines were supplied to Albania (4), Bulgaria (2), China (5), Egypt (7), Indonesia (14), North Korea (4) and Poland (4). In addition, China constructed 21 from Soviet-supplied parts, as Type 03. The class had a long life and 45 were still on the active list with the Soviet Navy in 1982. With the possible exception of some North Korean boats, all Whiskeys are now decommissioned.

Project 615, initiated in the late 1940s, was intended to provide the Soviet fleet with a coastal attack submarine of the most up-to-date type. Before the war, the Soviets had already been working on a closed-cycle engine that did not require to draw air from above the surface, and the experimental craft *M-401* had been launched in 1941 and tested in the secluded waters of the Caspian Sea. Liquid oxygen mixed with purified exhaust gases powered the underwater motor.

Although streamlined, the class, codenamed Quebec by NATO, carried a twin 45mm (1.8in) AA gun in its earlier versions, faired into the forward end of the tower. The Quebecs remained an under-armed type, with no spare torpedo capacity for the four bow-mounted tubes. Thirty were built between 1952 and 1957, out of an original 100 planned. At this time they were the only submarines in the world using air-independent propulsion. Although some notable performances were achieved, the fuel caused frequent problems because of its tendency to catch fire. Two boats were lost. The Soviet Navy's development of nuclear submarines overtook the Quebecs, although they were modernized in the later 1950s under Project M615. By the time the last was retired, in the 1970s, the AIP motor had been

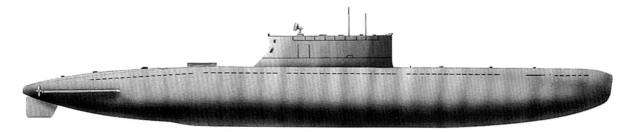

▲ **Whiskey class**

Soviet Navy patrol/missile submarine

Prefabrication and welded assembly were used to speed up production of the large numbers in this class. Between 1956 and 1963, 13 were converted to carry the Soviet Union's first guided missiles. Others were used as radar pickets and in intelligence-gathering missions.

Specifications

Crew: 50

Powerplant: Twin shaft; diesel-electric

Max Speed: (33.3/26km/hr (18/14kt) surf/sub

Surface Range: 15,890km (8580nm)

Displacement: 1066/1,371t (1050/1350 tons) surf/sub

Dimensions (length/beam/draught): 76 x 6.5 x 5m (294.3 x 21.3 x 16ft)

Commissioned: 1949 (1st unit)

Armament: Four 533mm (21in) and two 406mm (16in) torpedo tubes replaced by a conventional electric one. One of the Project 615 boats was used for research on developing an anechoic coating, with results that were to be applied to most Soviet combat submarines.

United States

USS *Cusk* (Balao class) and USS *Carbonero* (Gato class) were adapted in 1946–47 to fire air-breathing 'Loon' missiles, derived from the German V-1 pulse-jet rocket. A single missile was held in a tank-like hangar and fired from a rack mounted on the afterdeck. Both boats remained in service as guided-missile testing vehicles.

Parallel to the early missile operations, Project Guppy (Greater Underwater Propulsion Programme) was set up to enhance the capacities of the existing fleet. From June 1946, the programme passed through seven phases until 1963. It began with the intensive examination and testing of two Type XXI U-boats, *U-2513* and *U-3008*, but further refinements and improvements were soon being added. USS *Odax* and *Pomodon*, Tench class boats commissioned in 1945, were adapted in 1947. The deck guns were taken off, the bridge and shears structure adapted to reduce drag, capstans and deck cleats were made retractable, and the bow was redesigned from the sharp 'fleet bow' to a rounded 'Guppy bow'. Battery power was greatly increased and the boats were fitted with new sonar and radar equipment. The Guppy 1A programme was

THE LEGACY OF TYPE XX1	
Country	Derivative
France	E 48; Aréthuse
Great Britain	Explorer; Porpoise
Russia	Zulu; Whiskey; Romeo
United States	Guppy programme; Tench class

somewhat less comprehensive, fitted to nine Balao and one Tench boat in 1951. Guppy II included reconstruction of the sail to carry the array of masts required for snorkel induction, snorkel exhaust, periscopes and communication. A submarine sail might now support 12 or 13 separate antennas for range- and direction-finding, communications at different frequencies, and radar for both surface and air search. Guppy IIA also installed a new sail and a Guppy bow, as well as new motors. The 'Fleet Snorkel' conversion was a partial-Guppy, providing only snorkel equipment and an ESM mast. The pointed fleet bow was retained and the engines were not modernized, though the auxiliary motor was replaced by air-conditioning equipment. With the Guppy project, the conning tower ceased to hold a control station and came to be known as the sail (United States) or fin (Great Britain).

As a consequence of the development of rockets and with the increasing threat of the long-range bomber, radar detection was given a high priority and

▲ **Quebec class**

Soviet Navy coastal submarine, Black Sea

This was the only AIP-engined submarine to be in series production before the 1990s, but technical problems limited its usefulness. It had two main diesel engines plus the closed cycle engine and an electric 'creep motor'. Theoretically capable of remaining 14 days submerged, they suffered numerous accidents and the design was abandoned after 1957.

Specifications

Crew: 30

Powerplant: Three shafts; two diesel engines; one 900hp (670kW) AIP diesel; creep motor

Max. speeds: 33/30km/hr (18/16kt) surf/sub

Surface Range: 5090km (2750nm) at 9kt

Displacement: 460.4/548.6t (460/540 tons)

surf/sub

Dimensions (length/beam/draught): 56 x 5.1 x 3.8m (183.75 x 16.4 x 12.5ft)

Commissioned: 1952

Armament: Four 533mm (21in) torpedo tubes; eight torpedoes

a group of Gato, Balao and Tench class boats were fitted as 'radar-picket' boats in the Migraine Programme, which went through three phases between 1946 and 1952.

The Korean War

USS *Pickerel*, Tench class, was launched in December 1944 but not commissioned until 1949, benefitting from the Guppy II programme developments, including a snorkel and batteries with a total of 504 cells. *Pickerel* was then deployed in the Korean War zone, but submarines played relatively little part in the conflict. No US boat fired a a shot, but they were intensively used for reconnaissance and surveillance,

occasionally catching sight of Soviet submarines engaged in similar activities. *Pickerel* would be further modernized in 1962 under the Guppy III programme; and, during the Vietnam War in the later 1960s, it provided support for the carrier group based on 'Yankee Station' in the Gulf of Tonkin. On 18 August 1972, *Pickerel* was transferred to the Italian Navy, where it served as *Primo Longobardo* until 1980.

The first post-war design was closely related to the Guppy programme. USS *Tang* and its five sisters, commissioned between 1951 and 1952, were intended as fast attack boats, following on from the Tench class. Submerged speed was 18.3 knots

▲ USS Volador

US Navy, Tench class attack submarine, Pacific 1949–70

Commissioned on 1 October 1948, *Volador* was with the Pacific Fleet until 1970, on reconnaissance patrols in the Korean War and earning three campaign stars in the Vietnam War. Note the three housings for PUFFS (BQG-4) passive underwater fire-control feasibility study. In 1980, it was transferred to Italy as *Gianfranco Gazzana Priaroggia*.

Specifications

Crew: 81	surf/sub
Powerplant: Twin shaft; four diesel engines; two electric motors	Dimensions (length/beam/draught): 95.2 x 8.32 x 4.65m (311.75 x 27.25 x 15.25ft)
Max Speed: 37.4/53km/hr (20.2/8.7kt) surf/sub	Commissioned: 1 October 1948
Surface Range: 20,372km (11,000nm) at 10kt	Armament: 28 x 533mm (21in) torpedoes; 10 tubes
Displacement: 1595/2,453t (1570/2415 tons)	

Specifications

Crew: 83	Displacement: 1585/2296t (1560/2260 tons) surf/sub
Powerplant: Twin shaft; diesel-electric	Dimensions (length/beam/draught): 82 x 8.3 x 5.2m (269.2 x 27.2 x 17ft)
Max. speeds: 28.7/34km/hr (15.5/18.3kt) surf/sub	Commissioned: 25 October 1951
Surface Range:18,530km (10,000nm) at 10kt	Armament: Eight 533mm (21in) torpedo tubes

▲ USS Tang

US Navy, patrol submarine

The design was intended to keep the hull length as short as possible and to be adaptable to a future closed-cycle power plant. When *Tang* was transferred to Turkey in 1980, successive modifications meant the boat was 609.6 tonnes (600 tons) heavier and 22ft (6.5m) longer than on its launch in 1951.

compared to 15.5 knots on the surface. The six forward torpedo tubes were the prime armament, with the two aft tubes intended for ASW countermeasures weapons. The original four General Motors 'pancake' engines, with radial cylinders arranged round a vertical crankshaft, were not successful and were replaced in 1956 by three conventional Fairbanks-Morse 10-cylinder opposed-piston diesels. The Tang class carried 26 torpedoes. Diving capacity was 213m (700ft).

USS *Tang* was retired in 1980 as the oldest diesel-electric submarine in the Navy and the last to serve in the Atlantic Fleet, to which it was transferred in 1978 after long service in the Pacific. Even then it still had more than 20 years of active life ahead, being transferred to the Turkish Navy as *Pirireis* and serving until 2004.

Operational requirements stiffened as the Cold War intensified. On the Atlantic side, boats patrolled the GIUK Gap, the area between Greenland, Iceland and the British Isles through which Soviet ships had to pass to reach the open Atlantic; also the exits from the Baltic and Black Seas, and from the Mediterranean. Despite the investment in the Guppy programme and the Tang class, and the undoubted improvements they brought, certain US Navy officers felt that a more radical approach was needed, starting from a blank sheet and using every device of modern design and technology to produce a true underwater warship. This resulted in the one-off experimental

THE GUPPY PROGRAMME			
Phase	Year	No. of boats	Note
1	1946–47	2	
II	1947–51	24	
IA	1951	10	
Fleet Snorkel		28	
IIA	1952–54	17	
IB	1953–55	4	Allied Navy boats
III	1959–63	9	

boat *Albacore*, built at the naval yard at Kittery, Maine, and commissioned on 5 December 1953. Ostensibly designed as a 'target boat' for hunter-killer practice, it immediately became clear that *Albacore* was virtually uncatchable. With a submerged speed of 33 knots and an unprecedented ability for steep dives and tight turns, it outperformed any existing submarine.

Aircraft technology was freely drawn on for control systems. Built as a testbed, *Albacore* went through a succession of modifications and conversions through the 1960s. These included sound-proofing contra-rotating propellers on the shaft, dive brakes, a redesigned bow and new battery systems, as well as underwater drag-chutes (not a success). The US Navy and its allies learned a great deal from *Albacore*, and vindication of the project came in 1956 when the combination of teardrop hull and nuclear propulsion was established with USS

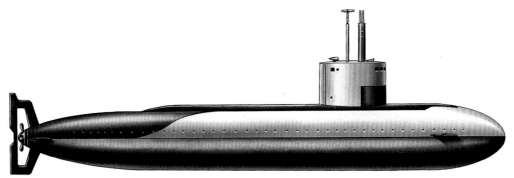

▲ USS Albacore
US Navy, test submarine, 1953
After many experiments and wind-tunnel tests, the teardrop hull had an intriguing resemblance to some of the earliest submarines. The pressure hull was constructed from new HY-80 high-yield steel. The single screw was originally incorporated with the rudder and stern planes, but in 1955–56 was relocated behind them.

Specifications
Crew: 52–60

Powerplant: Single shaft; two diesel engines; one electric motor,

Max Speed: 46.3/61km/hr (25/33kt) surf/sub

Surface Range: Not released

Displacement: 1524/1880t (1500/1850 tons) surf/sub

Dimensions (length/beam/draught): 62.2 x 8.4 x 5.6m (204 x 27.6 x 15.6ft)

Commissioned: 5 December 1953

Armament: nil

US POST-WAR DIESEL-ELECTRIC SUBMARINES				
Class	Type	Number	Year	Note
Barracuda	ASW	3	1944–51	Retired in 1950s
Tang	Attack	6	1949–52	Retired by 1975
Albacore	Experimental	1	1953	Retired 1972
Grayback	SSG	2	1954–58	Withdrawn as SSG 1964
Barbel	Attack	3	1956–59	Retired by 1990

Skipjack, and has remained the basis of submarine design since. *Albacore* was decommissioned in 1972 and stricken in 1980; it remains as a memorial boat in Portsmouth, New Hampshire.

USS *Mackerel*, with sister boat *Marlin*, were the smallest American submarines to be built since the 'C' class of 1909, intended as training craft for personnel who would then transfer to the fleet boats. Originally nameless, known as T-1 and T-2, they were commissioned in 1953 and named in 1956. *Marlin* was assigned to the submarine base at Key West, Florida (SubRon 12) from January 1954 and served as a training boat and target ship. Both were decommissioned on 31 January 1973. *Marlin* is preserved far from the sea at Omaha, Bebraska.

Converging Lines of Development

In the early 1950s, the US Navy was following two lines of submarine development that would ultimately converge. One was typified by the design and building of USS *Albacore*, where a traditional form of propulsion was used with a revolutionary hull and controls. The other kept to the long-established torpedo-boat hull-form but with a wholly new and equally revolutionary form of power plant: the nuclear reactor. Once the construction of the compact reactor became technically feasible, its application to submarines was only a matter of time, although it did not seem like that to the pioneers who had to persuade the naval supremos and the US Congress. In July 1951, the Congress authorized

▲ **USS *Skate***

USS *Skate* was the nuclear-powered submarine to transit the North Pole and also made the first entirely submerged crossing of the Atlantic.

construction of a nuclear-powered submarine, the keel was laid at the Electric Boat yard in Groton Connecticut on 14 June 1952, it was launched as *Nautilus* on 21 January 1954, and commissioned on 30 September of that year. Apart from its nuclear drive, *Nautilus* was modelled on the Tang class. The naval reactors programme had been running since 1948, and by March 1953 a viable compact reactor had been constructed. The S2W naval reactor, a pressurized water reactor, was built by the Westinghouse Corporation. On 17 January 1955, *Nautilus* went to sea for the first time and in the next

two years covered distances unthinkable for a conventional submarine. On 3 August 1958, it became the first vessel to pass beneath the North Pole, using an inertial navigation system developed by North American Aviation. *Nautilus* served with US naval units in the Atlantic and Mediterranean. In 1960, it was assigned to the Sixth Fleet. By the mid-1960s, a range of more advanced nuclear submarines was in operation and *Nautilus* spent its final active years as a training boat. It was decommissioned on 3 March 1980, by which time it had travelled over half a million nautical miles.

Specifications

Crew: 18

Powerplant: Single shaft; diesel-electric

Max Speed: 14.8/17.6km/hr (8/9.5kt) surf/sub

Surface Range: 3706km (2000nm) at 8kt

Displacement: 308/353t (303/347 tons) surf/sub

Dimensions (length/beam/draught): 40 x 4.1 x 3.7m (131.2 x 13.5 x 12.2in)

Commissioned: 20 November 1953

Armament: One 533mm (21in) torpedo tube

▲ USS Marlin

US Navy, coastal submarine

In 1966–67, *Mackerel* was adapted to test deep-sea rescue equipment, including keel-mounted wheels for moving on the ocean floor, thrusters, TV cameras and extensible arms, all of which were eventually used on the deep submergence vehicle NR-1. *Marlin* had a more conventional career participating in ASW training and exercises.

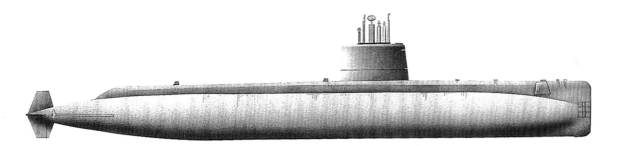

Specifications

Crew: 105

Powerplant: Twin shaft; one S2W pwr; turbines

Max Speed: 37/42.6km/hr (20/23kt) surf/sub

Surface Range: Unlimited

Displacement: 3589.7/4,167.8t (3533/4102 tons) surf/sub

Dimensions: 97 x 8.4 x 6.6m (323.55 x 27.8 x 21.75ft)

Commissioned: 30 September 1954

Armament: Six 533mm (21in) torpedo tubes

▲ USS Nautilus

US Navy, nuclear submarine, 1954

An extraordinary range of technical challenges were solved between 1951 and 1954 to make the US nuclear submarine a safe and effective vessel. Unlike any previous submarine, *Nautilus* had only one engine, and the absence of fuel tanks, batteries and double motors meant a welcome increase of crew space.

New roles for submarines
1955–64

For most navies, nuclear power was not an option. But all took an interest in the new capacity of submarines to fire tactical missiles.

APART FROM TWO BRITISH BOATS acquired in the immediate post-war period, China's first submarine classes originated in the Soviet Union. In 1956, China began construction of 21 boats identical to the Whiskey class. The Soviet Union then developed an advance on the Whiskey classes, Project 633, a diesel-electric attack boat given the name *Romeo* by NATO.

China

After 20 Soviet boats had been built, the designs were passed to China, under the Friendship and Mutual Assistance Treaty, and production began in 1962 at the Jiangnan yard in Shanghai. In China it was known as Type 033 and the first was launched in December 1965. Between 1962 and 1984 a total of 84 were built for the People's Liberation Army Navy, plus others for other countries. Over that period the Chinese made a range of modifications to the design. From the start, the Type 033 had eight torpedo tubes compared to the *Romeo*'s six. It could also carry 28 mines as an alternative to its 14 533mm (21in) torpedoes. A slightly greater displacement made it

roomier and increased fuel capacity gave it a range of almost double the original Romeos. Now obsolete, the Romeos survive perhaps only in the North Korean fleet, though other navies may have mothballed versions.

China went on to develop its Type 035 (Ming class) submarine from the Type 033. Of similar hull dimensions, it is a more advanced boat in all respects. Twenty were built from the early 1970s. The final six, commissioned between 1996 and 2001, were intended as a stopgap because of delays with the new generation Type 039, and are classed Type 035B. With an improved fire control system, and damping tiles to reduce noise, they carry 18 Yu-4 (SAET-60) passive homing surface-target torpedoes, capable of travelling 15km (9.3 miles) at 40 knots.

France

Requin was one of six boats of the Narval class completed between 1957 and 1960, intended as long-range patrol/attack submarines. They stand in line from the German Type XXI but were a more advanced design in many respects. The snorkel

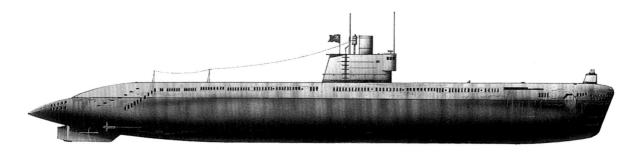

▲ **Romeo class**

Soviet/Chinese patrol-attack submarine

Type 033 boats were built for Algeria, Bulgaria, Egypt and Syria. In addition, 22 were built in North Korea. They also provided the basis of the Chinese-designed Type 035 Ming class, of which 21 were built from 1971, most of them in the 1990s.

Specifications

Crew: 60

Powerplant: Twin shaft; diesel-electric

Max Speed: 29.6/24 km/hr (16/13kt) surf/sub

Surface Range: 29,632km (16,000nm) at 10kt

Displacement: 1351/1727t (1330/1700 tons) surf/sub

Dimensions (length/beam/draught): 77 x 6.7 x 4.9m (252.65 x 22 x 16.1ft)

Commissioned: 1958 (Russia), 1962 (China); first units

Armament: Eight 533mm (21in) torpedo tubes

system was entirely new, and increased electrical power gave them a submerged range of 740km (400 nautical miles) compared to the Type XXIs' 537km (290 nautical miles). They could operate at a depth of 400m (1300ft) and were significantly quieter. The least satisfactory aspect was the Schneider 2-stroke diesels, which were replaced in 1966–70 by diesel-electric motors based on the SEMT-Pielstick 12PA4-185 type. Major refits at the same time resulted in the removal of the two stern tubes, and the fitting of a new fin based on the Daphné class, as well as updating of sensory equipment. Later, *Requin* and *Dauphin* were used as testbeds for sonar and other electronic equipment to be installed on the nuclear-powered Triomphant class. *Requin* was finally disposed of as a target in 1992.

The India–Pakistan War

In 1958–60, France built four small boats of the Aréthuse class, modelled on the German Type XXIII, for use as hunter-killer boats in the Mediterranean. They were followed by a larger boat, the Daphné class of patrol/attack submarines, 11-strong, all completed between 1961 and 1970. Two were lost, in 1968 and 1970, the blame being attached to faults in the snorkel design.

Numerous boats of this type were sold to other countries. The Portuguese Navy acquired four in 1967–69 (one sold on to Pakistan in 1975), the South African Navy got three in 1970–71, and the Spanish got four in 1973–75. The best known are perhaps the trio sold to Pakistan in 1970, particularly PNS *Hangor*, which torpedoed the Indian ASW

Specifications

Crew: 45	Displacement: 884/1062t (870/1045 tons) surf/sub
Powerplant: Two diesel engines: two electric motors	Dimensions: 58 x 7 x 4.6m (189.77 x 22.45 x 15ft)
Max Speed: 25/29.6km/hr (13.5/16kt) surf/sub	Commissioned: 20 Jun 1959
Surface Range: 8334km (400nm) at 5kt	Armament: 12 552mm (21.7in) torpedo tubes

▲ **Daphné**

French Navy, attack submarine, also Pakistan Navy, 1971

The four stern torpedo tubes were externally mounted and not reloadable while submerged. Based first at Lorient, then Toulon from 1972, *Daphné* underwent a major refit in 1967–68 and was last used in 1989 to test the new French Murène torpedo. It was sunk as a missile target in November 1994.

▲ **Requin**

French Navy, Narval-class patrol submarine

The Narval class owes its origin to *U-2518*, renamed *Roland Morillot*. They were built in seven 10m (33ft) sections that were then welded together, the first French construction of this kind. After the 1966–70 refits, they joined the 2nd squadron at Lorient.

Specifications

Crew: 63	
Powerplant:Twin shaft; diesel-electric	Dimensions (length/beam/draught): 78.4 x 7.8 x 5.2m (257 x 26 x 17ft)
Max Speed: 29.6/33.3 km/hr (16/18kt) surf/sub	Commissioned: 3 December 1955
Surface Range: 27,795km (15,000nm) at 8kt	Armament: Eight 550mm (21.7in) torpedo tubes
Displacement:1661/1941t (1635/1910 tons) surf/sub	

FRENCH POST WAR SUBMARINES (DIESEL-ELECTRIC)				
Class	Type	Number	Year	Note
Aurore	Patrol	5	1949–54	Pre-war class; modernized
E 48		2	1948	Experimental
Narval	Patrol	6	1957–86	
Aréthuse	Attack	4	1958–81	
Daphné	Attack	11	1964–70	Also for Pakistan (4), Portugal (4), South Africa (3), Spain (4)
Agosta	Attack	4	1977–2001	4 for Spain, 3 for Pakistan
Scorpène	Multi-role		2005	French/Spanish
Marlin	Multi-role		2008	French-only

frigate *Khukri* during the brief India–Pakistan war in November to December 1971.

This was the first submarine 'kill' since World War II. The engagement happened off India's west coast on 9 December 1971, when *Khukri* and a sister frigate *Kirpan* were sent to intercept *Hangor*. *Kirpan* was fired at, but the torpedo missed. *Khukri*, coming to attack, was struck and rapidly sank. Evading depth charges from *Kirpan* (and damaging its stern with a torpedo), *Hangor* eventually returned to base despite intense efforts by Indian air and surface craft to destroy it.

On 4 December, *Hangor*'s sister boat *Ghazi* had sunk in the Bay of Bengal, perhaps from an explosion of one of its own mines. *Hangor* was withdrawn in 2006 and is now a museum boat. France struck its remaining Daphné class boats in the 1990s.

Great Britain

In the 1950s, it was assumed that the Royal Navy would continue to play a worldwide role, extending to Far Eastern waters. Two almost identical long-range patrol/attack submarines, the Porpoise and Oberon classes, were introduced in 1959. Endurance was built in, with glass-reinforced plastic used in construction of the casing. Their quietness compared to contemporary US and Soviet boats made them very useful in clandestine operations, when it might be necessary to lurk very close to a potentially hostile coastline or harbour in order to gather intelligence or to land special forces. Payload for the forward tubes was 20 Tigerfish torpedoes, the stern tubes were pre-loaded for anti-submarine defence. Electronics, sonar and radar were upgraded during the class's 30-year-plus career.

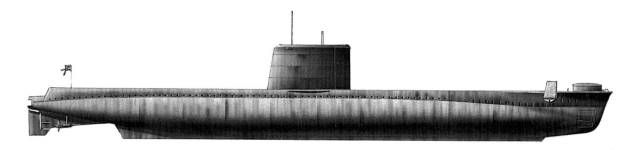

▲ **HMS Oberon**

Royal Navy, O-class patrol submarine

Thirteen of the class were commissioned into the RN. The prime difference to the Porpoise boats was better internal soundproofing and hulls constructed of high-strength QT28 steel, increasing diving capacity to 340m (1115ft). Two Admiralty V16 diesels of 3680hp (2744kW) powered two 3000hp (2237kW) electric motors.

Specifications

Crew: 69

Powerplant: Twin shaft; two diesel-electric motors

Max Speed: 22.2/31.5 km/hr (12/17.5kt) surf/sub

Surface Range: 11,118km (6000nm) at 10kt

Displacement: 2,063/2,449t (2,030/2,410 tons) surf/sub

Dimensions (length/beam/draught): 90 x 8.1 x 5.5m (295.25 x 26.5 x 18ft)

Commissioned: 18 July 1959

Armament: Eight 533mm (21in) torpedo tubes

Six Oberons were built for the Royal Australian Navy. These used American Mark 48 torpedoes, and the radar and sonar systems were Sperry Micropuffs passive ranging sonar and Krupp CSU3-41 attack sonar. Their stern tubes were sealed off and in the 1980s they were fitted with subsonic Harpoon missiles and designated as SSGs. Three were also built for Canada, three for Brazil and two for Chile. The Oberons were generally regarded as a very effective submarine. In effect, they were the last diesel-electric class to be in regular use by the Royal Navy.

Britain had experimented with hydrogen-peroxide drive, but by 1956 it was evident that any first-class naval power needed to have nuclear submarines on a par with those being built by the United States and the Soviets. HMS *Dreadnought* was the first, launched on 21 October 1960 and powered by a US S5W pressurized water reactor, designed for the US Skipjack class (the aft machinery area was known as 'the American sector'). The hull design also resembled *Skipjack*'s, though navigational and combat systems were largely based on British technology. Commissioned on 17 April 1963,

Specifications

Crew: 71	Displacement: 2062/2444t (2030/2405 tons) surf/sub
Powerplant: Twin shaft; two diesel-electric motors	Dimensions (length/beam/draught): 73.5 x 8.1 x 5.5m (241 x 26.5 x 18ft)
Max Speed: 22.2/31.5 km/hr (12/17kt) surf/sub	Commissioned: 22 September 1959
Surface Range: 16,677km (9000nm) at 10kt	Armament: Eight 533mm (21in) torpedo tubes

▲ HMS Walrus

Royal Navy, Porpoise-class patrol submarine

Eight of this class were built. The 'Snort' air-breathing system, shared with the Oberons, was a robust but efficient one intended to operate in rough sea conditions. Diving depth was 300m (984ft). Air and surface radar warning systems operated from periscope depth. All were decommissioned by 1988.

Specifications

Crew: 88	Displacement: 3556/4064t (3500/4000 tons) surf/sub
Powerplant: Single shaft; S5W pwr; steam turbines	Dimensions (length/beam/draught): 81 x 9.8 x 8m (265.75 x 32.25 x 26.25ft)
Max Speed: 37/55.5km/hr (20/30kt) surf/sub	Commissioned: 17 April 1963
Surface Range: Unlimited	Armament: Six 533mm (21in) torpedo tubes

▲ HMS Dreadnought

Royal Navy, nuclear patrol submarine (SSN)

To obtain a new US reactor design was a considerable achievement for the British, though future Royal Navy nuclear boats would have British reactors. A major refit and refuelling was carried out in 1970. *Dreadnought* surfaced at the North Pole on 34 March 1971.

BRITISH POST-WAR SUBMARINES (DIESEL-ELECTRIC)

Class	Type	Number	Year	Note
Explorer	Test boat	2	1958	Experimental, HTP motor
Stickleback	Midget	4	1954–55	Improved XE-class
Porpoise	Patrol	8	1956–59	
Oberon	Multi-role	13	1960–67	14 built for export
Upholder	Patrol	4	199–93	Transferred to Canada 1998

DUTCH POST-WAR SUBMARINES

Class	Type	Number	Year	Note
Dolfijn	Patrol	2	1954–60	Decommissioned
Zwaardvis	Patrol	2	1966–72	Decommissioned by 1995
Walrus	Patrol	4	1985–94	

Dreadnought was inevitably used as a training and testing boat, though it was a fully effective SSN (fast attack), whose high underwater speed of 30 knots made it suitable for use as an escort to fast carrier groups. In 1980 it was withdrawn following damage to the machinery, which was not considered repairable, and the hulk remains at Rosyth naval dockyard. *Dreadnought*, built rapidly with US help, remained a one-off. Next to come was HMS *Valiant*, commissioned 18 July 1966, one of two hunter-killer boats (*Warspite* being the other, commissioned April 1967). Though based in many ways on *Dreadnought*, apart from being somewhat larger, there were two major differences: the pressurized-water reactor was built by Rolls-Royce, and the two steam turbines by English Electric, and a 'rafting' system was used to install the machinery so that it did not bear directly on the hull, with a great improvement in quiet running. Rafting later became a common feature of nuclear submarines.

In Cold War operations, the two Valiant class served primarily in ASW roles, shadowing Soviet SSBNs (ballistic missile submarines) or task force groups and patrolling the lanes through which Soviet submarines passed into the open Atlantic. *Warspite* was decommissioned in 1991 and *Valiant* in 1994, because of cracks in the primary-to-secondary cooling system.

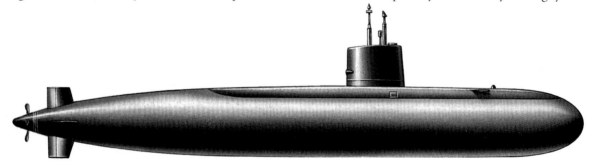

Specifications

Crew: 116

Powerplant: Single shaft; one pwr; steam turbines

Max Speed: 37/53.7km/hr (20/29kt) surf/sub

Surface Range: Unlimited

Displacement: 4470/4979t (4400/4900 tons)

surf/sub

Dimensions (length/beam/draught): 86.9 x 10.1 x 8.2m (285 x 33.25 x 27ft)

Commissioned: 18 July 1966

Armament: Six 533mm (21in) torpedo tubes

▲ **HMS Valiant**

Royal Navy, SSN, South Atlantic 1982

Unlike *Dreadnought*, *Valiant* had a Paxman diesel-electric auxiliary drive for silent running. In 1967, it made a 28-day submerged transit from Singapore to Britain, of 19,312km (12,000 miles). It spent 101 days patrolling the Argentinian coast in 1982, on surveillance and air-warning reconnaissance duty. Refits were undertaken in 1970, 1977 and 1989.

Netherlands

On 16 December 1960, *Dolfijn* was commissioned into the Royal Dutch Navy, after six years construction. The four boats of this ocean-going patrol-attack class were the first home-built submarines for the Dutch Navy since World War II. The design was a unique one incorporating three separate pressure hulls in a triangular arrangement, inside an external casing. The crew inhabited the top one; the other two contained the engines, batteries and storage space. The arrangement, complex and expensive to build, allowed a maximum diving depth of 300m (984ft), unusual for the late 1950s. The boats were commissioned between 1960 and 1966, the second pair having been held back while the possibility of nuclear propulsion was considered, and rejected.

Another unusual feature was an even division of the eight torpedo tubes between bow and stern. Minelaying via the tubes was also possible. *Dolfijn* was broken up in 1985; the others in the class survived into the 1990s, with *Zeehond* being used as a demonstrator for AIP propulsion by the RBM shipyard in Rotterdam between 1990 and 1994.

The Soviet Union

Project 641 was intended to provide a more up-to-date patrol/attack boat than the Whiskey class and the subsequent 1952 Zulu class, both World War II derivatives, and the resultant design, noted as Foxtrot by NATO, fulfilled the objective. The first of the class was laid down in 1957 and commissioned in 1958: construction continued until 1983. In all, 58 were built for the Soviet Navy, and a further 20 or so for other countries. The Foxtrots were powered by three Kolomna diesel engines and three electric motors, driving three propeller shafts. These made the boats relatively noisy, and their submerged speed of 15 knots did not allow for rapid chasing or shadowing. Nevertheless, the Foxtrot class played an important role in the Soviet Navy for more than 20 years, as a submarine that could be deployed almost anywhere. That included the North and West Atlantic Oceans.

The Cuban Missile Crisis

Foxtrot submarines were involved in the tense encounters that took place during the Cuban missile crisis of 16–28 October 1962. Four of the class were deployed to Cuban waters on 1 October. Although they did not have combat orders, all (unknown to the United States) were carrying a torpedo with a nuclear warhead. A Zulu-class boat, *B-75*, armed with two nuclear warheads, was also in the Atlantic under instruction to protect Soviet shipping between the Soviet Union and Cuba. Aware of the presence of Soviet submarines in the North Atlantic, the Pentagon ordered US Navy units on 23 October to track them and 'induce' them to surface and identify themselves. This involved the use of small-size practice depth charges.

Three Foxtrots, *B-36*, *B-59*, and *B-130,* were forced to the surface either by depth-charges or

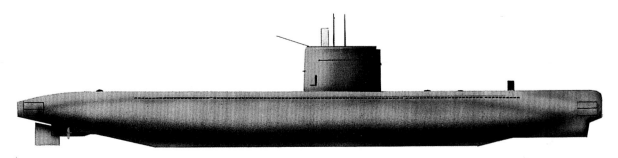

▲ Dolfijn

Netherlands Navy, patrol submarine

The triple hull formation was not continued by the Dutch Navy in future submarine classes, due to the later use of higher-grade steel and the improvement of welding techniques, which gave monohulled boats equivalent performance at less cost.

Specifications

Crew: 64

Powerplant: Twin shaft; two diesel engines; two electric motors

Max Speed: 26.8/31.5km/hr (14.5/17kt) surf/sub

Surface Range: Details not available

Displacement: 1518/1855t (1494/1826 tons) surf/sub

Dimensions (length/beam/draught): 80 x 8 x 4.8m (260.8 x 25.75 x 15.75ft)

Commissioned: 16 December 1960

Armament: Eight 533mm (21in) torpedo tubes

through battery exhaustion. A fourth, *B-4*, evaded US efforts to make it surface. The *Zulu* was recalled by Moscow when US President Kennedy announced the 'quarantine' zone around Cuba on 22 October. Meanwhile, in the Pacific, *Zulu B-88*, also with atomic warheads, was sent on patrol close to Pearl Harbor, with instructions to attack if war should break out. For a few days world security was on a knife-edge and submarines were on the brink of losing their deterrent role and unleashing a nuclear war. US submarines were put into a state of battle readiness at every East Coast base and submarines monitored the movements of Soviet shipping. On both sides, nuclear submarines, armed with ICBMs, were on full alert.

The Golf submarines had an unmistakable profile, with the sail extended into a long missile silo. Designated as Project 629, this was the first purpose-built Soviet ballistic missile submarine. Design began in the mid-1950s, after six Zulu boats had been modified to carry Scud missiles. Twenty-three were commissioned between 1958 and 1962. The first design allowed for carrying three R-11FM (SS-N-4) missiles with a range of around 150km (93 miles), and which had to be launched from the surface.

Sixteen of the class were modified in 1966–72 (Project 629A) to carry R-21 (SS-N-5) Sark missiles with a range of 1400km (870 miles), which could be launched while the submarine was submerged and

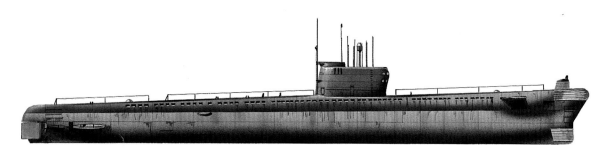

Specifications

Crew: 80	Displacement: 1950/2500t (1191/2540 tons)
Powerplant: Triple shaft; three diesels engines;	surf/sub
three electric motors	Dimensions (length/beam/draught): 91.5 x 8 x
Max Speed: 33.3/29.6km/hr (18/16kt) surf/sub	6.1m (300.18 x 26.25 x 20ft)
Surface Range:10,190km (5500nm) at 8kt	Commissioned: 1959 (first units)
	Armament: 10 533mm (21in) torpedo tubes

▲ Foxtrot

Soviet Navy, patrol-attack submarine

Foxtrots carried the Soviet ensign in every ocean region. They were the last Soviet submarines to be constructed with old-style hulls, though the sail was of streamlined design. Their successors would be given the teardrop hull format.

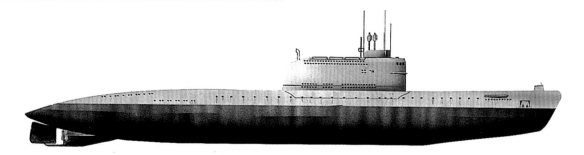

▲ Golf I

Soviet Navy, missile submarine

The keel was deepened in mid-section to accommodate the tubes of the missile silo. Like the Foxtrots, they had triple diesel-electric motors driving three propeller shafts and were not quiet in the water, except when using their slow-speed creep motor.

Specifications

Crew: 86	surf/sub
Powerplant: Triple shaft; three diesel-electric	Dimensions (length/beam/draught): 100 x 8.5 x
motors	6.6m (328 x 27.9 x 21.6ft)
Max Speed: 31.5/26km/hr (17/14kt) surf/sub	Commissioned: 1958
Surface Range: 36,510km (19,700nm) at 10kt	Armament: Three SS-N-4 SLBM; 10 533mm
Displacement: 2336/2743t (2300/2700 tons)	(21in) torpedo tubes

moving. These were known as Golf II. One of these, *K-129*, sank northwest of Oahu in the Pacific on 8 March 1968, with the loss of all its crew. Three R-21 nuclear missiles and two nuclear torpedoes were on board. SOSUS detector equipment registered the incident and the United States ran a semi-secret operation, Project Azorian, in 1974 to retrieve the wreck, using the SSNs *Halibut* and *Seawolf* as search vehicles. Part of the wreck was retrieved, but the details of the operation remain cloaked in secrecy.

By 1990, the Soviet Navy had withdrawn all its Golf class boats. Ten were sold to North Korea in 1993, for scrapping. A Chinese version of the *Golf I* was built in 1966 and may still be in commission as a missile-testing platform.

On 16 September 1955, the Zulu class *B-67* launched the first submarine-launched ballistic missile (SLBM), the R-11FM. From 1956, some Whiskey class submarines were adapted to carry guided missiles, initially the SS-N-3 Shaddock cruise missile. The first prototype, identified by NATO as Whiskey single-cylinder, carried only one missile, but six more were converted between 1958 and 1960 to carry two (Whiskey two-cylinder). The missile tubes were fitted aft of the sail. A further six were fitted with a lengthened sail to hold four vertically mounted Shaddocks (Whiskey long bin). *B-67* was the first Soviet submarine to fire from a submerged position, on 10 September 1960, only two months after USS SSBN *George Washington* made a submerged launch of a Polaris A1. The first

launch of a nuclear-armed SLBM was on 20 October 1961 from a Project 629 submarine on the Novaya Zemlya Arctic test ground.

United States

In the United States, the Guppy programme was entering its final phase. Guppy III (1959–63) was a major operation that involved fitting a new 4.5m (15ft) central section to nine boats that had already been through Guppy II. This accommodated the increasing amount of electronic support measures (ESM), sonar and fire control equipment. The sail was heightened to raise the bridge and allow it to be manned in severe weather. Numerous Guppy boats were transferred to other navies between the 1950s and the mid-70s, and two survived into the twenty-first century: *Thornback* (Turkish *Uluc Ali Reis*) decommissioned in 2000, and *Greenfish* (Brazilian *Amazonas*) scrapped in 2004.

Many early missile experiments were made with adapted fleet submarines. USS *Grayback* was commissioned at Mare Island, California, on 7 March 1958. Originally intended as attack submarines, it and USS *Growler* were converted on the slip to carry Regulus I sea-to-surface missiles. Four missiles were mounted in a hangar set in the bulbous bow. In September 1958, *Grayback* carried out the first successful launch of a Regulus missile from a submarine, establishing the role of the submarine as a vessel capable of striking land targets. *Grayback* subsequently went on Pacific operational

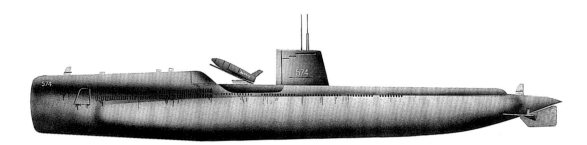

Specifications

Crew: 84

Powerplant: Twin shaft; two diesel-electric motors

Max Speed: 37/31.5km/hr (20/17kt) surf/sub

Surface Range: 14,825km (8000nm) at 10kt

Displacement: 2712/3708t (2670/3650 tons)

surf/sub

Dimensions (length/beam/draught): 98.2 x 9.1 x 5.8m (322.3 x 30 x 19ft)

Commissioned: 7 March 1958

Armament: Four Regulus I missiles; eight 533mm (21in) torpedo tubes

▲ USS Grayback

US Navy, missile submarine

The large missile hangar is the defining feature. For designers, its size and danger of flooding in a following sea was a major problem. The launcher was mounted on a turntable. The Regulus boats formed SubRon I at Pearl Harbor from 1958 to 1964.

patrols as an SSG, its rockets armed with nuclear warheads, inaugurating the concept of the 'strategic deterrent' that was to govern Cold War thinking and planning for 30 years. It was active until 25 May 1964, when it was decommissioned, with the abandonment of the Regulus programme. In 1967–68 it was converted to an amphibious transport submarine (LPSS) , with the former missile chambers used to hold troops and SEAL swimmer delivery craft. In this configuration it was used in Vietnam War operations, including Operation Thunderhead in June 1972, intended to rescue US prisoners of war from North Vietnam. *Grayback* was finally decommissioned on 15 January 1984, and sunk as a target on 13 April 1986. *Growler* is preserved as a museum boat in Brooklyn.

Nuclear Program

The progress of nuclear technology and the performance of the first nuclear submarines determined the US Navy to press on with nuclear propulsion. An order was placed in July 1955 for USS *Skate*, lead ship of a class of four, and it was commissioned on 23 December 1957. The design was based on the Tang class and they were among the smallest nuclear powered attack submarines. At the time, however, they were considered large boats, and were certainly effective in operation. *Skate* went on sub-Arctic patrols and was the first boat to surface at the North Pole (17 March 1959). Most of its almost 30-year career was spent with Atlantic Fleet, based at

New London, Connecticut. Before the Skate class had completed building, a new hunter-killer class, led by USS *Skipjack*, was built between 1956 and 1961. Constructed from HY-80 steel, these six boats had the teardrop hull design that had also been used in the Navy's final diesel-electric class, the three Barbel fast attack boats, built simultaneously (1956–59). In both classes, the command centre was located not in the tower but within the hull.

The S5W pressurized-water reactor, first installed in this class, became the standard for future classes until the 1970s. The Skipjack boats were very fast, with a submerged speed in excess of 29 knots, and were widely deployed, including Arctic patrols on the Soviet exit-route from Murmansk. Some were deployed in tactical forces during the Vietnam War. One of the class, USS *Scorpion*, was lost on 5 June 1968 off the Azores, returning from a patrol in the Mediterranean Sea. The cause of the disaster remains unidentified, but was most probably a mechanical failure. Skipjack was decommissioned and struck from the register on 19 April 1990.

Up to 1962, submarines played a key strategic role as radar picket boats, equipped with air search radar to give early warning of missile or aircraft attacks aimed at land bases or at fleet groups. Designated SSR or SSRN for nuclear boats, these had begun with the conversion of fleet submarines under the Migraine Programme, but the speed and endurance of the nuclear submarine made it much more suitable for the picket role, attached to fast carrier groups.

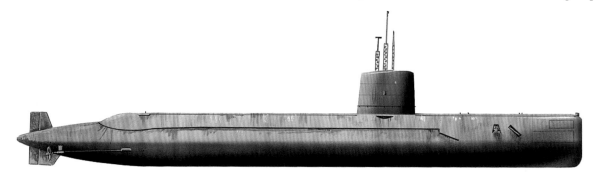

Specifications	
Crew: 95	surf/sub
Powerplant: Twin shaft; one pwr	Dimensions (length/beam/draught): 81.5 x 7.6 x
Max Speed: 37/46.3km/hr (20/25kt) surf/sub	6.4m (267.6 x 25 x 21ft)
Surface Range: Unlimited	Commissioned: 23 December 1957
Displacement: 2611/2907t (2570/2681 tons)	Armament: Six 533mm (21in) torpedo tubes

▲ **USS Skate**

US Navy, first series-production SSN

The world's first production-line nuclear submarine, *Skate* had dimensions similar to the Tang class; its greater weight was caused by the need for radiation shielding of its S3W reactor. Towed sonar was at first of the 'clip-on' kind, but two of the class later had integral reeled arrays installed.

▲ **Submarine launcher**
Halibut launching a Regulus missile from the deck. The streamlined hangar can clearly be seen.

USS *Triton*, commissioned on 10 November 1959, was built for radar picket duty, and assigned to SubRon 10, an all-nuclear unit based at New London, Connecticut. *Triton* fielded a range of detection equipment, not only AN/SPS-26 3-D long-range air search radar but also towed sonar gear. But only two years after commissioning, the $109 million craft was obsolete, its picket role taken over by carrier-based aircraft.

Triton was converted to SSN status as an attack submarine. It has been suggested that it was also considered as a NECPA (National Emergency Command Post Afloat) for use as a mobile command centre. But its career was short and it was decommissioned in 1969, the first US nuclear submarine to be taken out of service.

Polaris Deployed

Caught at a disadvantage by Soviet development of missile-carrying submarines, the United States mounted a powerful response in the late 1950s. The crucial weapon was a new missile, the Polaris A1, a relatively lightweight (13,063kg/28,800lb) two-stage solid-fuel rocket that had been developed with remarkable speed since December 1956, with a first test launch in September 1958, the first submerged launch on 20 July 1960 and the first operational patrol in November 1960. Intended from the start as an SLBM, while Polaris was being tested, a Skipjack class nuclear submarine then under construction, USS *Scorpion* (which was intended as an SSN), was extended with a new 40m (130ft) centre section to carry 16 missile launch tubes, and renamed *George Washington*, the first SSBN.

The Polaris A1's range of 2200km (1370 miles) and the quantity carried by the new SSBNs placed the United States firmly in the lead of missile development. In 1964–65, the Polaris missile was upgraded to A3. Later, *George Washington* was assigned to the Pacific Fleet's Pearl Harbor base. In 1983 it completed the last of 55 patrols as an SSBN, its missiles were removed, as were those of two others of the class, and it served for two years as an SSN before being decommissioned on 24 January 1985.

Commissioned a few days after *George Washington*, on 4 January 1960, USS *Halibut* was the first submarine specifically designed to launch guided missiles. Laid down as a conventionally powered boat, it was completed as a nuclear-powered one. It carried five Regulus I missiles, with a single launcher, and worked through 1961–64 with the Pacific Fleet. Overhauled at Pearl Harbor in 1965, with Regulus now obsolete, *Halibut* was redesignated an SSN, participating in ASW patrols and exercises until 1968. At Mare Island yard it was transformed into an undersea reconnaissance and retrieval vessel, and in this role participated in the attempted raising of the Soviet *K-129* as well as engaging in seabed espionage. *Halibut* was decommissioned on 30 June 1976.

In January 1958, the construction order was given for the SSN USS *Thresher*, lead boat of a class of SSNs, an advance on the Skipjacks, with many new

technological features, including deep-diving mechanisms, with a test depth of 400m (1300ft), advanced sonars, four midships-angled torpedo tubes also capable of launching the SUBROC ASW missile, and a high level of machinery-quieting, with the turbines supported on British-type 'rafts'.

Commissioned on 3 August 1961, *Thresher* was extensively tested and exercised through 1962. On 10 April 1963, it failed to surface from deep diving tests and was lost with all hands in the ocean east of Cape Cod. Intensive research followed the disaster, resulting in the SUBSAFE programme, providing the maximum reasonable assurance of quality in all systems exposed to sea pressure, or critical to recovery from flooding. A further 13 submarines of the class

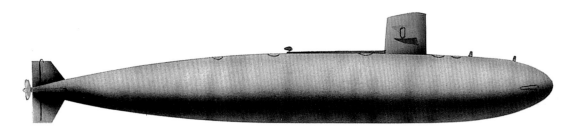

▲ **USS Skipjack**

US Navy, SSN, 1965

Skipjack had a single-hull design, with the sail set well forward, carrying the diving planes. This transference from bow-mounting reduced flow-noise past the bow sonar and made it much more effective. It was also the first single-shaft nuclear submarine, with the propeller set aft of the rudder and diving plane gear.

Specifications

Crew: 106

Powerplant: Single shaft; one S5W pwr; steam turbines

Max Speed: 33.3/55.5km/hr (18/30kt) surf/sub

Surface Range: Unlimited

Displacement: 3124/3556t (3075/3500 tons) surf/sub

Dimensions (length/beam/draught): 76.7 x 9.6 x 8.5m (251.75 x 31.5 x 27.8ft)

Commissioned: 15 April 1959

Armament: Five 533mm (21in) torpedo tubes

Specifications

Crew: 172

Powerplant: Twin shaft; one S4G pwr; steam turbines

Max Speed: 50/37km/hr (27/20kt) surf/sub

Surface Range: Unlimited

Displacement: 6035/7905t (5940/7780 tons) surf/sub

Dimensions (length/beam/draught): 136.3 x 11.3 x 7.3m (447.5 x 37 x 24ft)

Commissioned: 10 November 1959

Armament: Six 533mm (21in) torpedo tubes

▲ **USS Triton**

US Navy, radar/reconnaissance nuclear submarine

The largest submarine yet built, it was the only US nuclear submarine with two reactors: it had two S4G pressurized-water reactors driving twin propellers. Each reactor could function independently of the other. In early 1960, it was the first vessel to circumnavigate the globe underwater.

were built between 1958 and 1967, and the class name was passed to the second boat, *Permit*. All shared the forward-set sail, though some were given an enlarged version, as well as heavier machinery, under the SUBSAFE programme, adding 3m (9ft 10in) to their length. The class was distributed between the Atlantic and Pacific Fleets, serving on a mixture of routine patrols and special intelligence-gathering and surveillance missions.

The 10 James Madison SSBNs, which were built from 1962 to 1964, marked a new step in missile, rather than submarine, development, being almost identical in dimensions to the 19 boats of the preceding Lafayette class. They were armed, however, with 16 Polaris A3 missiles, whose range

was 1900km (1180 miles) greater than that of the A2, and which had three re-entry vehicles for each warhead, the first multiple re-entry vehicle missile. Guidance, fire control and navigational systems were all improved from the Lafayettes. Built at Mare Island, California, *Daniel Boone* served first with the Pacific Fleet at Guam, then later with Submarine Squadron 14 at the forward base of Holy Loch, Scotland. It was modified in 1976–78 to carry Poseidon C-3 missiles with the Mark 88 fire-control system, and in 1980 was the first of the Madison class to go on patrol with the new Trident C-4. After almost 30 years of service and 75 patrols, *Daniel Boone* was decommissioned on 18 February 1994.

▲ USS Halibut

US Navy, guided missile submarine (SSGN)

This was the first boat fitted with the SINS inertial navigation system designed for ballistic submarines. The bulging single-shell hangar was in effect a secondary pressure hull, later adapted as a hangar, with a sea-lock, for a towed underwater search vehicle.

Specifications

Crew: 99	Dimensions (length/beam/draught): 106.7 x 8.9 x
Powerplant: Single shaft; one S3W pwr; turbines	6.3m (350 x 29.5 x 20.75ft)
Max Speed: 27.8/26km/hr (15/14kt)	Commissioned: 4 January 1960
Surface Range: Unlimited	Armament: Five Regulus I or four Regulus II
Displacement: (2670/3650 tons) surf/sub	missiles; six 533mm (21in) torpedo tubes

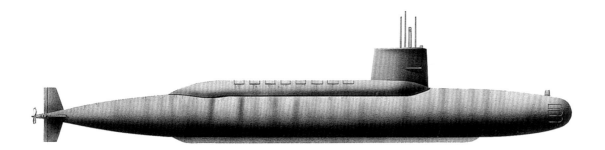

Specifications

Crew: 112	Dimensions (length/beam/draught): 116.3 x 10 x
Powerplant: Single shaft; one S5W pwr; turbines,	8.8m (381.7 x 33 x 28.8ft)
Max Speed: 37/56.5km/hr (20/30.5kt) surf/sub	Commissioned: 30 December 1959
Surface Range: Unlimited	Armament: 16 Polaris Al SBM; six 533mm (21in)
Displacement: 6115/6998t (6019/6888 tons)	torpedo tubes
surf/sub	

▲ USS George Washington

US Navy, ballistic missile submarine (SSBN)

George Washington was commissioned on 30 December 1959, the first of a class of five SSBNs, each with two crews, to ensure full utilization of the boat's capacity. Between 28 October 1960 and 21 January 1961 it made its first patrol, and from April 1961 was based at the Holy Loch, Scotland.

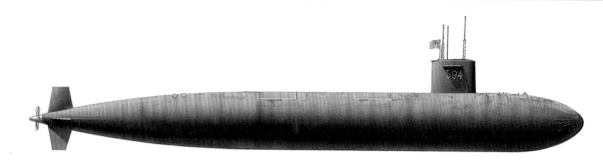

Specifications

Crew: 134

Powerplant: Single shaft; one S5W pwr; steam
  turbines,

Max Speed: 33.3/50km/hr (18/27kt) surf/sub

Surface Range: Unlimited

Displacement: 3810/4380t (3750/4311 tons)
  surf/sub

Dimensions (length/beam/draught): 84.9 x 9.6 x
  8.8m (278.5 x 31.65 x 28.8ft)

Commissioned: 3 August 1961

Armament: Four 533mm (21in) torpedo tubes

▲ USS Thresher

US Navy, Thresher/Permit class SSN

The loss of *Thresher* was a major shock, as this was considered the best nuclear submarine yet. The class was the first to carry the spherical sonar array that could track fast submarines in all three dimensions. These boats could detect the the standard Mk 37 ASW torpedo, and outrun it.

Specifications

Crew: 140

Powerplant: Single shaft; one S5W pwr; steam
  turbines,

Max Speed: 37/64.8km/hr (20/35kt) surf/sub

Surface Range: Unlimited

Displacement: 7366/8382t (7250/8250 tons)

surf/sub

Dimensions (length/beam/draught): 130 x 10 x
  10m (425 x 33 x 33ft)

Commissioned: 23 April 1964

Armament: 16 Polaris A2/A3 SBM; four 533mm
  (21in) torpedo tubes

▲ USS Daniel Boone

US Navy, James Madison class SSBN

The James Madison class submarines were in direct line from the Ethan Allen class of 1960, through the Lafayettes (1963), but had improved guidance, fire-control, navigational and missile-launching systems. Gas generators had already replaced compressed-air launchers with the Lafayette class.

The race for missile superiority
1965–74

The deep-sea lanes are now patrolled by ICBM-carrying SSBN 'Boomers'. But conventional submarines have not lost their attack role.

CHINA'S FIRST NUCLEAR submarine class, Type 091 or Han, had a hull design closely resembling the US 'teardrop' form, with diving planes fitted to the sail. Five were commissioned between 1974 and 1990. Propulsion was by a single pressurized-water reactor. Although little is known for certain about

Chinese nuclear submarine development, the long construction period indicates that the later boats may differ considerably in internal layout and weapons and other systems.

In successive refits all have been modernized to a degree, with the most essential feature being improved radiation shielding. Three are believed to remain in service, fitted with anechoic tiles to dampen their (considerable) noise and with Type H/SQ2-262B sonar replacing the original Type 603. The class can fire C-801 anti-ship missiles in addition to SET-65E and Type 53-51 torpedoes; or carry 36 mines.

Despite their limitations, the Chinese Han class brought China into the club of nuclear submarine operators and provided a solid base for further development.

Denmark

Though constructed by the Copenhagen Naval Dockyard, the Danish submarines *Narhvalen* and *Nordkaperen* were German designs, based on the Type 205, with certain differences and modifications. The hulls were formed of magnetic steel, as the non-magnetic steel used on the Type 205 had serious corrosion problems.

Narhvalen was commissioned on 27 February 1970, and with its sister ship was used as a patrol/attack submarine to police the sensitive

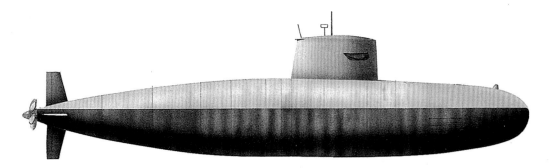

▲ Han

Chinese Navy, Type O91 SSN

Han-class deployments are believed to be infrequent, although in the past they have shadowed US Naval groups and one boat infringed territorial limits off a Japanese island in 2004. They are assigned to the PLA Navy's North Sea Fleet, at the the Qingdao naval base.

Specifications

Crew: 120	Dimensions (length/beam/draught): 90 x 8 x
Powerplant: Single shaft; one pwr	8.2m (295.25 x 26.25 x 27ft)
Max Speed: 37/51.8km/hr (20/28kt) surf/sub	Commissioned: 1972
Surface Range: Unlimited	Armament: Six 533mm (21in) torpedo tubes;
Displacement: 4572/5588.25t (4500/5500 tons)	18 torpedoes; 36 mines
surf/sub	

▲ Narhvalen

Danish Navy, patrol submarine, Skagerrak 1970

Failure to communicate with its command base, due to a radio failure, caused fears that *Narhvalen* had sunk in the *Skagerrak* in September 1970. In 1994, it and *Nordkaperen* went through a major refit, and it continued with coastal and NATO patrols until decommissioned in October 2003.

Specifications

Crew: 19	Displacement: 442/517t (453/509 tons) surf/sub
Powerplant: Twin shaft; two diesel engines;	Dimensions (length/beam/draught): 44 x 4.55
two electric motors	x 3.98m (144.35 x 14.9 x 13ft)
Max Speed: 18/31.5km/hr (10/17kt) surf/sub	Commissioned: 27 February 1970
Surface Range: Details not available	Armament: Eight 533mm (21in) torpedo
	tubes

Kattegat and Skagerrak waters as well as participating in wider-scale NATO exercises. Their longest known patrol is a 41-day cruise from the Baltic Sea to the Faeroe Islands and back, with only 5 per cent of the time spent on the surface.

France

Laid down in 1964, commissioned in December 1971 after lengthy trials, *Redoutable* was France's first SSBN (known to the French as SNLE), and lead-boat of a class of six. Four were completed by 1976, and the final two in 1980 and 1985. The first two carried France's M1 SLBMs; the others had the much

superior M4, a three-stage missile with a range of 5300km (3290 miles). Each has six 150kT MIRV warheads. *Redoutable* and its sisters formed part of the Force Océanique Stratégique (FOST) set up to ensure at least one French SSBN was operational at any time. *Redoutable* made 51 operational patrols over 20 years before being decommissioned in 1991. All the class are now withdrawn.

France did not abandon the diesel-electric submarine and in 1977 introduced the Agosta class for patrol/attack duties. Four were built at Cherbourg for the French Navy in 1977–78 and four at Cartagena for the Spanish Navy in 1983–85. A

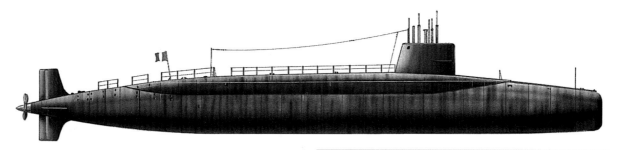

▲ **Le Redoutable**

French Navy, SSBN

Redoutable carried 18 L5 dual-purpose and F17 anti-ship torpedoes in addition to the missile armament. It was the only member of its class not to be retrofitted with Aerospatiale M4 ballistic missiles. Following its withdrawal, the five remaining boats were officially designated as the Inflexible class.

Specifications

Crew: 142

Powerplant: Single shaft; one pwr; turbines

Max Speed: 37/51.8km/hr (20/28kt) surf/sub

Surface Range: Unlimited

Displacement: 7620/9144t (7500/9000 tons) surf/sub

Dimensions (length/beam/draught): 128 x 10.6 x 10m (420 x 34.8 x 32.8ft)

Commissioned: 1 December 1971

Armament: 16 SLBM; SM-39 Exocet; four 533mm (21in) torpedo tubes

Specifications

Crew: 54

Powerplant: Single shaft; two diesel engines; one electric motor

Max Speed: 23.1/32.4km/hr (12.5/17.5kt) surf/sub

Surface Range: 15,750km (8500nm) at 9kt

Displacement: 1514/1768t (1490/1740 tons) surf/sub

Dimensions (length/beam/draught): 67.6 x 6.8 x 5.4m (221.75 x 22.45 x 17.75ft)

Commissioned: 11 February 1978

Armament: Four 550mm (21.7in) tubes; 40 mines

▲ **Agosta**

French Navy, patrol-attack submarine

The class was designed with Mediterranean deployment in mind. Use of HLES 80 steel enabled it to dive to 350m (1150ft). Its torpedo tubes were a new design, with rapid pneumatic-ram reload, which could fire at any speed and depth. It carried 23 torpedoes.

further two, originally ordered by South Africa, were sold to Pakistan in 1979–80.

Pakistan also has three Agosta 90B or Khalid class boats, built between 1999 and 2006, to a modernized design with upgraded weapons and sensor systems. Automated systems require a crew of only 36 compared to the Agosta's 54. The French Agosta boats have been decommissioned.

Germany

Eleven boats, numbered *U1* to *U12* (excluding *U3*) formed this class of attack submarines, which were intended for use in the Baltic Sea. This sea is shallow, which explains why they had a test depth of 100m (330ft), not very great for a modern submarine. The hulls were formed of a non-magnetic steel that turned out to have severe corrosion problems, though the problem was resolved by the time *U9* to *U12* were built, in 1967–69. *U1* and *U2*, originally Type 201, were rebuilt as Type 205s with normal steel. In the Baltic, accurate sensory equipment is of vital importance and the first sea trials of the Bundesmarine CSU90 sonar array were conducted by a Type 205. *U4* to *U8* had brief careers, all being

▲ U-12

Specifications

Crew: 21	Dimensions (length/beam/draught): 43.9 x 4.6 x 4.3m (144 x 15 x 14ft)
Powerplant: Single screw; diesel-electric	
Max Speed: 18/.5/32.4km/hr (10/17.5kt) surf/sub	Commissioned: 10 September 1968
Surface Range: 7040km (3800nm) at 10kt	Armament: Eight 533mm (21in) torpedo tubes
Displacement: 425.457t (419/450 tons) surf/sub	

Federal German Navy, Type 205 coastal submarine, Baltic Sea, 1968

A clear line of development can be traced from the Type 201 to the Type 205 and beyond. Working from the FGR submarine base at Eckernförde, *U-12* was reclassified as Type 205B while trialling new sonar systems. *U-1* was used as a test-boat for AIP propulsion in 1988.

▲ U-20

Specifications

Crew: 21	Dimensions (length/beam/draught): 48.6 x 4./6 x 4.5m (159.45 x 15.16 x 14.8ft)
Powerplant: Single shaft; diesel-electric	
Max Speed: 18.5/31.5km/hr (10/17kt) surf/sub	Commissioned: 1974
Surface Range: 7.040km (3800nm) at 10kt	Armament: Eight 533mm (21in) torpedo tubes
Displacement: 457/508t (450/500 tons) surf/sub	

Federal German Navy, Type 206 coastal submarine, 1974

Mines have always been a major element in Baltic naval operations, and the Type 206 was designed both to avoid them and to lay them. The compact hull design allows for eight bow tubes, for wire-guided torpedoes, Type DM2A1 (Seeaal) on the Type 206 boats, and DM2A3 (Seehecht) on the 206As. Diving depth was 200m (656ft).

BRITISH NUCLEAR SUBMARINES				
Class	Type	Number	Year	Note
Dreadnought	Hunter-killer	1	1960	Stricken 1982
Valiant	Hunter-killer	5	1963–70	Stricken 1990–92
Resolution	SSBN	4	1966–68	Stricken 1990s
Swiftsure	Hunter-killer	6	1971–79	
Trafalgar	Hunter-killer	7	1981–91	
Vanguard	SSBN	4	1992–99	
Astute	SSN	2	2006–	

scrapped by 1974, while *U12* was not decommissioned until 2005.

The follow-on class, Type 206, was built between 1968 and 1975, and like the 205s had hulls of high-strength non-magnetic steel. Twelve were modernized in the early 1990s as Type 206A. New features included the DBQS-21D sonar, new periscopes, a new LEWA weapons control system and GPS navigation. External containers enabling the boats to carry 24 ground mines were fitted. From 2010, all 206 and 206A boats have been decommissioned.

Great Britain

With the introduction of the Resolution class of SSBN, the role of maintaining Britain's weapons of nuclear deterrence passed from the Air Force to the Navy. Four suitable submarines were ordered, and the first to be commissioned was HMS *Resolution* on 2 October 1967. Bow and stern sections were constructed separately, and the US-designed missile compartment inserted between them. Resemblances to the US Navy's Lafayette class were clear, though the British boats had bow-mounted hydroplanes, and other specifically British features included the 'rafting' of the main machinery, an automated hovering system and welded hull valves.

Like the Valiant class, it had a Rolls Royce pressurized-water reactor and English Electric turbines. Sixteen Polaris A3 were carried. Operational patrols did not begin until 15 June 1968, with the class based with the 10th Submarine Squadron at Faslane, Scotland. As with other SSBNs, each boat had two crews serving alternate missions. In the course of the 1980s they were converted to carry the Polaris AT-K missile, with the British Chevaline MRV warhead. All were decommissioned between 1992 and 1996.

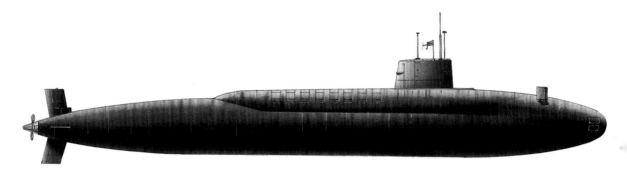

▲ **HMS Resolution**

Royal Navy, SSBN

HMS *Resolution* made its first Polaris launch on 15 February 1968, and remained in service for another 26 years, with a major upgrading of weapons and other systems in 1984. In 1991, it made the Royal Navy's longest Polaris patrol, of 108 days.

Specifications

Crew: 154

Powerplant: Single shaft; one pwr; steam turbines

Max Speed: 37/46.3km/hr (20/25kt) surf/sub

Surface Range: Unlimited

Displacement: 7620/8535t (7500/8400 tons)

surf/sub

Dimensions: 129.5 x 10.1 x 9.1m (425 x 33 x 30ft)

Commissioned: 2 October 1967

Armament: 16 Polaris A3TK SBM; six 533mm (21in) torpedo tubes

An updated version of the Valiant fleet submarine class, the Churchill class was formed of three SSNs commissioned in 1970–71. HMS *Churchill* was the first. As built, they were fitted with a Type 21 sonar array, replaced in the late 1970s by a Type 2020 hull-mounted array and a Type 2026 towed array. The six 533mm (21in) tubes could fire Mark 8 and Tigerfish torpedoes. From 1981, Harpoon anti-ship missiles were also carried. The Churchills were propelled by a shrouded pump-jet propulsor, quieter than any propeller and which produced the same speed for fewer revolutions. This feature was maintained in the next class of fleet submarines, the six Swiftsure boats, except for *Swiftsure* itself.

This class, commissioned between 1973 and 1981, showed a change in hull design, more cylindrical than its predecessors and 4m (13ft) shorter than the Churchills. The fin was reduced and retractable diving planes were placed below the water-line. They had a maximum diving depth of 600m (1980ft) and an underwater speed in excess of 30 knots. Both anti-submarine and anti-surface attack was envisaged,

Specifications

Crew: 116	surf/sub
Powerplant: Single shaft; one pwr; steam	Dimensions (length/beam/draught): 86.9 x 10.1 x
turbines	8.2m (285 x 33.25 x 27ft)
Max Speed: 37/53.7km/hr (20/29kt) surf/sub	Commissioned: 9 November 1971
Surface Range: Unlimited	Armament: Six 533mm torpedo tubes; Tigerfish
Displacement: 4470/4979t (4400/4900 tons)	torpedoes

▲ HMS Conqueror
Royal Navy, Churchill class SSN, Falklands, 1982

The Churchill class was essentially an improved version of the two Valiant boats. HMS *Conqueror* sank the Argentinian cruiser *General Belgrano* with Mk 8 torpedoes of World War II type on 2 May 1982 during the Falklands/Malvinas War. Later the class's torpedo armament was modernized.

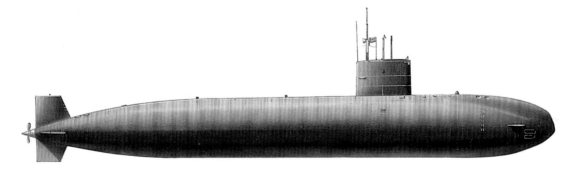

Specifications

Crew: 116	surf/sub
Powerplant: Single shaft; one pwr; steam	Dimensions (length/beam/draught): 82.9 x 9.8 x
turbines	8.5m (272 x 32.4 x 28ft)
Max Speed: 37/55.5km/hr (20/30kt) surf/sub	Commissioned: 17 April 1973
Surface Range: Unlimited	Armament: Five 533mm torpedo tubes;
Displacement: 4471/4979t (4400/4900 tons)	Tomahawk and Sub Harpoon SSMs

▲ HMS Swiftsure
Royal Navy, SSN

The class were deployed both for ASW screening duties with task-force groups and on independent patrol with anti-ship and anti-submarine capability. Like the Valiant and Churchill classes, they had an auxiliary diesel generator, 112-cell battery and electric motor. *Spartan* and *Splendid* were involved in the Falklands campaign of 1982. *Swiftsure* was decommissioned in 1992.

with the Mk 24 Tigerfish torpedo and the Sub Harpoon missile.

The comprehensive sonar suite featured the Type 2074 (active/passive search and attack), Type 2007 (passive), Type 2046 (towed array), 2019 (intercept and ranging) and Type 2077 (short range classification). HMS *Splendid* was the first British submarine to be fitted with Tomahawk cruise missiles, and fired them at land targets during the 1999 NATO strikes against Serbia. Last to be decommissioned was HMS *Sceptre* in 2010.

Italy

After training experience with ex-US submarines, Italy completed its first home-built submarines in 1968. These formed the four-strong Enrico Toti class, small vessels that were intended as interceptors and attack boats. The four torpedo tubes could fire the Whitehead Motofides A184 wire-guided torpedo, intended both for anti-ship and anti-submarine engagements, with a range of some 25km (15.5 miles) and an active/passive acoustic homing head with advanced countermeasures to spot enemy decoys.

Enrico Toti served in the Mediterranean Sea, achieving 220,480km (137,000 miles) on patrol duty round the coasts of Italy. All were decommissioned in 1991–93. *Enrico Toti* is preserved as a museum boat at Milan.

Japan

Japan's first fleet submarines since World War II were the Oshio class of 1967. In fact, *Oshio* itself differed significantly from the other four, with a larger bow structure and with a preliminary sonar fit. Also, the others were built of NS46 high-tensile steel and could operate at greater depths. *Harushio*, third to be commissioned, was more typical. They were multi-purpose boats, for patrol, surveillance, reconnaissance and crew training. The two stern torpedo tubes, intended for ASW defence, were later removed. All in the class were decommissioned by 1986.

The Soviet Union

The Echo class of SSGN falls into two groups: Project 659, the first five boats, was designated Echo I by NATO, and Project 675, the following 29, were Echo II. The Echo I boats, completed between 1960 and 1962, carried six launchers for the P-5 Pyatyorka (SS-N-3C Shaddock B) cruise missile. Their role was essentially a strategic one as they did not possess the fire-control and radar-detection equipment needed for attack boats.

Between 1969 and 1974, the cruise missiles were removed and the submarines converted to SSNs. All were deployed in the Pacific Fleet. Echo II were built at Severodvinsk and Komsomolsk between 1962 and 1967 for anti-ship warfare, with aircraft carriers particularly in mind. They carried eight P-6 (SS-N-

Specifications

Crew: 26	surf/sub
Powerplant: Single shaft; diesel engines; electric motor	Dimensions (length/beam/draught): 46.2 x 4.7 x 4m (151.66 x 15.46 x 13ft)
Max Speed: 25.8/27.8km/hr (14/15kt) surf/sub	Commissioned: 12 March 1967
Surface Range: 5556km (3000nm) at 5kt	Armament: Four 533mm (21in) torpedo tubes
Displacement: 532/591t (524/582 tons)	

▲ **Enrico Toti**

Italian Navy, coastal patrol submarine, 1967

Two Fiat MB820 diesels generated 2220hp (1640kW). Only six torpedoes were carried, but they were of a highly efficient kind. Built by Fincantieri in Monfalcone, the Toti class can be compared to the French Aréthuse and the German Type 205 classes in size and functions.

ITALIAN POST-WAR SUBMARINES				
Class	Type	Number	Year	Note
Da Vinci	Attack	3	1954–66	ex-US Gato class, 1942–43
Torricelli	Attack	2	1955–75	ex-US Balao class, 1944–45
Longobardo	Attack	2	1974–87	ex-US Tench class, 1948
Piomarta	Attack	2	1975–87	ex-US Tang class, 1952
Enrico Toti	Attack	4	1965–97	
Nazario Sauro	Attack	8	1970–93	4 in service (III and IV Sauro)
U-212A	Patrol	2	2006–09	Co-built with Germany

JAPANESE POST-WAR SUBMARINES				
Class	Type	Number	Year	Note
Kuroshio	Patrol	1	1955	ex USS *Mingo;* stricken 1966
Oyashio	Patrol	1	1960	Stricken 1976
Asashio	Attack	4	1964–69	In service to 1986
Uzushio	Attack	7	1968–78	Teardrop hull; in service 1971–96
Yushio	Attack	10	1980–89	In service to 2006
Harushio	Patrol	7	1987–97	4 used in training
Oyashio	Patrol	11	1994–2006	In service
Soryu	Patrol		2009	

3a Shaddock A) anti-ship cruise missiles, which could only be fired from a surfaced position. In order to effect guidance of a fired missile, the boat had to remain surfaced until mid-course correction and final target selection had been made: the element of vulnerability is clear.

Fourteen boats were modified to carry the P-500 Bazalt (SS-N-12 Sandbox) anti-ship cruise missile.

Specifications

Crew: 80

Powerplant: Twin shaft; two diesel engines; two electric motors

Max Speed: 25.8/33.3km/hr (14/18kt) surf/sub

Surface Range: 16,677km (9000nm) at 10kt

Displacement: 1650/2150t (1624/2116 tons)

surf/sub

Dimensions (length/beam/draught): 88 x 8.2 4.9m (288.65 x 27 x 16.18ft)

Commissioned: 25 February 1967

Armament: Eight 533mm (21in) torpedo tubes

▲ **Harushio**

Japanese Maritime Self-Defence Force, Oshio class patrol submarine, 1967

The Oshio class were built by Mitsubishi and Kawasaki at Kobe. Two Kawasaki diesels produced 2900hp each (2162kW) and the two electric motors developed 6300hp (4698kW). Innovations included aircraft-type controls and a five-bladed propeller.

This had a range of 550km (340 miles) and three were further upgraded with the P-1000 Vulkan (GRAU 3M70) with a 700km (430-mile) range. But by the early 1980s, the Echo I and II were becoming obsolete. All of Echo I were decommissioned by 1989; Echo II were decommissioned between 1989 and 1995.

Project 667A began in 1962 and the first submarine, *K-137*, was launched in 1964 and commissioned into the Northern Fleet at the end of 1967. Between 1967 and 1974, 33 more were added. The hull was cylinder-shaped and the front hydroplanes were re-sited on the sail. There was a touch of irony in their NATO designation of 'Yankee', as the Soviets were considered to have used stolen US plans in designing the class. As usual with Soviet practice, two reactors were installed, of the pressurized-water type. To reduce noise, new propellers were devised, the pressure hull was covered with sound-absorbing rubber and the external hull with antihydroacoustic coating. The footings under the propulsion systems were also isolated by rubber buffers. The Yankee I SSBNs were equipped with the 'Cloud' battle management system, which could receive signals up to a depth of 50m (165ft) with the help of a Paravan towed antenna. The first four employed the Sigma navigation system, whereas the follow-on ships were

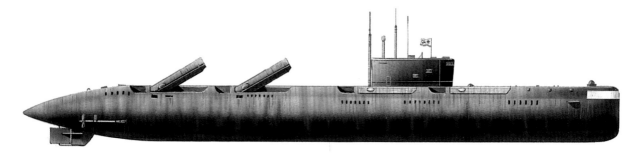

▲ Echo class
Soviet Navy, SSGN/SSN

The launch tubes, installed above the pressure hull, are shown in erected mode. Six missiles were carried. Echo II submarines carried eight and were 5 metres (16.5ft) longer to accommodate the additional tubes. At least four Echo class boats are believed to have suffered serious accidents.

Specifications
Crew: 90	surf/sub
Powerplant: Twin shaft; one pwr; two steam turbines	Dimensions (length/beam/draught): 110 x 9 x 7.5m (360.9 x 29.5 x 24.58ft)
Max Speed: 37/51.8km/hr (20/28kt) surf/sub	Commissioned: 1960
Surface Range: Unlimited	Armament: As SSGN, six SS-N-3C cruise missiles; two 406mm (16in) torpedo tubes
Displacement: 4572/5588t (4500/5500 tons)	

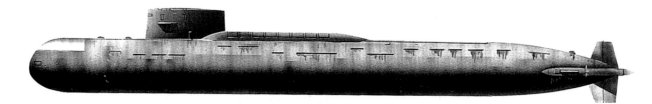

Specifications
Crew: 120	Dimensions (length/beam/draught): 129.5 x 11.6 x 7.8m (424.9 x 38 x 25.6ft)
Powerplant: Two shaft; two pwr; turbines	Commissioned: 1967
Max Speed: 37/55.5km/hr (20/30kt) surf/sub	Armament: 16 SS-N-6 SBM; six 533mm (21in) torpedo tubes
Surface Range: Unlimited	
Displacement: 7925/9450t (7800/9300 tons) surf/sub	

▲ Yankee class
Soviet Navy, SSBN

Through the 1970s, at least three Yankee submarines were stationed at strategic distances from the US mainland, with one or two on the way out or home, some of which must have passed close to US submarines on similar missions in the opposite direction.

SOVIET POST-WAR DIESEL-ELECTRIC SUBMARINES				
Project/(NATO name)	Type	Number	Year	Note
613, 664, 665 (Whiskey)	Coastal	236	1949–58	5 variants; retired by 1989
611 (Zulu)	Attack	26	1952–57	
615 (Quebec)	Coastal	30	1952–57	Retired in 1970s
633 (Romeo)	Attack	20	1957–61	560 planned; 113 exported
641 (Foxtrot)	Attack	74	1957–83	Retired by 2000
651 (Juliet)	Missile	16	1967–69	Retired by 1994
641B (Tango)	Attack	18	1972–82	
877 (Kilo)	Attack		1980–82	Some still active
636 (Improved Kilo)	Attack	49	1982–	Some still active; 30+ for export
677 Lada/Petersburg	Patrol	1	2004	Project suspended

▲ Charlie I

Soviet Navy, SSGN

This was the first Soviet SSGN capable of launching surface-to-surface missiles without having to surface first. With a high submerged speed and armed with SS-N-15 anti-submarine missiles, it also had hunter-killer capabilities.

Specifications

Crew: 100

Powerplant: Single shaft; one pwr; steam turbine

Max Speed: 37/50km/hr (20/27kt) surf/sub

Surface Range: Unlimited

Displacement: 4064/4877t (4000/4800 tons) surf/sub

Dimensions (length/beam/draught): 94 x 10 x 7.6m (308 x 32.75 x 25ft)

Commissioned: 1967

Armament: Eight SS-N-7 cruise missiles; six 533mm (21in) torpedo tubes

Specifications

Crew: 31

Powerplant: Single shaft; liquid-metal reactor; two steam turbines,

Max Speed: 37/77.8km/hr (20/42kt) surf/sub

Surface Range: Unlimited

Displacement: 2845/3739t (2800/3680 tons)

surf/sub

Dimensions (length/beam/draught): 81 x 9.5 x 8m (265.75 x 31.18 x 26.25ft)

Commissioned: 1970

Armament: Six 533mm (21in) torpedoes, nuclear warheads; 36 mines

▲ Alfa class

Soviet Navy, high-speed SSN

The appearance of this class caused hurried rethinking in the US submarine command, which assumed, incorrectly, that it was capable of operating at very deep levels. Faster submarines, and deep-running torpedoes, were made a high priority.

equipped with the Tobol – the first Soviet satellite-linked navigational system.

The Yankee class were armed with 16 R-27 (SS-N-6 Serb) missiles, carried within the hull, unlike their predecessors. They had to come relatively close to the United States to target inland centres like Chicago or Kansas City. Nevertheless, they were a powerful threat, and the first Soviet SSBN to seriously challenge US boats. As a result of changing strategic requirements, and the arms limitation agreements, a number of variant Yankee types appeared, in most cases without ballistic missiles, and carrying cruise missiles or converted to SSN. Decommissioning of the class, in all configurations, began in the late 1980s and was complete by 1995.

Between 1968 and 1972, 11 Project 670A Charlie I submarines were commissioned. A compact SSGN, it was unique among Soviet boats at the time by having a single reactor and propeller. The Charlie I was originally designed to carry the SS-N-9 anti-shipping cruise missile. When this was not ready in time, the SS-N-7, a modified version of the SS-N-2 Styx, was substituted. Either 11 or 12 Charlie I submarines, carrying eight SS-N-7s of approximately 48km (30-mile) range, were built between 1967 and 1972 at a rate of about two a year.

Six Charlie II submarines, each with 8 SS-N-9s of 96km (60-mile) range, followed between 1972 and 1980. Charlie II carried the SS-N-9 missile originally planned for the Charlie I class, along with an

Specifications

Crew: 60	surf/sub
Powerplant: Twin shaft; diesel-electric	Dimensions (length/beam/draught): 92 x 9 x 7m
Max. speeds: 37/29.6km/hr (20/16kt) surf/sub	(301.85 x 29.5 x 24ft)
Surface Range: 22,236km (12,000nm) at 10kt	Commissioned: 1971
Displacement: 3251/3962t (3200/3900 tons)	Armament: Six 533mm (21in) torpedo tubes

▲ **Tango class**

Soviet Navy, patrol-attack submarine

Unprecedentedly high battery capacity enabled the Tango class to run submerged for a week before requiring to use their snorkels. A rubberized hull coating helped to make them hard to detect. They carried 24 torpedoes. The fin design is distinctive.

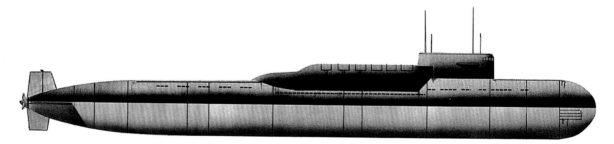

Specifications

Crew: 120	Dimensions (length/beam/draught): 150 x 12 x
Powerplant: Single shaft; two pwr; turbines	10.2m (492 x 39.33 x 33.5ft)
Max Speed: 35.2/46.3km/hr (19/25kt) surf/sub	Commissioned: 1971
Surface Range: Unlimited	Armament: 12 SS-N-8 SBM; six 457mm (18in)
Displacement: 7925/10,160t (7800/10,000 tons)	torpedo tubes
surf/sub	

▲ **Delta class**

Soviet Navy, SSBN

The Delta class reverted to the Soviet two-reactor arrangement (pressurized water-cooled system), with twin propellers. Capable of operating under the Arctic ice-cap, it was equipped with the Tobol-B navigation system and the Cyclone-B satellite navigation system.

improved fire control system. In January 1988, the Soviets leased a Charlie I to India, where it served until January 1991 as the *Chakra*. Since the mid-1990s, all Charlie I and Charlie II have been on the reserve list.

In 1972, the Soviet Union completed the world's first titanium-hulled submarine, which was also the fastest, with a maximum underwater speed believed to be 44.7 knots. Numbered *K-222*, it remained a one-off, known as the Papa class by NATO, but was followed by the Lira class submarine (Project 705). Known as *Alfa*, no one could say this was lifted from US designs.

The profile, with the sail blending smoothly into the hull, was unique. Its hull was also made of titanium, stronger and lighter than steel. It could travel at 41 knots and, it was believed, could outdive the US Mk 48 torpedo. As a high-speed interceptor craft, the Alfa class was really ahead of its time, and only seven were built, between 1971 and 1981. Its level of automation made it complex to operate, and there were difficulties with the reduced crew levels, especially in problematic situations. Its reactor (a single one) was a new design with a lead-bismuth liquid-metal cooling system, which despite its power gave numerous operating difficulties. All were decommissioned by 1990.

The Soviets, however, had not given up on building conventionally powered boats, and so, between 1972 and 1982, 18 diesel-electric submarines of Project 641B Som (Catfish; Tango class to NATO) were built. These were large attack submarines; their size being dictated by the need for ever-more complex electronic systems as well as more sophisticated weaponry. The diesel powerplant was identical to that of the later Foxtrots. Tango boats were deployed with the Black Sea and Northern fleets and were capable of long-range reconnaissance and intelligence-gathering missions.

After the shock of the Alfa class, the Soviet Navy unveiled what was perhaps a more serious threat to the security of the NATO powers, Project 667B Murena (Eel), or the Delta 1 class. This large SSBN was a major step forward from the Yankees, equipped with R-29 (SS-N-8 Sawfly) missiles with a range of 7800km (4846 miles).

The United States' new Poseidon missiles did have such a range. The first Delta I, K279, was completed in 1972, and a further 17 were built up to 1980. All the Delta I boats were decommissioned by the end of the twentieth century.

Spain

By the 1970s, the Spanish Navy was badly in need of modern submarines. It had five ex-US Balao class boats of World War II vintage, all ready for retirement. To replace them, it acquired four submarines of the French Daphné design, built under licence in Cartagena in 1973–75, and known as the Delfin class after the first to be commissioned.

The sonar suite comprised DUUA-2B, DSUV 22A, and DUUX-2A, and a DLT-D-3 fire control

▲ **Marsopa**

Spanish Navy, Delfin/Daphné class patrol submarine

Marsopa's last major outing was to take part in the Spontex 3 exercise in May 2003, a NATO combined-operations test with ships of many nations, to see whether the 'Blues' could effect a troop landing against the opposition of the 'Orange' vessels. It was decommissioned in 2006.

Specifications

Crew: 45	surf/sub
Powerplant: Twin shaft; two diesel engines; two electric motors	Dimensions (length/beam/draught): 58 x 7 x 4.6m (189.66 x 22.33 x 15ft)
Max Speed: 24.9/29.6km/hr (13.5/16kt) surf/sub	Commissioned: 1975
Surface Range: 8338km (4300nm) at 5kt	Armament: 12 552mm (21.7in) torpedo tubes
Displacement: 884/1062t (870/1045 tons)	

SWEDISH POST-WAR SUBMARINES				
Class	Type	Number	Year	Note
Hajen	Patrol	6	1954–58	Decommissioned
Draken	Patrol	6	1960–61	Decommissioned
Sjöörmen	Patrol	5	1967–68	Decommissioned
Näcken	Patrol	3	1978–79	Decommissioned
Västergötland	Patrol	2	1983–90	Active
Gotland	Patrol	3	1992–97	Active
Södermanland	Patrol	2	2003–04	Improved Västergötland

system was installed. In general, the electronics were an improvement on the French boats. Based at Cartagena, though deployed at different times both on Spain's Atlantic and Mediterranean coasts, the Delfin class participated in exercises with US Naval groups. All are now decommissioned.

Sweden

With the Sjöörmen class, Sweden once again claimed a place among the leaders of diesel-electric submarine design. Five boats formed the class, commissioned between July 1968 and September 1969. They incorporated numerous features developed by the Kockums shipbuilding form and the Swedish Navy, including a form of the x-rudder first seen on USS *Albacore*. Anechoic tiles damped the sound and the submerged speed of 20 knots was

fast for a conventional submarine of the time. In Swedish service until the early 1990s, they were modernized and refitted for tropical waters and became Singapore's Challenger class, four for service plus one for spare parts.

United States

The United States launched 41 SSBNs between 1960 and 1966. This massive force fielded 656 Polaris nuclear missiles, and comprised five classes, all generally similar in size, appearance and performance, but each one incorporating successive improvements in electronic systems.

Many were adapted for roles other than that of missile submarine. Benjamin Franklin class USS *George Washington Carver* was commissioned on 15 June 1966 and was deployed from the forward base at

Specifications

Crew: 18

Powerplant: Single shaft; four diesel engines; one electric motor

Max Speed: 27.8/37km/hr (15/20kt) surf/sub

Surface Range: Not available

Displacement: 1143/1422t (1125/1400 tons)

surf/sub

Dimensions (length/beam/draught): 51 x 6.1 x 5.8m (167.25 x 20 x 19ft)

Commissioned: 31 July 1976

Armament: Four 533mm (21in) and two 400mm (15.75in) torpedo tubes

▲ **Sjoormen**

Swedish Navy, ASW patrol submarine

Anti-submarine action was the prime purpose of the class, and its short length and round Albacore-type hull make it highly manoeuvrable. It is also very quiet-running. In 1984–85, all were upgraded with new Ericsson IBS-A17 combat data and fire-control systems.

Rota, Spain. The prime difference between the Franklins and the preceding James Madison class was quieter machinery, giving them a low acoustic signal for the time. All were powered by the well-tried S5W pressurized-water reactor. Following overhaul in 1977, its Polaris A3 missiles were replaced by Poseidon C-3, but it was not among those further converted to carry Trident-1 missiles. *George Washington Carver* was decommissioned on 18 March 1993.

On 12 July 1969, USS *Narwhal* was commissioned. This was a one-off SSN, built to hold the new S5G reactor, a pressurized-water reactor but with a different cooling system to the S5W. Based on 'natural circulation', with the reactor set low and steam generators set high, its advantage was greater quietness in operation.

Narwhal was indeed a very quiet boat and was used in many stealth operations off the Soviet coasts. Some of its innovatory systems were adopted for the subsequent Ohio class, but the Navy did not adopt the 'natural cooling' system. It was deactivated on 16 January 1999.

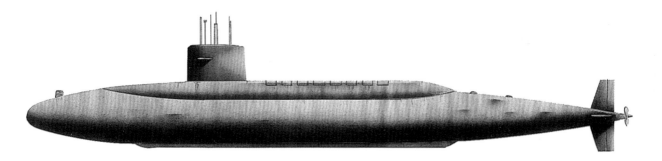

▲ USS George Washington Carver

US Navy, Lafayette class SSBN

Built at Newport News, Virginia, *George Washington Carver* made 73 patrols as a 'Boomer' up to 1991. Conversion to SSN of a large submarine with only four torpedo tubes and a large sealed missile silo can hardly have been very effective, even though it could fire Mk45 nuclear-tipped torpedoes.

Specifications

Crew: 140

Powerplant: Single shaft; one S5W pwr; steam turbines

Max Speed: 37/55.5km/hr(20/30kt) surf/sub

Surface Range: Unlimited

Displacement: 7366/8382t (7250/8250 tons)

surf/sub

Dimensions (length/beam/draught): 129.5 x 10 x 9.6m (425.8 x 32.8 x 31.8ft)

Commissioned: 15 June 1966

Armament: 16 Trident C4 SLBM and four 533mm (21in) torpedo tubes

Specifications

Crew: 141

Powerplant: Single shaft; one SSG natural circulation pwr; turbines

Max Speed: 33.3/48.2km/hr (18/26kt) surf/sub

Surface Range: Unlimited

Displacement: 4251/5436t (4450/5350 tons)

surf/sub

Dimensions (length/beam/draught): 95.9 x 11.6 x 7.9m (314.66 x 38 x 25.9ft)

Commissioned: 12 July 1969

Armament: SUBROC and Sub Harpoon missiles; four 533mm (21in) torpedo tubes

▲ USS Narwhal

US Navy, reconnaissance SSN

The four torpedo tubes were mounted amidships to allow for a bow-mounted sonar system in addition to a towed sonar array. Many of *Narwhal*'s features remain classified; it could probably hold remote-control underwater vehicles, and had sophisticated detection equipment for eavesdropping on Soviet communications.

Last years of the Cold War
1975–89

The long stand-off gradually begins to ease, but nuclear submarines remain the key elements in global strategy and gain new tactical roles.

ALTHOUGH PLANNED and ordered before the Falkland/Malvinas War of 1982, the Argentinian Navy did not take delivery of the TR-1700 Santa Cruz class submarine until 1984. Designed by Thyssen-Nordseewerke, they are the biggest submarines built in Germany since World War II.

Originally six boats were provided for: two to be built in Germany and four others under licence in Argentina – two more TR-1700s and two smaller TR-1400 types (later revised back to TR-1700). In the event, construction on the remaining four was suspended in the 1990s, though plans exist to restart the programme. The TR-1700 class is a long-range, high-speed SSK with a diving depth of 300m (990ft), and operating endurance of 30 days, extendable to 70 days. While intended as attack boats, they also have the capacity to carry and land small parties of special forces. *Santa Cruz* was modernized in 1999–2001 in a Brazilian yard, and its sister *San Juan* is also undergoing a refit. The Argentinian Navy still states an intention to develop nuclear submarines.

Brazil

Brazil's Tupi class patrol submarine was inaugurated in 1989. Designed and built by Howaldtswerke-Deutsche Werft (HDW) in Kiel, Germany, a variant on the German U-209 class, it was followed by three others built at the Arsenal de Marinha at Rio in 1994–99. Operating from the Almirante Castro e Silva base on Moncague Island, the Tupi boats are armed with British Tigerfish wire-guided torpedoes and Brazilian anti-submarine torpedoes developed by the Naval Research Institute (IPqM). An 'improved Tupi' boat, *Tikuna*, was launched in March 2005, and there is a long-term plan for nuclear propulsion to be installed in this hull design.

China

The Type 092 (NATO codename *Xia*) was China's first ballistic missile submarine. Laid down in September 1970, it shared the hull form of the Type 091 but lengthened to hold the missile compartment, under a raised deck behind the sail. The pressurized-

▲ **Santa Cruz**

Argentinian Navy, TR-1700 type patrol-attack submarine

Based at Mar del Plata, this high-performance boat has four MTU diesels driving a single shaft, and a Varta-made battery of 8 x 120 cells. A diver's lockout is fitted. Sonar is an STW Atlas Elektronik CSU-83 suite with Thales DUUX-5 passive array, and an integrated battle and data system, with plotting table, is fitted.

Specifications

Crew: 29

Powerplant: Single shaft; diesel-electric

Max Speed: 27.8/46.3km/hr (15/25kt) surf/sub

Surface Range: 22,224km (12,000nm) at 8kt

Displacement: 2150/2,300t (2116/2264 tons) surf/sub

Dimensions (length/beam/draught): 66 x 7.3 x 6.5m (216.58 x 23.9 x 21.25ft)

Commissioned: October 1984

Armament: Six 533mm (21in) torpedo tubes

water reactor and turbo-electric drive are also taken from the Type 091.

Launch did not take place until 1981 and it was officially commissioned in August 1983. The *Xia* initially carried 12 JuLang I (CSS-N-3) single-warhead ballistic missiles, first tested on 30 April 1982, though successful submerged firing from the *Xia* was not made until September 1987. During a major refit between 1995 and 2001, longer-range JuLang 1A SLBMs were installed. Since the mid-1980s, the *Xia* has been based at Qingdao naval base, and remains technically on the active list.

France

Having established its nuclear striking force with the Redoutable class, the French Navy began to develop

CHINESE NUCLEAR SUBMARINES			
Class	Type	Number	Year
Han, Type 091	Patrol/attack	5	1970s
Xia, Type 092	SSBN	1	1983
Jin, Type 094	SSBN	2+	2006
Shang, Type 093	Attack	2+	2006

an SSN from 1974 and the class leader *Rubis* was laid down in December 1976. Eight boats were planned and six were eventually completed. *Rubis* was commissioned on 23 February 1983. Substantial redesign was made with the final two boats, incorporating a rounded bow rather than the original blunt front, and the first four boats were rebuilt

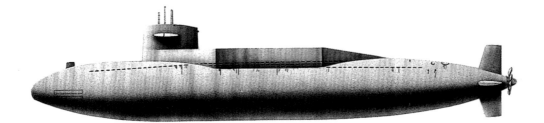

Specifications

Crew: 30

Powerplant: Four diesel engines; four alternators; single electric motor

Max Speed:18/44.4km/hr (10/24kt) surf/sub

Surface Range: 20,000km (11,000nm) at 10kt

Displacement: 1422.4/1586t (1400/1550 tons)

surf/sub

Dimensions (length/beam/draught): 61.2 x 6.25 x 5.5m (200.8 x 20.5 x 18ft)

Commissioned: 1989

Armament: Eight 533mm (21in) torpedo tubes; 16 torpedoes

▲ Tupi

Brazilian Navy, Type 209/1400 patrol-attack submarine

Brazil shares with Argentina a stated desire to develop a nuclear reactor to power submarines. Meanwhile, the Tupi class is powered by four German 12V 493 A280 GAA 31L diesels from MTU, driving four Siemens alternators rated at 1.8mW, giving a total output of 9655hp.

▲ Xia

Chinese Navy, SSBN

The prime value of the *Xia* to the PNLA has been in solving technical problems whose solutions can be applied to the following Type 094 class. To mount an effective nuclear deterrent requires at least three SSBNs, of which at least one has to be at sea at any given time.

Specifications

Crew: 140

Powerplant: Single shaft; one pwr; turbo-electric drive

Max Speed: 40.6km/hr (22kt) submerged

Surface Range: Unlimited

Displacement: Not released

Dimensions (length/beam/draught): 120 x 10 x 8m (393.58 x 33 x 26.16ft)

Commissioned: April 1961

Armament: 12 JL1 SBM; six 533mm (21in) torpedo tubes

between 1989 and 1995 to the same shape, which considerably reduced their noise level and also provided space for upgraded sonar equipment. The relatively light weight of the French-designed K48 pressurized-water reactor helped to keep the boats to an exceptionally compact size for SSNs, though they were provided with diesel-electric auxiliary motors. The weapons control system is the DLA 2B and DLA 3, with the SAT ('système d'armes tactique') tactical data system. Based at Toulon, the class is set to be displaced over the next few years by the Barracuda class SSN.

Great Britain

From 1983, the Trafalgar class has formed the basis of the Royal Navy's hunter-killer submarine capacity. Ordered in April 1977, *Trafalgar* was completed in 1983 and all seven were in service by July 1986. Developed from the Swiftsure class, the Trafalgars have a new reactor core, pump-jet propulsion and

anechoic-tiled hulls. Technical problems have dogged the class and in August 2000 only one boat was operational while others underwent refit or repair. HMS *Tireless* was stranded at Gibraltar for much of 2000 with a leak in the reactor primary cooling circuit. By 2005, it was officially stated that the problems had been resolved.

In 2001, HMS *Trafalgar* took part in Operation Veritas, launching Tomahawk missiles against targets in Afghanistan. HMS *Triumph* was part of the support fleet for the invasion of Iraq in 2003, again firing Tomahawks against land targets. During the Libyan campaign of 2011, *Triumph* fired six Tomahawks against Libyan air defence systems. HMS *Trafalgar* was decommissioned in 2009; the others are scheduled to be gradually replaced as the Astute class joins the Royal Navy.

In the early 1980s, British naval planners considered that there was still a role for conventionally powered submarines, and in 1983

FRENCH NUCLEAR SUBMARINES				
Class	Type	Number	Year	Note
Le Redoutable	SSBN	5	1972–80	Decommissioned
Rubis	SSN	6	1988	Decommissioned
Amethyste	SSN	2	1992–93	Improved Rubis
Le Triomphant	SSBN	4	1997–2010	
Barracuda	SSN	3+	2016	In progress

▲ **Rubis**

French Navy, Saphir class SSGN

The Saphir class carry Exocet SM39 anti-ship missiles, fired from the torpedo tubes; ECAN L5 mod three torpedoes equipped with active and passive homing to a range of 9.5km (6 miles); and ECAN F17 mod two torpedoes, wire-guided, with active and passive homing to a range of 20km (12 miles). They can carry 14 missiles/torpedoes.

Specifications

Crew: 67

Powerplant: Single shaft; one auxiliary diesel-
electric motor

Max Speed: 46.3km/hr25/25kt)

Surface Range: Unlimited

Displacement: 2423 /2713t (2385/2670 tons)

surf/sub

Dimensions (length/beam/draught): 72.1 x 7.6 x
6.4m (236.5 x 24.9 x 21ft)

Commissioned: 23 February 1983

Armament: Exocet SSM; four 533mm (21in)
torpedo tubes

orders were placed for four Type 2400 boats, beginning with HMS *Upholder*; plans for a further eight were cancelled. *Upholder* was finally commissioned in June 1990 and all four were in service by 1993. Despite initial problems with the torpedo firing systems, they were regarded as an effective class, though the hoped-for export sales did not happen. By the early 1990s, it was decided that diesel-electric submarines were not to form part of the British fleet and the Upholders were decommissioned. In 1998, they were sold to Canada and commissioned as the Victoria class in the Royal Canadian Navy between 2000 and 2004, two stationed at Esquimalt, British Columbia, and two at Halifax, Nova Scotia.

Israel

The first Israeli Navy submarines were former British S- and T-class boats of World War II, and the Gal class were its first modern boats. Based on the German Type 206A, they were built for the specific needs of Israel as a small, manoeuvrable boat intended for coastal and inshore operations. Although a German design, they were built in the British yard of Vickers at Barrow in Furness. *Gal* grounded on its way from England to Israel, but was repaired, and was commissioned in 1976, followed by two others. The full mission history of these boats has not been published, but they were undoubtedly involved in many clandestine landing operations, especially during periods of hostilities such as the 1982 Lebanon

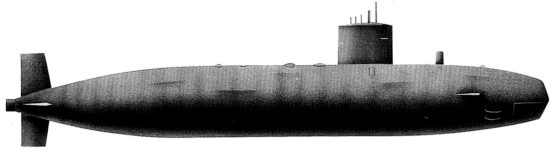

Specifications

Crew: 130	Dimensions (length/beam/draught): 85.4 x 10 x
Powerplant: One pwr; turbines; pump-jet	8.2m (280.16 x 33.16 x 27ft)
Max Speed: 37/59.1km/hr (20/32kt) surf/sub	Commissioned: 7 February 1987
Surface Range: Unlimited	Armament: Tomahawk and Sub Harpoon SSM,
Displacement: 4877/5384t (4800/5300 tons)	five 533mm (21in) torpedo tubes
surf/sub	

▲ **HMS Torbay**

Royal Navy, Trafalgar class SSN

The class was first fitted with Type 2020 sonar, but Torbay was re-equipped with Type 2076 passive search towed array, claimed to be the most advanced and effective in the world. Electronic warfare and decoy systems are: two SSE Mk8 launchers for Type 2066 and Type 2071 torpedo decoys; RESM Racaul UAP passive intercept; CESM Outfit CXA; and SAWCS decoys.

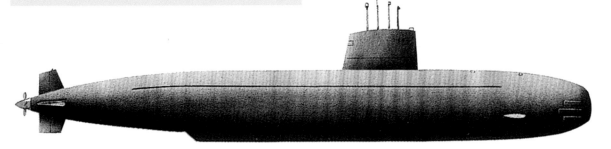

Specifications

Crew: 47	Dimensions (length/beam/draught): 70.3 x 7.6 x
Powerplant: Single shaft; diesel-electric	5.5m (230.6 x 25 x 17.6ft)
Max Speed: 22.2/37km/hr (12/20kt) surf/sub	Commissioned: June 1990
Surface Range: 14,816km (8000nm) at 8kt	Armament: Sub harpoon SSM; six 533mm (21in)
Displacement: 2203/2494t (2168/2455 tons)	torpedo tubes
surf/sub	

▲ **HMS Upholder**

Royal Navy, patrol submarine

The streamlined teardrop-form single hull is of NQ 1 high-tensile steel. Glass-fibre fins reduce both weight and noise and enable a 20-knot underwater speed. Much of the technology of the nuclear fleet was incorporated, with high levels of automation. A five-man lockout chamber is fitted in the fin.

war. In 1983, they were upgraded to carry the UGM-84 Harpoon missile and its fire-control system. The original Mk37 torpedoes were replaced in 1987 by NT37E types. Further overhauls in 1994–95 provided improved sensors and fire-control systems. The class was decommissioned in 2003. *Gal* is kept as a museum boat in Haifa.

Italy

After the Enrico Toti boats of the 1960s, the next class was the four Sauro patrol submarines, completed between 1980 and 1982, Italy's last home design. The Sauros were much larger, with a wider range and greater versatility than their predecessors. The tall sail had wide hydroplanes and an extended rear lip. Test diving depth for the class was 300m (984ft), though the hull strength can withstand pressures down to 600m (1970ft) for a brief period. In the 1980s and 1990s, two improved Sauro classes appeared, each of two boats.

Giuliano Prini was the second boat of the Salvatore Pelosi class of 1988–89. The Primo Longobardo class of 1993 had improved combat systems, and were significantly upgraded in 2004, being given new acoustic sensors, Harpoon anti-ship missiles, the ATLAS Elektronik ISUS 90-20

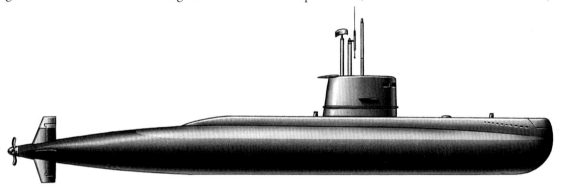

▲ Nazario Sauro

Italian Navy, patrol-attack submarine

Problems with the batteries caused delay in commissioning *Nazario Sauro*, and the second unit, *Carlo Fecia de Cossato*, was commissioned before it (1979 and 1980 respectively). Anti-ship and ASW operations were the designers' prime concern. The Sauros carried 12 torpedoes.

Specifications

Crew: 45

Powerplant: Single shaft; diesel-electric

Max Speed: 20.3/37km/hr (11/20kt) surf/sub

Surface Range: 12,970km (7000nm) at 10kt

Displacement: 1479/1657t (1456/1631 tons) surf/sub

Dimensions (length/beam/draught): 63.9 x 6.8 x 5.7m (209.6 x 22.33 x 18.66ft)

Commissioned: 1980

Armament: Six 533mm (21in) torpedo tubes

Specifications

Crew: 22

Powerplant: Single shaft; two diesel engines; one electric motor

Max Speed: 20.3/31.5km/hr (11/17kt) surf/sub

Surface Range: 7038km (3800nm) at 10kt

Displacement: 427/610t (420/600 tons) surf/sub

Dimensions (length/beam/draught): 45 x 4.7 x 3.7m (147.7 x 15.4 x 12.18ft)

Commissioned: December 1976

Armament: Eight 533mm (21in) torpedo tubes

▲ Gal

Israeli Navy, Type 206 patrol-attack submarine

It is likely that Israel's submarines have been used more often and intensively than any others in coastal and offshore operations, including much activity along the Lebanese coast in the late 1970s and 1980s. Short but intensive patrols and missions are the normal pattern.

weapons control system, and new communications. The improved Sauros are expected to serve until 2015 and 2030 respectively. Only one of the original Sauros remains, as a training boat. A proposal to sell them to the United States for refurbishment and onward sale to Taiwan came to nothing.

Japan

Japan's 10-strong Yuushio class of attack submarine is a development of the preceding Uzushio class, larger and with enhanced diving capacity, the test diving depth being 275m (902ft). Commissioned between 1980 and 1989, they are of double-hull construction and follow the US practice of midship-mounted, outward-angled torpedo tubes in order not to impede the operation of the bow sonar array. From 1984, new boats were fitted to carry the Sub-Harpoon anti-ship missile, and all but *Yuushio* were retrofitted for this weapon. *Yuushio* was used as a training boat from 1996, and the last of the class to be in service was withdrawn in 2008.

The Harushio class, which progressively took over from the Yuushios, is slightly larger than the Yuushios and with improved noise reduction, anechoic material being applied to the hull and fin surfaces. The profiles are very similar, though the Harushio class sail is somewhat higher and shorter. Greater hull strength, using NS 110 high-strength steel, enables a diving depth of at least 300m (984ft) and perhaps as great as 500m (1640ft). Seven boats were built

between 1989 and 1997, with the last, *Asashio*, built to a modified design and with greater systems automation, reducing its crew to 71. It also has AIP propulsion.

Netherlands

The Dutch Navy began evaluation of a new class of modern diesel-electric attack submarines in 1972, but it was 1990 before the first was commissioned, and four were in service by July 1994. They have an X-configuration of four combined rudders and stern diving planes, used also on the Swedish Sjöormen class, the Australian Collins class and the German Type 212A, which is a major aid to quiet operation. Diving depth, officially 300m (984ft), is probably nearer 400m (1310ft), due to a hull fabricated from French MAREI high-tensile steel. The Dutch submarines lead active lives, on regular patrols and also operating in the North Sea and Atlantic with other NATO vessels, but going as far afield as the Caribbean and the Somali coast in joint ventures against piracy and drug-running.

Peru

One of the most widely used submarine types is the German-designed Type 209. Development work began in the late 1960s and the first boats were launched in 1971. The Type 209 has never been used by the German Navy, but between 1971 and 2008, 61 were commissioned for 13 other navies. It is

▲ Giuliano Prini
Italian Navy, 'improved Sauro' class patrol submarine

Very little different to the Sauros in dimensions, outline and internal layout, the Pelosi class have the same armament but improved sonar, with IPD-703 active/passive, MD1005 passive flank and M5 intercept. Operational endurance is 45 days. They are based with the Second Submarine Group at Augusta, Sicily.

Specifications

Crew: 50	Dimensions (length/beam/draught): 64.4 x 6.8 x 5.6m (211.16 x 22.25 x 18.4ft)
Powerplant: Single shaft; diesel-electric	
Max Speed: 20.3/35.2km/hr (11/19kt) surf/sub	Commissioned: 1989
Surface Range: 17,692km (9548nm) at 11kt	Armament: Six 533mm (21in) torpedo tubes
Displacement: 1500/1689t (1476/1662 tonnes) surf/sub	

closely based on the IKL Type 206 design. Single-hulled, with a test depth of 500m (1640ft), it is a versatile craft that lends itself to many tasks and can carry a variety of different armaments. In 1975, the Peruvian Navy acquired two Type 209/1100 submarines, and between 1980 and 1983 a further four of Type 209/1200. The Peruvian Navy's aim was to keep four boats in service at any one time, but it is unclear whether this is being maintained, as its Type 209/1200s are due for refitting.

The Soviet Union

From 1972, Soviet Russia developed the Project 667 BDR Kalmar class, codenamed Delta III by NATO. Fourteen were built between 1976 and 1982, double-hulled, with a large, broad turtle-back missile silo set behind the sail. The 16 missiles were R-29R (SS-N-18, Stingray), the first multiple-warhead rockets to be carried on Soviet submarines. Delta III boats were assigned both to the Northern Fleet (at Sayda and Olyenya, then Yagyelnaya from the early 1990s) and the Pacific Fleet based on the Kamchatka Peninsula. Rather than operate in the Atlantic, they were often stationed under thinner sections of the Arctic ice cap. The sail-mounted hydroplanes could be rotated to vertical when breaking through ice. Withdrawal began in the mid-1990s, and in 2010 it was estimated that four were still active. Between 1985 and 1992, seven Delta IV boats were built, under Project 667BDRM. Very similar to the Delta IIIs, they are

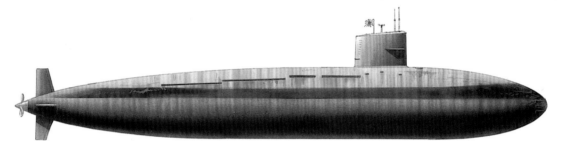

Specifications

Crew: 75	surf/sub
Powerplant: Single shaft; diesel-electric	Dimensions (length/beam/draught): 76 x 9.9 x
Max Speed: 22.2/37km/hr (12/20kt) surf/sub	7.5m (249.25 x 32.5 x 24.6ft)
Surface Range: 17,603km (9500nm) at 10kt	Commissioned: 1980
Displacement: 2235/2774t (2200/2730 tons)	Armament: Six 533mm (21in) torpedo tubes

▲ **Yuushio**

Japanese Maritime Self-Defence Force, patrol submarine

The Japanese Maritime Self-Defence Force is more reticent than some navies about its submarines. The torpedoes carried on the Yuushio class were Type 89 active-passive with a maximum range of 50km (31 miles). Electronic equipment included ZQQ-5 bow sonar (modification of the US BQS-4) and the ZQR towed array.

▲ **Harushio**

Japanese Maritime Self-Defence Force, long-range patrol submarine

This class has a 4630km (2877-mile) greater range than the Yuushio, giving it a longer sea endurance. Its greater displacement is accounted for by increased fuel capacity and more electronic equipment. Crew levels in both classes are the same. Japan keeps submarines permanently on patrol.

Specifications

Crew: 75	Dimensions (length/beam/draught): 77 x 10 x
Powerplant: Single shaft; diesel-electric	7.75m (252.6 x 32.8 x 25.33ft)
Max Speed: 22.2/37km/hr (12/20kt) surf/sub	Commissioned: 1990
Surface Range: 22,236km (12,000nm) at 10kt	Armament: Sub Harpoon SSM; six 533mm (21in)
Displacement: surfaced 2489t (2450/2750 tons)	torpedo tubes
surf/sub	

quieter in operation, with more effective hydroacoustic coating and new five-bladed propellers. All were in service with the Northern Fleet at the end of 2011, though one was damaged in a dockyard fire on 29 December 2011.

Simultaneous with the Delta III class was a new fast attack boat in the form of Project 671RTM, Shchuka (Pike), known to NATO as Victor III. Between 1978 and 1992, a total of 26 were added to the fleet. The Victor IIIs have a 6m (20ft) hull extension forward of the fin and a pod mounted above the upper rudder, from which a towed sonar array could be extended. This enlargement provided

for the additional electronic equipment required to process data from the towed array and two new flank arrays. Another prime requirement of the design was quiet running: the Victor I and Victor II classes had been shown to be too easily traceable. Clusterguard anechoic coatings decrease noise levels and bow hydroplanes retract into the hull at high underwater speeds or when surfaced. Very few, if any, Victor III boats remain in service as of 2011.

In the late 1970s, the Rubin Design Bureau was working on Project 941, *Akula*, an SSBN that could carry 20 long-range missiles, each with up to 10 MIRV nuclear warheads – a total of 200 nuclear

▲ Walrus

Netherlands Navy, patrol-attack submarine

In 2000, the entire class was temporarily withdrawn while problems with the closing valves on the diesel exhaust system were dealt with. From 2007, the four Walrus boats have been refitted and upgraded and can now fire the Mk 48 mod-7 torpedo.

Specifications

Crew: 49	surf/sub
Powerplant: Single shaft; diesel-electric	Dimensions (length/beam/draught): 67.5 x 8.4 x
Max Speed: 24/37km/hr (13/20kt) surf/sub	6.6m (222 x 27.6 x 21.66ft)
Surface Range: 18,520km (10,000nm) at 9kt	Commissioned: 1990
Displacement: 2490/2800t (2450/2775 tons)	Armament: Four 533mm (21in) torpedo tubes

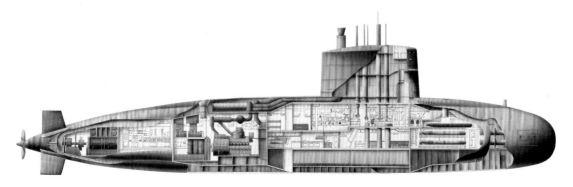

Specifications

Crew: 49	surf/sub
Powerplant: Single shaft; diesel-electric	Dimensions (length/beam/draught): 67.5 x 8.4 x
Max Speed: 24/37km/hr (13/20kt) surf/sub	6.6m (222 x 27.6 x 21.66ft)
Surface Range: 18,520km (10,000nm) at 9kt	Commissioned: 1988
Displacement: 2490/2800t (2450/2775 tons)	Armament: Four 533mm (21in) torpedo tubes

▲ Zeeleeuw

Netherlands Navy, Walrus class patrol-attack submarine

The hull form is based on the *Zwaardvis* (1972), but with ESM radar systems upgraded in 2000; Thomson Sintra TSM 2272 Eledone Octopus, GEC Avionics Type 2026 towed array, Thomson Sintra DUUX 5B passive ranging and intercept sonar; and DECCA 1229 surface search radar. Fire Control is HSA SEWACO VIII action data automation, GTHW integrated.

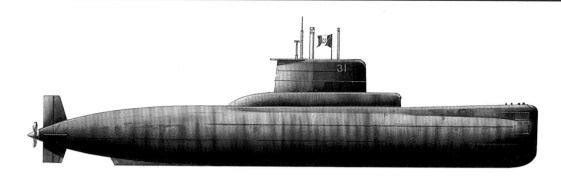

Specifications

Crew: 35	Displacement: 1122/1249t (1105/12340 tons)
Powerplant: Single shaft; four diesel engines;	surf/sub
one electric motor	Dimensions: 56 x 6.2 x 5.5m (183.75 x 20.25 x
Max Speed: 18/40.6km/hr (10/22kt) surf/sub	18ft)
Surface Range: 4447km (2400nm) at 8kt	Commissioned: 19 December 1980
	Armament: Eight 533mm (21in) torpedo tubes

▲ **Angamos**

Peruvian Navy, Type 209 patrol-attack submarine

They are intended for coastal operations rather than oceanic patrols. *CSU-83* active/passive sonar is fitted as well as DUUX 2 intercept sonar. They carry 14 A-184 SST (Special Surface Target) torpedoes. The two 209/1100 boats were upgraded in Peru in 2008. The Type 209/1200 *Angamos* was formerly named *Casma*.

weapons. This was comparable with the US Ohio class, but Trident missiles were much lighter than the the Soviet RSM-52 (SS-N-20 Sturgeon), and the submarine had to be scaled accordingly. Given the reporting name Typhoon by NATO, it was the largest submarine yet to be constructed. The design includes features for travelling under ice and ice-breaking through ice cover up to 3m (9ft 10in) thick. The new-design stern fin has horizontal hydroplane fitted behind the screws, and the nose horizontal hydroplanes are retractable into the hull. In the main body, two pressure hulls lie parallel with a third, smaller pressure hull above them, producing the bulge just below the sail; and two other pressure hulls for torpedoes and steering gear. Maximum diving depth is 400m (1312ft). *Typhoon* can spend at least 120 days submerged.

From September and December 2005, the Typhoon *Dmitriy Donskoy* has been carrying out flight tests of a new solid fuel SLBM, the SS-N-30 Bulava, reported to have a range of more than 8000km (5000 miles). Six Typhoons were commissioned, with a seventh launched but never completed. Three have been scrapped, with two on reserve. Current deployment is limited to the *Dmitriy Donskoy*.

The Oscar class nuclear-powered cruise missile attack submarine, displacing around 18,289 tonnes (18,000 tons) submerged, was designed, as with earlier SSGNs, primarily to attack US aircraft carrier

battle groups. Though said to be slow to dive and cumbersome in manoeuvre, they are credited with a submerged speed of about 30 knots – sufficient to keep pace with their targets. *Oscar II* is about 10m (33ft) longer than *Oscar I*, with a substantially enlarged fin, and replaces *Oscar I*'s four-bladed propeller with a seven-bladed screw. It carries three times as many anti-ship cruise missiles as earlier Charlie and Echo II class submarines. The missiles are launched underwater from tubes fixed at an angle of approximately 400 and arranged in two rows of 12 each, on each side of the sail. The two Oscar I boats were stricken in 1996. Around five Oscar II remained active at the end of 2011, three with the Northern Fleet and two with the Pacific Fleet.

Rubin Bureau designed a new diesel-electric submarine in the late 1970s, Project 877 Paltus (*Halibut*), or *Kilo*. The first entered service with the Soviet Navy in 1980, and 23 others were added up to 1992. Exports were made to Algeria, China, India, Iran, Poland, Romania and Vietnam. It was superseded by Type 636, Improved Kilo, one of the quietest diesel submarines yet built, and equipped with a multi-purpose combat and command system. Most of the Type 636 boats are still active or in reserve. Orders from other countries include 10 for the People's Republic of China, delivered 1997–2005, and two for Algeria (2009), with others ordered for Vietnam with delivery dates post-2013. Sales to Egypt and Venezuela are also being explored.

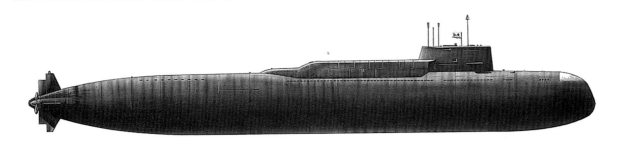

Specifications

Crew: 130

Powerplant: Twin shaft; two pwr; turbines

Max Speed: 26/44.4km/hr (14/24kt) surf/sub

Surface Range: Unlimited

Displacement: 10,791/13.463t (10,550/
13,250 tons) surf/sub

Dimensions (length/beam/draught): 160 x 12 x
8.7 (524.9 x 39.4 x 28.5ft)

Commissioned: 30 December 1976

Armament: 16 SS-N-8 SLBM; four 533mm (21in)
torpedo tubes

▲ Delta III

Soviet Navy, Kalmar class SSBN

The Delta III were fitted with the Almaz-BDR battle-management system for firing deep-water torpedoes. They had the Tobo-M-1 and then the Tobol-M-2 inertial navigation systems and a hydroacoustic navigational system codenamed by NATO as 'Bumblebee', using hydroacoustic buoys to determine position.

▲ Victor III

Soviet Navy, SSN

The class is powered by two OK-300 pressurized water reactors with two turbine generators, driving a single shaft. Two auxiliary diesel-electric motors are provided. The radiated noise level is very low, comparable with the US Los Angeles boats. Maximum diving depth is 400m (1312ft).

Specifications

Crew: 100

Powerplant: Single shaft; two VM-4T pwr; steam
turbine

Max Speed: 44.4/55.5km/hr (24/30kt) surf/sub

Surface Range: Unlimited

Displacement: 4775 x 7305t (4700/7190 tons)

surf/sub

Dimensions (length/beam/draught): 104 x 10 x
7m (347.75 x 32.8 x 23ft)

Commissioned: 1972

Armament: SS-N-15/16/21 SSM; six 533mm
(21in) torpedo tubes

Specifications

Crew: 175

Powerplant: Twin shaft; two pwr; turbines

Max Speed: 44.4/46.3km/hr (12/25kt) surf/sub

Surface Range: Unlimited

Displacement: 18,797/26,925t (18,500/
26,500 tons) surf/sub

Dimensions (length/beam/draught): 171.5 x 24.6
x 13m (562.6 x 80.6 x 42.5ft)

Commissioned: 12 December 1981

Armament: 20 SS-N-20 SLBM; four 630mm
(25in) and two 533mm (21in) torpedo tubes

▲ Typhoon

Soviet Navy, SSBN

The two reactors drive two 50,000hp steam turbines and four 3200kW turbogenerators. Twin propellers are seven-blade, fixed-pitch shrouded. The two built-in thrusters on the bow and stern are telescopic turning screw rudders, powered by a 750kW motor. Despite their huge bulk, these are perhaps the quietest Soviet submarines yet built.

▲ Oscar I

Soviet Navy, SSGN

Like most Soviet submarines, the *Oscar* has a double hull – an inner pressure hull and an outer hydrodynamic hull, with 20cm (8in) of rubber between them to muffle sounds. The 3.5m (11.5ft) separation between the *Oscar*'s inner and outer hulls provides significant reserve buoyancy and improved survivability against conventional torpedoes.

Specifications

Crew: 130	Dimensions (length/beam/draught): 143 x 18.2 x
Powerplant: Twin shaft; two pwr; turbines,	9m (469.18 x 59.66 x 29.5ft)
Max Speed: 40.7/55.5km/hr (22/30kt) surf/sub	Commissioned: April 1980
Surface Range: Unlimited	Armament: SS-N-15/16/19 SSM; four 650mm
Displacement: 11,685/13,615t (11,500/13,400	(25.6in) and four 533mm (21in) torpedo tubes
tons) surf/sub	

▲ Kilo

Soviet Navy, patrol-attack submarine

Kilo is formed of six watertight compartments separated by transverse bulkheads in a pressurized double-hull. This design and the submarine's good reserve buoyancy lead to increased survivability if the boat is holed, even with one compartment and two adjacent ballast tanks flooded.

Specifications

Crew: 45	surf/sub
Powerplant: Single shaft; three diesels; three	Dimensions (length/beam/draught): 69 x 9 x 7m
electric motors,	(226.4 x 29.5 x 23ft)
Max Speed: 27.8/44.4km/hr (15/24kt) surf/sub	Commissioned: 1980 (first units)
Surface Range: 11,112km (6000nm) at 7kt	Armament: Six 533mm (21in) torpedo tubes
Displacement: 2494/393t (2455/3143 tons)	

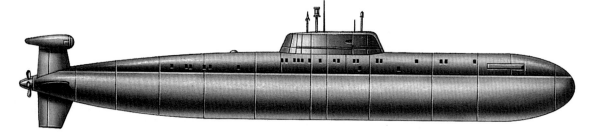

Specifications

Crew: 61	Dimensions (length/beam/draught): 107 x 12.5 x
Powerplant: Single shaft; one pwr; single turbine	8.8m (351 x 41 x 28.9ft)
Max Speed: 18/59.2km/hr (10/32kt) surf/sub	Commissioned: 1987
Surface Range: Unlimited	Armament: SS-N-15 and SS-N-21 SSMs; four
Displacement: 7112/8230t (7000/8100 tons)	650mm (25.6in) and four 533mm (21in)
surf/sub	torpedo tubes

▲ Sierra

Soviet Navy, SSN

The hull has six major compartments: torpedo room and battery; crew quarters, officers' mess and galley; command centre, computer complex and diesel generators; reactor; main switchboard, pumps and geared turbines; and electric motors, steering gear and pumps. A crew escape chamber is capable of bringing up the entire crew from a depth of 460m (1510ft).

▲ Kilo class

A Kilo class submarine makes contact with warships from the Indian Navy. The Kilo class can be easily identified by their teardrop-shaped hull.

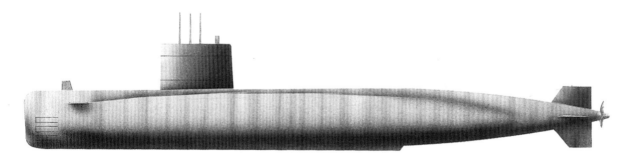

▲ Galerna

Spanish Navy, Agosta-type patrol-attack submarine

Two of *Galerna*'s sister boats, *Tramontana* and *Mistral*, were engaged in Operation Protector off the coast of Libya during March to June 2011. *Mistral* is currently undergoing a major refit at Cartagena, intended to keep it viable until 2020, leaving two of the class in service; the fourth has been withdrawn.

Specifications

Crew: 54	surf/sub
Powerplant: Single shaft; diesel-electric	Dimensions (length/beam/draught): 67.6 x 6.8 x
Max Speed: 22.2/37km/hr (12/20kt) surf/sub	5.4m (221.75 x 22.33 x 17.75ft)
Surface Range: 13,672km (7378nm) at 9kt	Commissioned: 1983
Displacement: 1473/1753t (1450/1725 tons)	Armament: Four 551mm (21.7in) torpedo tubes

For 10 years, Project 945 had been working on an attack submarine that could outfight any other, resulting in a single SSN, commissioned in September 1984, with a second in 1987, both classified by NATO as Sierra I. With some different features, two more Project 945A Kondor (Sierra II) were completed in 1992 and 1993, after the fall of the Soviet Union.

Hull construction is of titanium alloy, providing very deep diving capability, to 700m (2300ft) with an outer maximum of 800m (2625ft) and the ability to avoid magnetic anomaly detection. Further

additions to the class were cancelled in favour of of the new Project 971 Akula class. The first Sierra I, named first *Karp*, then *Tula*, has been withdrawn. Its sister, *Krab*, is on the active list, as are the two Sierra II, *Nizhniy Novgorod* and *Pskov*.

Spain

Four submarines of the French Agosta class, built at Cartagena, were commissioned in 1983–86. Designated SSK, they are versatile and adaptable boats, forming the main element of the Spanish Navy's submarine arm into the twenty-first century.

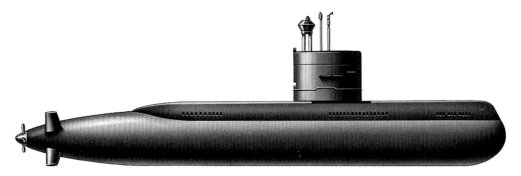

▲ **Näcken**

Swedish Navy, patrol-attack submarine

US Kollmorgen periscopes were fitted and all boats had the Data Saab NEDPS combined ship control and action information system. Wire-guided torpedoes of passive Type 613 for anti-ship strikes were fitted, as well as Type 431 active/passive anti-submarine torpedoes fired from the 400mm (15.7in) tubes.

Specifications

Crew: 19	Dimensions (length/beam/draught): 44 x 5.7 x
Powerplant: Single shaft; diesel-electric	5.5m (144.33 x 18.66 x 18ft)
Max Speed: 37/46.3km/hr (20/25kt) surf/sub	Commissioned: 25 April 1980
Surface Range: 3335km (1800nm) at 10kt	Armament: Six 533mm (21in) and two 400mm
Displacement: 996/1168t (980/1150 tons)	(15.7in) torpedo tubes
surf/sub	

Specifications

Crew: 28	Dimensions (length/beam/draught): 48.5 x 6.1 x
Powerplant: Single shaft; diesel-electric	5.6m (159.18 x 20 x 18.4ft))
Max Speed: 19.8/37km/hr (11/20kt) surf/sub	Commissioned: 27 November 1987
Surface Range: Not released	Armament: Six 533mm (21in) and three 400mm
Displacement: 1087/1161t (1070/1143 tons)	(15.75in) torpedo tubes
surf/sub	

▲ **Västergotland**

Swedish Navy, patrol-attack submarine

A high-performance single-hulled patrol-attack submarine. Bow and stern parts were built at the Karlskrona yard, and the central section by Kockums at Malmö. They have x-format stern control planes and other features include a Pilkington Optronics search periscope with night vision.

Sea endurance range is 45 days and diving depth is 300m (984ft). Sensors and processing equipment include Thomson CSF DRUA 33 radar, Thomson Sintra DSUV 22, DUUA 2D, DUU 1D, DUUX 2 sonar plus DSUV 62A towed array. Updating and upgrading of equipment has taken place. In 2011, *Galerna* was fitted with a WECDIS NAV/C2S system, which integrates information from the navigation sensors with official ENC (electronic nautical cartography) data.

Sweden

Sweden ordered three new submarines in 1972, from Kockums at Karlskrona. Commissioned in 1980–81, officially the A-14 type, they were usually known as the Näcken class, after the lead boat. Of compact design, with teardrop hull and two internal decks, their prime function was to intercept incursions into Swedish territorial waters. Deep diving was not required and maximum operational depth was 150m (490ft), but they were highly manoeuvrable. In 1987–88, *Näcken* was lengthened by 8m (26ft 3in) to accommodate two United Stirling Type V4 closed-cycle engines, with liquid-oxygen fuel. The AIP drive gave it a submerged endurance of 14 days. The electronics were updated in the early 1990s, but were all withdrawn later in the decade, except *Näcken*, transferred to Denmark as *Kronborg* on a buy-or-lease arrangement between 2001 and 2005, and currently stored at Karlskrona.

Four SSK boats of the A-17 or Västergotland class were commissioned between 1987 and 1989. In 2003–04, the second two were refitted, extended by 12m (37ft), and provided with Stirling-type AIP engines as tested on *Nacken*. New weapons systems and stealth improvements were incorporated, and in this form they were redesignated as the Södermanland class, considered by many experts to be the quietest and most effective 'conventional' submarines in service anywhere. The first two boats were refitted for service in high-salinity tropical waters and sold to Singapore in 2008 as the Archer class. Sweden's two Södermanland class boats remain in service.

Taiwan

At times during the Cold War, relations between Taiwan (Republic of China) and the People's Republic of China were extremely tense. For coastal defence, Taiwan ordered two SSK type boats from the Netherlands. As the Hai Lung (Sea-dragon) class, a modified version of the Dutch *Zwaardvis* attack submarine, they were commissioned in October 1987 and April 1988.

Beijing's diplomatic pressure prevented a further sale of four boats in 1992, and so far Taiwan has been unable to enlarge its submarine fleet. In 2008, the United States allowed the sale of UGM-84 Harpoon Block II missiles to Taiwan and it is believed that the

▲ Hai Lung

Taiwanese Navy, improved Zwaardvis type patrol submarine

The Zwaardvis type teardrop hull design was in turn based on that of USS *Barbel*, the last US diesel-electric submarine. *Hai Lung*'s dimensions were almost identical. Power came from three diesel engines rated at 42,000hp (3100kW) driving a Holec electric motor of 5100hp (3800kW) and a single shaft.

Specifications

Crew: 67

Powerplant: single shaft; three diesel engines; one electric motor

Max Speed: 19.8/37km/hr (11/20kt) surf/sub

Surface Range: 19,000km (10,241nm) at 9kt

Displacement: 2414/2702t (2376/2660 tons)

surf/sub

Dimensions (length/beam/draught): 66 x 8.4 x 7.1m (216.5 x 27.6 x 23.33ft)

Commissioned: 1987

Armament: Six 533mm (21in) torpedo tubes

two Hai Lung boats have the capacity to deploy these, in addition to their AEG SUT dual-purpose wire-guided, active/passive homing torpedoes. Late in 2011, it was reported that the Taiwanese Government is now considering construction of its own submarines.

United States

The Los Angeles or 688 class of fast attack submarine is numerically the largest in the world, with 62 commissioned between 1976 and 1996. They are equipped for anti-submarine warfare, intelligence gathering, show-of-force missions, insertion of special forces, strike missions, mining, and search and rescue. The last 23 boats, built since 1982, beginning with USS *San Juan,* known as Improved 688, incorporate upgraded weapons and electronic systems, are quieter in operation and are configured for under-ice operation, with the diving planes moved from the sail to the bow.

Other developments include an improved propulsion system and Navstar Global Positioning System (GPS) guidance capability. The LA class has participated in all US global operations. Nine were deployed in the Gulf War in 1991, during which Tomahawk missiles were launched from two of the submarines. Twelve were deployed in support of Operation Iraqi Freedom in March to April 2003. All launched Tomahawk TLAM missiles. Later operations have included strikes on targets in Yemen (2009) and Libya (2011). Forty-three remain on active duty.

▲ **USS *Los Angeles***

Submarines of this class were used in 'indication and warning' service, running ahead of nuclear-powered carriers in the build-up to the Gulf War.

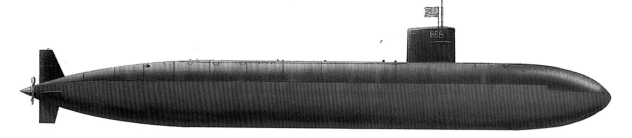

▲ **USS Los Angeles**

US Navy, SSN

The hull contains two separate watertight compartments, with crew, weapons and control space forward, and most machinery systems aft. The GE PWR S6G reactor needs refuelling only after 30 years' operation. Maximum diving depth is at least 450m (1475ft). Five have been adapted with Dry Dock shelters to allow entrance and exit of SEAL forces.

Specifications

Crew: 133

Powerplant: Single shaft; one S6G pwr; turbines

Max Speed: 37/59.2km/hr (20/32kt) surf/sub

Surface Range: Unlimited

Displacement: 6180/7038t (6082/6.927 tons) surf/sub

Dimensions (length/beam/draught): 110.3 x 10.1 x 9.9m (362 x 33 x 32.25ft)

Commissioned: 13 November 1976

Armament: Tomahawk Land Attack missiles; Harpoon SSM; four 533mm (21in) torpedo tubes

USS *San Francisco*, commissioned on 24 April 1981, was stationed from 1981 to 1986 at Pearl Harbor. Following a modernization there in 1989–90, it was deployed in the Western Pacific and from 2002 was based at Apra Harbor, Guam. On 8 January 2005, travelling submerged at approximately 61m (200ft) and at full speed of 25 knots, it struck an uncharted undersea mountain. The forward ballast tanks ruptured and the sonar dome was wrecked, but the inner hull was not breached and the crew were able to bring the boat to the surface. A number of failures in procedures were later identified. *San Francisco*, with a normal life expectancy to 2017, was repaired, its bow section replaced by that of the about-to-be-retired USS *Honolulu*; and in 2009 it resumed service based at San Diego, California.

The basis of the United States' strategic nuclear deterrent remains the Ohio class of SSBN, the largest submarines built for the US Navy, with 18 commissioned between 1981 and 1997.

They carry up to 24 submarine-launched ballistic missiles with multiple independently targeted warheads. Originally, these were Trident I C4, but from the ninth boat, USS *Tennessee*, they carry the Trident II D5, and older boats have been retrofitted. Following the START II arms limitation treaty of June 1992, four were altered from SSBN to SSGN, carrying Tomahawk missiles and capable of tactical operations with special operations forces. Conversion was not completed until 2008. All in this class carry highly sophisticated countermeasures systems, including AN/WLY-1 from Northrop Grumman, providing automatic response against torpedo attack.

Fourteen Ohio class SSBNs were on the active list in November 2011. The four SSGN boats are also still in service.

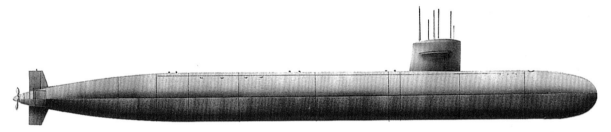

Specifications

Crew: 133

Powerplant: Single shaft; one S6G pwr;, turbines

Max Speed: 37/59.2km/hr (20/32kt) surf/sub

Surface Range: Unlimited

Displacement: 6180/7038t (6082/6.927 tons) surf/sub

Dimensions (length/beam/draught): 110.3 x 10.1 x 9.9m (362 x 33 x 32.25ft)

Commissioned: 24 April 1981

Armament: Tomahawk Land Attack missiles; Harpoon SSM; four 533mm (21in) torpedo tubes

▲ USS San Francisco
US Navy, Los Angeles class SSN

As of 2011, 42 of the Los Angeles class were on the active list, assigned to home ports at Groton, Connecticut; Norfolk, Virginia; Pearl Harbor, Hawaii; San Diego, California; Apra Harbor, Guam; and Bremerton, Washington. The class is evenly divided between the Atlantic and Pacific Fleets.

▲ USS Ohio
US Navy, SSBN

The Ohio class like all SSBNs is designed for long-term patrols and they can remain submerged for up to 70 days. The main machinery is the GE PWR S8G reactor with two turbines providing 60,000hp (44,740kW) and driving a single shaft. Major overhauls are required only at 15-year intervals.

Specifications

Crew: 155

Powerplant: Single shaft; one S8G pwr;, two turbines

Max Speed: 44.4/51.8km/hr (24/28kt) surf/sub

Surface Range: Unlimited

Displacement: 16,360/19,050t (16,764/ 18,750 tons) surf/sub

Dimensions (length/beam/draught): 170.7 x 12.8 x 11m (560 x 42 x 36.4ft)

Commissioned: 11 November 1981

Armament: 24 Trident C4 SLBMs; four 533mm (21in) torpedo tubes

Chapter 5

Post-Cold War:
1990–Present

While the US and Russian submarine fleets
continued their patrols and exercises, the end of the Soviet
Union signalled a lower level of rivalry and tension, and the
numbers of nuclear submarines carrying long-range missiles
were greatly reduced. In submarine deployment, attention
switched from oceanic strategy to regional hot spots and
theatres of localized action. China, France, Great Britain,
Russia and the United States all developed new classes
of nuclear submarines, with the emphasis on hunter-killer
abilities, and other nations announced their intention to
join the nuclear club. Meanwhile, new self-contained
power systems and a high level of 'stealth' qualities
also brought about renewed interest in the potential
of the non-nuclear submarine.

◀ USS *Seawolf*

Seen here on trials in 1997, *Seawolf* proved quieter and more manoeuvrable than the Los
Angeles class. But its high cost ruled out further development.

Introduction

With the ending of the Cold War, international naval issues switched from superpower confrontation to the problems raised by regional rivalries and instabilities. This brought a focus on the tactical deployment of submarines in combined and shoreline operations.

AT A STEADY 25 KNOTS, a typical SSN (fast-attack submarine) will cover 1110km (690 miles) in 24 hours, and 7773km (4830 miles) in seven days. Anywhere on the open seas is within a few days' reach, at most, of a nuclear submarine. By contrast, the diesel-engined British submarine *Onyx* took almost four weeks to reach the Falklands war zone in 1982.

From 1990, the world political scene has been typified by localized hot spots and problem areas. Although all the nuclear-armed powers kept missile submarines at sea on secret patrol, the number of US and Russian active 'boomers' was greatly reduced. In

1989, over 400 nuclear submarines were operational or under construction. By 2011, three quarters had been decommissioned or dismantled. The majority of remaining boats, and of new builds, were designated SSN, or hunter-killers, though this plays down their versatility in intelligence-gathering, special operations and in firing missiles at static land targets, in the course of regional operations. SSNs' roles in operations like the Libyan campaign in 2011 and the Iraq War of 2005 have been largely restricted to providing defence and support to task force groups. Bombardment of land targets from submarines was a

▲ **Collins class**

The Australian Navy Collins class consists of six diesel-electric submarines armed with torpedoes and Harpoon anti-shipping missiles. The blunt-ended bow and the hydroplanes set forward on the fin are trademarks of the class.

EVOLUTION OF THE GERMAN SUBMARINE FROM TYPE 201 TO TYPE 206

Type	Year	Surface displacement tons/tonnes	Submerged displacement tons/tonnes	Speed knots	Range km/miles	Propulsion	Armament
201	1962–64	450/457	443/450	17.5	4800/2982	D/E	Torpedoes/mines
205	1967–70	450/456	500/508	17	7800/4847	D/E	Torpedoes/mines
206	1968–75		490/498	17	8300/5157	D/E	Torpedoes/mines

EVOLUTION OF THE GERMAN SUBMARINE FROM TYPE 209 TO TYPE 214

Type	Year	Surface displacement tons/tonnes	Submerged displacement tons/tonnes	Speed knots	Range km/miles	Propulsion	Armament
209	1971–	1427/1,450	1781/1810	22.5	20,000/12,427	D/E	Torpedoes; UGM-84 missile
212	2002	1663/1,690	1801/1830	20	14,800/9196	D/E +AIP	Torpedoes; short-range missiles
214	2007–		1830/1860	20	19,300/11,992	D/E +AIP	Torpedoes; UGM-84 missile

minor aspect. Possibly secret operations along coastlines were also involved.

By 2010, the US Navy had 71 active nuclear submarines, of which 18 carried ballistic or guided missiles and the rest were SSNs (the US SSN force has been cut by almost 40 per cent since 1994; one consequence of reduction has been to extend crew deployment from six to seven months at a time, from March 2007). The Russian Navy had approximately 13 SSN-type nuclear boats and eight missile carriers. Great Britain had eight SSN and four SSBN, while France had six SSN and four SSBN, and China was believed to have some 12 nuclear submarines, mostly of SSN type. India is about to join the nuclear submarine club, and Argentina and Brazil have announced the same ambition or intention.

Important advances have also been made with non-nuclear submarines. On more than one occasion in the last two decades, a non-nuclear boat has shown itself capable of passing undetected through supposedly unerring detection systems. The US Navy got a shock in late 2007 when a Chinese Type 039 – completely undetected – surfaced in the middle of a carrier group, well within striking range of the nuclear carrier *Kitty Hawk*.

The ocean floor is nowadays mapped almost as extensively as the land surface. Highways and lurking areas are identified, followed and used. On one such route, the French missile boat *Le Triomphant* and the British SSN *Vanguard* were involved in a glancing collision in mid-Atlantic in February 2009 (both were repaired). Submarines can cut telephone cables and lay others, and plant 'road signs' either for their own use or to mis-route others.

In recent years, submarine construction has slowed, and not merely because of global economic downturn. Submarines and their attack, detection and defence systems have become hugely expensive. When a new one, even of conventional drive, costs in excess of $400 million, buyers hesitate. Yet world demand for reliable, effective and up-to-date submarines is greater than ever. The French Scorpène competes for orders against such rivals as the German Type 214 and the Russian Kilo.

Even the United States has had to introduce the Technology Barriers (TB or Tango Bravo) programme to lower the cost of attack submarines, and speed up the replacement rate. It includes: propulsion concepts not constrained by a centreline shaft; externally stowed and launched weapons (especially torpedoes); conformal alternatives to the existing spherical sonar array; technologies that eliminate or substantially simplify current hull, mechanical and electrical systems; and automation to reduce crew workload (and numbers) for standard tasks.

Submarines today
1990–2011

The submarine has come a long way from the submersible torpedo boats of a century ago.

POSSESSING MORE DESTRUCTIVE power than all the capital ships of World War I, whether seen as a weapon of aggression or an instrument of peace-keeping, the submarine is unquestionably a marvel of technology and a key piece in international power-play.

Australia

The Royal Australian Navy (RAN) contracted for six diesel electric SSK boats with the Swedish builders, Kockums in June 1987. Construction work was done partially in Sweden and partially at Adelaide, and the boats were commissioned into the RAN between 1996 and 2003. Australia's strategic concerns required a long-range boat, and the Collins class, with a range of 18,496km (11,500 miles) at 10 knots, and a sea endurance of 70 days, are capable of extended patrols.

Sophisticated electronic systems are standard, including the ES-5600 electronic support sensor. Two Strachan and Henshaw submerged signal and decoy ejectors (SSDE) are carried; the forged unit containing the ejector barrel and water ram is welded into the hull. *Collins* deploys the Thales Underwater Systems Scylla active and passive bow array sonar, and passive flank, intercept and ranging arrays.

The class has been subject to numerous problems and no more than two or three are operational at any one time. Their service life is expected to last until 2025, and further refitting with US assistance is in progress. Since 2007, a project for replacement by an Australian-designed submarine, with an enlarged fleet of 12 boats, has been under way to ensure continuity of RAN submarine capability.

China

China maintains development of diesel-electric submarines. The Type 039 (codenamed Song by NATO) was first commissioned in June 1999: an ocean-going SSK with a teardrop-shaped hull. Revisions to the design came early, and only the first boat has a sail with a stepped-up rear section; all subsequent boats are classed as 039G. A multi-role combat and command system provides all the data needed for control of the boat and for the firing of torpedoes and missiles. This is likely to be an updated derivative of the combat/command system used in the

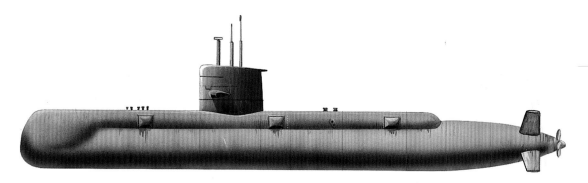

▲ **Collins**

Royal Australian Navy, patrol submarine

The *Collins* has a single skew-back propeller, powered by three Hedemora/Garden Island Type V18B/14 four-stroke turbo charged diesels, each providing 1475kW. Jeumont Schneider of France supplied the three 1400kW 440V DC generators. The main motor is a water cooled DC shunt, double armature motor with rated power of 5250kW.

Specifications

Crew: 42

Powerplant: Single shaft; Diesel-electric

Max Speed: 18/37km/hr (10/20kt) surf/sub

Surface Range: 18,496km (9982nm) at 1kt

Displacement: 3100/3407t (3051/3353 tons) surf/sub

Dimensions (length/beam/draught): 77.8 x 7.8 x 7m (255.18 x 25.6 x 23ft)

Commissioned: 27 July 1996

Armament: Sub Harpoon SSM; six 533mm (21in) torpedo tubes

Ming class submarines. The integrated sonar system comprises an active/passive medium-frequency spherical bow-mounted equipment and passive low-frequency reach arrays. The countermeasures suite comprises just the Type 921-A radar warning receiver and directional finder. The diesel-electric propulsion arrangement comprises four German MTU 16V396 SE diesel engines, four alternators and one electric motor, powering a single shaft.

Around 13 Song boats are in service, forming the basis of Beijing's modern conventional fleet, along with the 039A or Yuan class currently under development. Their prime use is likely to be in maintaining Chinese claims to islands like the Spratly group in the South China Sea, and monitoring the US observation-ships stationed just off China's territorial limits.

The next generation of Chinese attack submarines is the Type 093 (NATO codename Shang) replacement for the Han class. Two boats have been launched, and the first, after four years of trials, was commissioned into the PNLA Navy in 2006. The second may also be in service. Powered by a pressurized water reactor and with a new bow sonar and three flank arrays (H/SQG-207) on each side of the hull, it can fire wire-guided torpedoes and launch YJ-82 AshMs anti-ship missiles. It is likely that further Type 093 SSNs (six to eight are projected) will show many detail changes over the first two.

▲ Type 039 Song class

Chinese Navy, Type 039 multi-role submarine

The Song class is driven by one large seven-bladed propeller, and the primary machinery is located on shock-absorbent mountings for reduced vibration and minimized underwater noise radiation. The stealthiness of the design is further enhanced by the use of anechoic tiling similar to that used on the Russian Kilo class boats.

Specifications

Crew: 60
Powerplant: Single dhsft; three diesel engines
Max Speed: 27.8/41km/hr (15/22kt)
Surface Range: Not available
Displacement: 1700/2250t (1673/2215 tons) surf/sub

Dimensions (length/beam/draught): 74.9 x 8.4 x 5.3m (245.7 x 27.5 x 17.4ft)
Commissioned: June 1999
Armament: Six 533mm (21in) torpedo tubes; 18 torpedoes/missiles or 36 mines

▲ Shang class

Chinese Navy, Type 093 SSN

Few details are known for certain, but the Shang class is double-hulled and has six torpedo tubes, for anti-surface and anti-submarine torpedoes and also for anti-ship missiles. It may also be fitted to launch land-attack cruise missiles. Closed-loop fire control enables discharge of all missiles in two minutes.

Specifications

Crew: about 100
Powerplant: Single shaft; one gas-cooled reactor
Max Speed: 64.8km/hr (35kt) submerged
Surface Range: Unlimited
Displacement: c6090–7110t (6000-7000 tons) surf/sub

Dimensions (length/beam/draught): 110 x 11 x 10m (361 x 36 x 32.8ft)
Commissioned: 2006
Armament: Six launch tubes for torpedoes/ YJ-82 anti-ship missiles

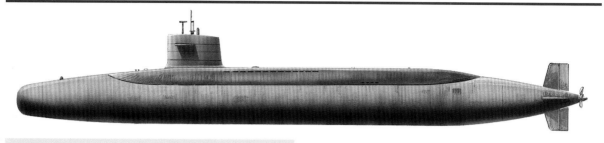

Specifications

Crew: 111

Powerplant: Single shaft; one pwr, pump-jet;
diesel auxiliary

Max Speed: 37/46.3km/hr (20/25kt) surf/sub

Surface Range: Unlimited

Displacement: 12,842/14,335t (12,640/

14,565 tons) surf/sub

Dimensions (length/beam/draught): 138 x 17 x
12.5m (453 x 77.75 x 41ft)

Commissioned: 21 March 1997

Armament: 16 M45/TN75 SLBM; four 533mm
(21in) torpedo tubes

▲ Le Triomphant

French Navy, SSBN

In line with French policy and planning, the electronic systems used are mostly of
French manufacture. Sensors and processing systems are Thales DMUX 80, Sonar
DUUX 5, Donar DSUV 61B VLF. Racal Decca navigation radar is installed. Thales
also supply the DR3000U electronic support system.

Specifications

Crew: 31

Powerplant: Diesel-electric motors; battery/AIP

Max Speed: 22/37km/hr (12/20kt) surf/sub

Surface Range: 12,000km (6500nm) at 8kt

Displacement: 1870t (1840.4 tons) submerged

Dimensions (length/beam/draught): 70 x 6.2 x
5.8m (229.6 x 20.3 x 19ft)

Commissioned: From 2005

Armament: Six 533mm (21in) launch tubes for
torpedoes/SM39 Exocet, or 30 mines

▲ Scorpène

French-Spanish CM-2000 patrol submarine

The *Scorpène* hull can carry 18 heavyweight torpedoes or missiles, or 30 mines. It
can fire the latest wire-guided torpedo types and can be adapted as an anti-ship,
anti-submarine or dual-purpose attack boat.

Specifications

Crew: 60

Powerplant: One K15 reactor; turboreductors;
pump jet

Max Speed: 26/46km/hr (14/25kt) surf/sub

Surface Range: Unlimited

Displacement: 4765/5300t (4689/5216.3 tons)

Dimensions (length/beam/draught): 99.4 x 8.8 x
7.3m (326 x 28.9 x 24ft)

Commissioned: Not yet in commission

Armament: Four 533mm (21in) launch tubes for
torpedoes; MDCN SCALP and Exocet SM39
Block2 missiles

▲ Barracuda

French Navy, new generation SSN

The high level of automation integrated into the submarine's operational and
mission systems will allow the submarine a complement of 60 (in two crews)
compared to 78 in the Rubis and Amethyste Classes. The operational cost will be
reduced by 30 per cent compared to that of the Rubis Class.

France

In 1997, *Le Triomphant* entered service as the first of the French Navy's new class of SSBN. Three more were commissioned between 2000 and 2010 and since then at least one has been permanently on patrol, armed with 16 M45 ballistic missiles. The final boat, *Le Terrible*, has been fitted with the enhanced M51 version as of 2010, with 12 multiple independently targetable re-entry vehicles (MIRVs) and a range of 8000km (5000 miles), and these will be fitted to the other members of the class by 2015. France's SSBNs are based at Ile Longue, Brest.

Through the DCNS (formerly DCN) company of Cherbourg, France is a contender in the export market market for non-nuclear submarines. In conjunction with the Spanish company Navantia, a new diesel-electric attack submarine, the Scorpène class, has been developed. The basic form is the CM-2000, with conventional diesel-electric engines, but also on offer are the AM-2000, with the French MESMA system of air-independent propulsion; the CA-2000, a smaller version for coastal work; and the S-BR, a larger version supplied to the Brazilian Navy, but without air-independent propulsion (AIP).

No Scorpène boat has been ordered by the French Navy, but the Spanish Government ordered four in 2003, then subsequently cancelled the order in favour of the similar S-80 Spanish-designed submarine, also built by Navantia in association with the US Lockheed-Martin Corporation.

It also has AIP, though of a different design. The future of the joint Scorpène project is uncertain, and DCNS have developed their own in-house design, known as Marlin. Meanwhile, two Scorpènes have been built for Chile, commissioned in 2005 and 2006, two for Malaysia, commissioned in 2009, three are under construction for India, with others under negotiation, and one under construction for Brazil, with three others to follow.

In France, the Barracuda project has been under way since 1998 in order to ensure availability of a state-of-the-art nuclear attack submarine from 2017. Six boats are planned. The Barracuda class will have a displacement of about 4100 tonnes (4035 tons) surfaced, an increase of 70 per cent compared to the Amethyste Class submarines.

The class (first boat to be named *Suffren*) incorporates a range of diving, safety and damage control technologies and an integrated platform

CURRENT CONVENTIONAL SUBMARINES (I)

Type	Year	Surface displacement tons/tonnes	Submerged displacement tons/tonnes	Speed knots	Range km/miles	Propulsion	Armament
Kilo Russia et al	1981	2300/2350	3000/3048	25	12,070/7,500	D/E	Torpedoes; missiles
Hai Lung Taiwan	1986	2338/2376	2618/2660	20	20,000/12,427	D/E	Torpedoes
Archer Singapore	1987/2011	1070/1050	1130/1150	20		D/E +AIP	Torpedoes; mines

CURRENT CONVENTIONAL SUBMARINES (II)

Type	Year	Surface displacement tons/tonnes	Submerged displacement tons/tonnes	Speed knots	Range km/miles	Propulsion	Armament
Collins Australia	1996	3003/3051	3300/3353	25	12,070/7,500	D/E	Torpedoes; UGM-84 Harpoon; mines
Victoria Canada	1990	2220/2255	2455/2494	20	20,000/12,427	D/E	Torpedoes
Dolphin Israel	1997–	1640/1666	1900/1930	20		D/E	Torpedoes; missiles (nuclear warheads)

CURRENT CONVENTIONAL SUBMARINES (IV)							
Type	Year	Surface displacement tons/tonnes	Submerged displacement tons/tonnes	Speed knots	Range km/miles	Propulsion	Armament
Type 214 Germany	2007	1663/1690	1830/1860	20		D/E + AIP	Torpedoes; UGM-84 torpedoes; missiles
Soryu Japan	2009	2854/2900	4134/4200	20		D/E + AIP	Torpedoes; UGM-84 Harpoon missiles
Lada/Petersburg Russia	2010	1737/1765	2657/2700	21	12,000/7,546	D/E + AIP	Torpedoes; RPK-6 missiles

The Vanguard submarines are based at Faslane on the Firth of Clyde. The oldest two have both undergone major refits, *Vanguard* in 2002–04 and *Victorious* in 2004–06. *Vigilant* is currently refitting. From 2017, they will be progressively withdrawn. Development work on a successor class is in progress.

Britain's new SSN class is named after HMS *Astute*, and is intended to be formed of seven boats, over a construction period extending towards 2020. The nuclear reactor is the PWR2, shared with the Vanguard SSBNs. Comprehensive countermeasures include decoys and electronic support measures (ESM). The ESM system is the Thales Sensors Outfit UAP(4). Outfit UAP(4) has two multifunction antenna arrays mounted on the two non-hull penetrating optronics masts from Thales Optronics and McTaggart Scott. The CM010 mast includes thermal imaging, low light TV and colour CCD TV sensors. The RN's Eddystone Communications band Electronic Support Measures (CESM) system provides advanced communications, signal intercept, recognition, direction-finding and monitoring capability.

Astute is fitted with I-band navigation radars. The sonar is the Thales Underwater Systems 2076 integrated passive/active search and attack suite with bow, intercept, flank and towed arrays; also the latest version of the Thales S2076 integrated suite. Atlas Hydrographic provided the DESO 25 high-precision echosounder, capable of precise depth measurements down to 10,000m (32,800ft). Raytheon Systems provide the Successor IFF (identification friend or foe) naval transponder system for the class.

India

Arihant, India's first home-constructed nuclear submarine, is expected to be commissioned in late 2012 or early 2013. Launched on 26 July 2009, it will be followed up by four others. The Indian Navy gained nuclear submarine experience with Russian help and the *Arihant* design owes a good deal to the Akula I class. It is powered by an 80MW pressurized water reactor. *Arihant* will be capable of carrying all types of missiles and will have underwater ballistic missile launch capability. It will carry 12 K-15 SLBMs that can be launched even under ice caps. Tested first in 2008, the K-15 will be replaced later by the 3500km (21,750-mile) range K-X missile. *Arihant* will also carry a range of anti-ship and land-attack cruise missiles and torpedoes.

Israel

Israel's Type 800 or Dolphin class submarine, based on the German Type 209, is modified to such an extent that it is really a class in its own right. The first of six boats was commissioned in 1999 and three were in service by 2000. A further three will enter service from 2012 on, equipped with AIP propulsion as used on German Type 214 boats and with other technical advances, including an even greater degree of automation. Patrol, surveillance, interception, attack, special operations and minelaying are all regular roles. Underwater swimmers can be deployed from a wet-and-dry compartment in the hull.

The US Navy recorded a cruise missile launched from an Israeli submarine in the Indian Ocean as travelling 1500km (930 miles). It is generally assumed, though unconfirmed officially, that Israel possesses nuclear weapons and tactical warheads that can be fitted to submarine-fired missiles. The Dolphin class uses the ISUS 90-1 TCS weapon control system supplied by STN Atlas Elektronik, for automatic sensor management, fire control, navigation, and operations. Radar warning and active surface search are fitted. The sonar suite includes the

Atlas Elektronik CSU 90 hull-mounted passive and active search and attack sonar.

The class is normally stationed at Haifa on the Mediterranean coast but is deployed in accordance with perceived security requirements and have been known to operate in the Red Sea from Eilat.

Japan

Japan's Oyashio class is a larger version of the *Harushio*, primarily to allow more space for flank-mounted sonar. The first of 11 boats was laid down at the Kawasaki

yard in Kobe in January 1994 and commissioned on 16 March 1998; the last was commissioned on 10 March 2008. All were built at Kobe by Kawasaki or Mitsubishi, and have capability both for anti-submarine and anti-surface operations. The propulsion system integrates two Kawasaki 12V25S diesel engines, two Kawasaki alternators and two Toshiba main motors, with a total power output of 7700hp (5742kW). From the late 1970s, an ever-increasing proportion of Japan Maritime Self-Defence Force (JMSDF) systems has been of Japanese origin, and the

▲ Arihant
Indian Navy, SSBN

Arihant is fitted with a combination of two sonar systems – Ushus and Panchendriya. Ushus is state-of-the-art sonar built for Kilo Class submarines. Panchendriya is a unified submarine sonar and tactical control system, which includes all types of sonar (passive, surveillance, ranging, intercept and active). It also features an underwater communications system.

Specifications

Crew: 96	Dimensions (length/beam/draught): 110 x 11 x
Powerplant: Single shaft; one pwr	9m (361 x 36 x 29.5ft)
Max Speed: 28/44km/hr (15/24kt) surf/sub	Commissioned: Due 2012
Surface Range: Unlimited	Armament: Six 533mm (21in) launch tubes; 12
Displacement: about 5800–7700/8200–13,000t	K-15 SLBM
(5708–7578/8070–12,795 tons)	

Specifications

Crew: 35	1900 tons) surf/sub
Powerplant: Single shaft; three diesel engines;	Dimensions (length/beam/draught): 57 x 6.8 x
diesel-electric	6.2m (187 x 22 x 20ft)
Max Speed: 37km/hr (20kt) submerged	Commissioned: 1999
Surface Range: Not released	Armament: Four 650mm (25.5in) and six 533mm
Displacement: 1666.3/1930.5t (1640/	(21in) launch tubes

▲ Dolphin
Israeli Navy, variant of German Type 209 patrol submarine

No less than 10 bow torpedo tubes are fitted, six of them 533mm (21in) for launching DM2A3 wire guided torpedoes. An unusual feature is the four 650mm (26in) torpedo tubes. These can be used to launch Israeli-built nuclear-armed Popeye Turbo cruise missiles (a variant of the Popeye standoff missile).

Oyashio class is equipped with Japanese-designed radar and electronics. Its sonar systems are based on US designs, but have been modified to suit Japanese requirements. The six HU-605 533mm tubes have 20 reloads for Type 89 wire-guided active/passive homing torpedoes or UGM-84D Harpoon anti-ship missiles.

None of the Oyashio class has AIP, but this feature is integral to the 16SS or Soryu class, the largest Japanese submarine since the World War II giants. Its functions are very much the same as those of the Oyashios, primarily patrol and interception, but its capacity for operating very close to the seabed, and

for long-term submergence, give it additional potential. While AIP and ultra-modern sensor equipment make these among the world's most advanced submarines, some observers have noted that the weapons deployed are less up to date, and this is an issue that the JMSDF is likely to address well before the 20-year life of the class comes to an end.

Russia

The cruise missile submarines of Project 949A, built between 1985 and 1996, known to NATO as Oscar II, are updated, quietened and enlarged versions of

▲ **Oyashio**

Japanese Maritime Self-Defence Force, patrol submarine

The new boats share the double hulls and anechoic coating of the previous class, but the revised outer casing, in 'leaf coil' rather than 'teardrop' form, gives them a slightly different appearance and the fin is of a more efficient hydrodynamic shape.

Specifications

Crew: 69

Powerplant: Single shaft; diesel-electric

Max Speed: 22.2/37km/hr (12/20kt) surf/sub

Surface Range: Not released

Displacement: 2743/3048t (2700/3000 tons) surf/sub

Dimensions (length/beam/draught): 81.7 x 8.9 x 7.4m (268.1 x 29.2 x 24.25ft)

Commissioned: 16 March 1998

Armament: Sub Harpoon SSM; six 533mm (21in) torpedo tubes

Specifications

Crew: 65

Powerplant: Two Kawasaki 12V diesels; four Kawasaki-Kockums V4-275R Stirling engines

Max Speed: 24/37km/hr (13/20kt) surf/sub

Surface Range: 11,297km (6100nm) at 6.5kt

Displacement: 2900/4200t (2854/4134 tons)

surf/sub

Dimensions (length/beam/draught): 84 x 9.1 x 8.5m (275.5 x 30 x 27.9ft)

Commissioned: 2009

Armament: Six 533mm (21in) launch tubes for torpedoes; Sub-Harpoon missiles; mines

▲ **Soryu**

Japanese Maritime Self-Defence Force, long-range patrol submarine

In addition to the twin Kawasaki 12V 25/25 SB-type diesels, it has four Kawasaki-Kockums V4-275R Stirling AIP engines. Lithium-ion batteries are fitted. Further Swedish influence can be seen in the X-format tailplanes. Seven are projected, with three in commission by the end of 2011 and two others under construction.

Oscar I. As standard with Soviet nuclear submarines, they have double hulls, two nuclear reactors and twin propeller shafts. An elongated sail reinforced for ice-breaking with multiple retractable masts has an open bridge as well as an enclosed bridge station beneath it. Missiles are launched from a submerged position, from tubes fixed at an angle of approximately 400. The tubes, arranged in two rows of 12, are each covered by six hatches on each side of the sail, with each hatch covering a pair of tubes. The launchers are placed between the inner pressure hull and the outer hydrodynamic hull.

As attack submarines, these are the largest to be built (only the Typhoon and Ohio class missile boats are bigger) and it is notable that construction went on after the collapse of the Soviet Union – a tribute to their general reliability as well as their versatility in uses ranging from shadowing carrier battle groups to attack on coastal and inland targets. Some of the later Oscar II boats remain on the active list in both the Northern and Pacific fleets, with three currently noted as in overhaul and three others in service.

K-141, *Kursk*, was commissioned on 30 December 1994 and deployed with the Northern Fleet. On 12 October 2000, it sank in the Barents Sea, with the loss of all 118 persons on board. It was raised in October 2001 in a salvage operation carried out by two Dutch companies, Mammoet Worldwide and Smit International, and towed to the naval shipyard in Murmansk. The forward weapons compartment was cut out prior to lifting and sections were later

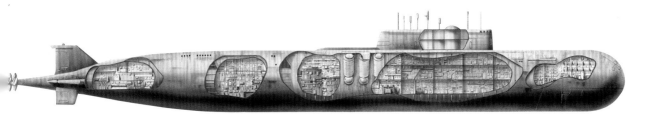

▲ Oscar II Kursk

Russian Navy, Oscar II class SSGN, Barents Sea, 2000

Oscar II is equipped with 24 SS-N-19 Granit cruise missiles with a range of 550km (342 miles). The missile weighs 6.9 tonnes (6.8 tons) with a warhead weighing 1000kg (2205lb). Its speed is Mach 1.5. Under the START arms limitation treaty, nuclear warheads for these missiles have been replaced with high explosive warheads.

Specifications

Crew: 112	(13,400–14,700/16,400–24,000 tons) surf/sub
Powerplant: Twin shaft; two OK-650b reactors;	Dimensions (length/beam/draught): 154 x 18.2 x
steam turbines	9m (505.2 x 60 x 29.5ft)
Max Speed: 30/59km/hr (16/32kt) surf/sub	Commissioned: December 1994
Surface Range: Unlimited	Armament: 24 SS-N-19 Granit missiles; two
Displacement: 13,615–14,935/16,663–24,835t	650mm and four 533mm (21in) launch tubes

Specifications

Crew: 107	Dimensions (length/beam/draught): 170 x 13.5 x
Powerplant: One OK-650B reactor; turbine;	10m (557.75 x 44.25 x 32.8ft)
pump-jet	Commissioned: Due 2012
Max Speed: 28/54km/hr (15/29kt) surf/sub	Armament: 16 RSM-56 Bulava SLBM; six 533mm
Surface Range: Unlimited	(21in) launch tubes for torpedoes/RPK-2 Viyuga
Displacement: 14,720/24,000t (14,488/	cruise missiles
23,621 tons) surf/sub	

▲ Borei

Russian Navy, new-generation SSBN

A single OK-650B nuclear reactor, also used on the preceding classes, provides power and these are the first Russian submarines to have pump-jet propulsion. The Borei class has a more compact and also more hydrodynamically efficient hull design compared to its SSBN predecessors. Diving depth is believed to be 450m (1480ft).

Specifications

Crew: about 95

Powerplant: Single shaft; one KPM pwr

Max Speed: 37/64.8km/hr (20/35kt) surf/sub

Surface Range: Unlimited

Displacement: 5800–7700/8200–13,000t

(5708–7578/8070–12,795 tons) surf/sub

Dimensions (length/beam/draught): 120 x 15 x

8.4m (393.7 x 49.2 x 27.5ft)

Commissioned: Not yet in commission

Armament: Eight vertical launch tubes for P-800

SSM or RK-55 LAM; eight 650mm (25.6in) and

two 533mm (21in) torpedo tubes

▲ **Granei**

Russian Navy, new generation Yasen class SSGN

It is known to be designed for a dive depth of up to 600m (1970ft) and for a maximum submerged speed in excess of 35 knots. This class is the first Russian submarine to be equipped with a spherical sonar, designated as Irytysh-Amfora. To accommodate this large-size array, the torpedo tubes are set at an angle.

lifted in May 2002. Wreckage remaining on the seabed was blown up. The nuclear reactors and Granit cruise missiles were all recovered. The cause of the disaster was revealed as the explosion of a Type 65 high-test peroxide (HTP) torpedo, triggering another explosion in the weapons compartment, causing the vessel to sink. The blast was caused by a leakage of the highly volatile torpedo propellant, which then came in contact with kerosene and metal. Although it was believed that *Kursk*, in common with other Oscar II boats, had an emergency crew escape capsule, it appears, unfortunately, to have been impossible to activate this rescue device.

Project 955, the Borei class of SSBN, is intended to replace the Delta IV and Typhoon classes. As the fourth generation of Russian nuclear submarine, this class is well endowed with new features. Eight boats are planned. The first of the class was

launched in 2007, but commissioning into active service has been delayed. A second boat is completed and two others are under construction – one for possible launch in 2012. Further boats will have design differences and have been referred to as Borei-A. None is likely to reach commissioning stage before 2020.

The class has been designed around the new RSM-56 Bulava missile (SS-NX-30), a three-stage missile using both solid (stages one and two) and liquid fuel (stage three). By far the most sophisticated missile design to emanate from Russia, it is understood to possess a range of defence-penetration systems including evasive manoeuvring, mid-course countermeasures and decoys, and warhead shielding against physical and electromagnetic pulse damage. It carries up to 10 hypersonic MIRV warheads with a range of 9000km (5592 miles) and a yield of 100–150kT. The first three Borei submarines will

FOURTH GENERATION AMERICAN AND RUSSIAN NUCLEAR SUBMARINES							
Class/Type	Year	Surface displacement tons/tonnes	Submerged displacement tons/tonnes	Speed knots	Test Depth m/feet	Propulsion	Armament
Borei SSBN	2010	14,488/14,720	23,621/24,000	29	450/1,476	1 OK-650B	16 RSM-56 Bulava
Granei/Yasen SSGN	2011	8600/8738	13,800/14021	35+	600/1,968	1 KPM PWR	24 Granat SLCM
Seawolf SSGN	2005	8600/8738	9,138/9284	35+	610/2,000	1 S6W PWR	50 Tomahawk
Virginia SSGN	2004	7800/7925		32	240/787	1 SNG PWR	12 Tomahawk

carry 16 Bulavas, but later boats will have 20. The missile was successfully fired from the first Borei, *Yuri Dolgorkiy*, in June 2011. The class is expected to be the mainstay of Russia's strategic missile capability into the 2040s.

Russia's fourth-generation SSN attack submarine is the subject of Project 885, also known as the Granei or Yasen class. Like its SSBN counterpart, it represents a large step forward. A new-type single KPM pressurized water reactor provides power to a single propeller shaft (it is not thought that the class has pump-jet propulsion). The first of the class, *Severodvinsk*, was launched on 15 June 2010 and is due to be commissioned into the Russian Navy by the end of 2012. A second was laid down on 24 July 2009 and is under construction, while a contract for a further four, to be delivered by 2016, was signed on

9 November 2011. The class will carry cruise missiles, of a type not yet specified.

United States

The Seawolf class, originally envisaged as the follow-on to the Los Angeles attack submarines, was the first completely new US submarine design for 30 years. But only three were built before new strategic requirements ended the programme in favour of developing the Virginia class. *Seawolf* is nevertheless a very advanced boat with many features that make it a formidable element in the US ocean armoury. Powered by a GE PWR S6W reactor and two turbines, it has a pump-jet propulsor and a secondary propulsion submerged motor.

The eight 660mm (26in) tubes enable silent 'swimout' torpedo launches, but also launch a variety

▲ USS Seawolf
US Navy, SSGN

Its hull, built of HY-100 steel, enables diving capability to 610m (2000ft); maximum submerged speed is 35 knots, and it is designed to operate below the ice cap. The bow diving planes are retractable. Full acoustic cladding is applied and at a 'silent' speed of 20 knots, it is virtually undetectable.

Specifications
Crew: 140	Dimensions (length/beam/draught): 107 x 12 x
Powerplant: Single shaft; one S6W pwr;	10.9m (353 x 40 x 35ft)
one secondary motor	Commissioned: 1997
Max Speed: 33/65km/hr (18/35kt) surf/sub	Armament: Eight 660mm (25.9in) launch tubes
Surface Range: Unlimited	for Mk 48; torpedoes; Tomahawk or Sub-
Displacement: 8738/9285t (8600/9138 tons)	Harpoon missiles; 50 weapons

Specifications
Crew: 135	Dimensions (length/beam): 115 x 10m (377 x
Powerplant: One S9G pwr; pump-jet propulsors	34ft)
Max Speed: 46km/hr (25kt) submerged	Commissioned: 23 October 2004
Surface Range: Unlimited	Armament: 12 vertical BGM-109 Tomahawk
Displacement: 7900t (7800 tons) submerged	cruise missile tubes; four 533mm (21in)
	torpedo tubes; 38 weapons

▲ USS Virginia
US Navy, new-generation SSGN

Instead of a traditional periscope, the class utilizes a pair of telescoping photonics masts located outside the pressure hull. Each mast contains high-resolution cameras, along with light-intensification and infrared sensors, an infrared laser rangefinder and an integrated Electronic Support Measures (ESM) array.

NATIONAL SUBMARINE STRENGTHS 2012			
Country	Number	Type/class	Note
Algeria	2	Kilo	Project 636
	2	Kilo	From 1980s
Argentina	1	Type 209	
	2	TR 1700	
Australia	6	Collins	2000
Brazil	5	Type 209	
	4	Scorpène	Under construction
Canada	4	Victoria class	Inactive
Chile	2	Scorpène	
	2	Type 209	Updated 2009
China	2	Han Type 091	SSN
	4	Shang Type 093	SSN
	4	Jin Type 094	SSBN
	1	Xia Type 092	SSGN
	17	Romeo	(Ming class)
	12	Kilo	
	20	Song Type 039	
	2	Yuan Type 041	
Colombia	2	Type 209/1200	
	2	Type SX-506	
Ecuador	2	Type 209	
Egypt	2	Oberon class	1989
	8	Romeo	Modernized
France	6	SSN	
	4	SSBN	

NATIONAL SUBMARINE STRENGTHS 2012			
Country	Number	Type/class	Note
Germany	4	Type 212	
Great Britain	2	Astute SSN	7 planned
	6	Trafalgar SSN	
	4	Vanguard SSBN	
Greece	3	U 214 type	
India	10	Kilo Type 877EM	
	4	Type 209/1500	
	2	Foxtrot	Training
	6	Scorpène	Under construction
	1	Arihant SSN	
	1	Nerpa SSN	Russian lease
Indonesia	2	Cakra class	Germany, 1980s
Iran	3	Kilo	
	1	Fateh	2011
	1	Nahang	2006
	14	Ghadir	Small boats
Israel	2	Type 212	
	3	Dolphin class	
Italy	2	Type 212	
	2	Sauro IV	
	2	Sauro III	
Japan	3	Soryu	3 in progress
	11	Oyashio	
	2	Harushio	

of other missiles and remotely operated vehicles. Combat data system, fire control, countermeasures and sonar equipment, all fully up to date when *Seawolf* was commissioned in 1997, have been upgraded. The third class member, USS *Jimmy Carter,* was adapted for seabed and special forces operations by the insertion of a 30m (99ft) 'multi-mission platform' section, allowing for deployment and recovery of remote-operating vehicle (ROV) units and SEAL forces. All three of the class remain in service as of 2012, based at Bangor, Washington.

Considerably smaller and less costly than the 'billion-dollar' *Seawolf,* the Virginia class was designed to assume the attack-submarine role in the post-Cold War context. Rather than deep-sea

encounters, coastal and hot-spot operations were considered most likely. Signals from the masts' sensors are transmitted through fibre optic data lines through signal processors to the control centre. Visual feeds from the masts are displayed on LCD interfaces in the command centre.

It is the first US submarine to employ a built-in Navy SEAL staging area allowing a team of nine men to enter and leave the submarine. With a newly designed anechoic coating, isolated deck structures and new design of propulsor to achieve low acoustic signature, it is claimed that the noise level of the *Virginia* is as low as that of the *Seawolf* class. Thirty boats are planned. As of early 2012, eight are in service and a further six are under construction or on order for delivery between 2013 and 2020.

NATIONAL SUBMARINE STRENGTHS 2012			
Country	Number	Type/class	Note
Malaysia	2	Scorpène	
Netherlands	4	Walrus	Undergoing upgrade
North Korea	4	Whiskey	ex-Russian, 1974
	c22	Romeo	
	c40	Yono	Small boats
	c22	Sang O	Coastal infiltration
Norway	6	Ula class	1987–92
Pakistan	3	Type 214	
	2	Agosta 70	
	3	Khalid	Agosta 90B
Peru	4	Type 209/1200	
	2	Type 209/1100	
Poland	1	Kilo	
	4	Kobben	From Norway, 2002–03
Portugal	2	Tridente	Type 214
Russia	7	Akula I	
	6	'Improved Akula'	
	1	Akula II	
	1	Akula III	
	1	Dmitri Donskoi	Testing Bulova missile
Singapore	4	Sjoormen type	
	2	Västergötland	Modernized
South Africa	3	Type 209/1400	From 2006

NATIONAL SUBMARINE STRENGTHS 2012			
Country	Number	Type/class	Note
South Korea	3	Son-Won-II	Type 214
	9	Chang-Bogo	Type 209/1200
Spain	4	S-70 Galerna	
	4	S-80	Under construction
Sweden	3	Gotland	AIP drive
	2	Sodermanland	AIP drive
Taiwan	2	Hai Lung	Zwaardvis class
	2	Hai Shih	Tench class
Turkey	6	U 214 type	Ordered 2011
	6	Ay class	Type 209/1200
	4	Preveze class	Type 209TI/1400
	4	Gür class	Type 209T2/1400
Ukraine	1	Foxtrot	
United States	18	Ohio SSBN	
	43	Los Angeles SSN	2 in reserve
	3	Seawolf SSN	
	7	Virginia SSN	3 under construction
Venezuela	2	Type 209	
Vietnam	6	Improved Kilo	On order for 2013

▼ **USS** *Connecticut*

The second of the three Seawolf class boats, *Connecticut* was commissioned on 11 December 1998. It is based at Bremerton in Washington State with Submarine Development Squadron Five.

Name Index

Page numbers in *italics* refer to illustrations and tables.

General Index

Page numbers in *italics* refer to illustrations and tables.